The Life We Were Given

The Life We Were Given

Operation Babylift, International Adoption,
and the Children of War in Vietnam

DANA SACHS

Beacon Press
Boston

Beacon Press
25 Beacon Street
Boston, Massachusetts 02108-2892
www.beacon.org

Beacon Press books
are published under the auspices of
the Unitarian Universalist Association of Congregations.

This book is printed on acid-free paper that meets the uncoated paper
ANSI/NISO specifications for permanence as revised in 1992.

Design and composition by Wilsted & Taylor Publishing Services

Library of Congress Cataloging-in-Publication Data

Sachs, Dana.
The life we were given : Operation Babylift, international adoption,
and the children of war in Vietnam / Dana Sachs.
p. cm.
Includes bibliographical references and index.
ISBN 978-0-8070-4241-0 (hardcover : alk. paper)
1. Vietnam War, 1961–1975—Children. 2. Vietnam War, 1961–1975—Refugees.
3. Airlift, Military—Vietnam—History—20th century. 4. Children and war—
Vietnam—History—20th century. 5. Refugee children—Vietnam—History—
20th century. 6. Orphans—Vietnam—History—20th century. 7. Intercountry
adoption—Vietnam—History—20th century. I. Title.

DS559.8.C53S23 2010
959.704'3086914—dc22   2009027662

The names and physical characteristics of some of the people in this work
have been changed to protect their identities.

For the adoptees

Author's Note

Between two thousand and three thousand children were airlifted out of Vietnam during the evacuation that came to be known as "Operation Babylift." Each of those lives touched many others: birth parents, adoptive parents, caregivers, adoption agency staff, airline employees, government officials, military personnel, evacuation volunteers, and, of course, the millions of people, both in Vietnam and around the world, who watched as these events transpired. Realizing that no account can ever be completely comprehensive, I chose to concentrate on those aspects of the story that will, I hope, give readers an understanding of the scope and complexity of what happened. For the most part, I have focused on the Vietnamese adoptees who were airlifted out of Vietnam, on both U.S. government–sponsored and private flights, during the April 1975 evacuation. I only briefly mention, then, the small number of Cambodian children who ended up on the Babylift and the several thousand Vietnamese children who were adopted in the years before the Babylift began. Also, the bulk of my research pertains to children who were adopted by families in the United States, although some 20 percent ended up in other countries. Finally, though seven adoption agencies—

Friends For All Children (FFAC), Friends of the Children of Viet Nam (FCVN), the Holt Adoption Program, the Pearl S. Buck Foundation, Traveler's Aid–International Social Services of America, the United States Catholic Conference, and the World Vision Relief Organization—and several private groups participated in the evacuations, I delve most deeply into the activities of three organizations: FCVN, FFAC, and the Holt Adoption Program, who, together, evacuated more than half the children. When I began this project in 2004, I quickly realized that I would have to balance my awareness of the breadth of this story with the recognition that I could never do it full justice. Much remains for others to tell, and it is my hope that this account will inspire anyone affected by the airlift to share their stories, particularly with the younger generations, who cannot themselves remember.

Contents

Introduction

The photograph shows a row of red-and-yellow striped seats inside the cabin of an airplane. They look like any seats on any commercial jet-liner, though the mod color scheme does help date them to the 1970s. What is odd about the photograph is not the seats themselves, but who occupies them: on each seat lies a tiny baby swaddled in white pajamas. As human beings, we view babies as vulnerable, and a solitary infant, in any context, seems strange and pathetic. These particular children look like dolls that some prankish three-year-old left forgotten on the sofa. A few of these children appear to be sleeping. One faces the camera, looking both curious and forlorn.

I first came across this picture in the spring of 2004, while reading about Vietnam on the Internet. I had been writing about the country for many years, but I had never seen the photograph or heard about the event it depicted. Now, on the Web site, I discovered that in April 1975, at the very end of the war in Vietnam, a group of foreign-run orphanages, with the help of the U.S. government, airlifted between two thousand and three thousand children out of Saigon and placed them with adoptive families overseas. The Web site showed photos from only one jet, but I learned that there had been many babies, and some four dozen flights that carried them out of Vietnam.

As a writer, my interest in Vietnam had, until that moment, consciously focused on the country as a *country*, not as a participant in a war. Too much attention had centered on the conflicts of the twentieth century and as a result, I believed, Americans knew little about the place except that we had fought a devastating war there. Now, looking at this puzzling photograph of babies on an airplane, I reminded myself that every war produces its own set of bizarre situations. Apparently, Operation Babylift had been one such situation that emerged from the war in Vietnam. I moved along in my research and told myself to forget about it.

I couldn't get my mind off those babies, though. April 1975 marked the end of the war in Southeast Asia, the moment that, after three decades of conflict, Vietnam finally emerged into a time of peace. Right at that moment, however, thousands of children were airlifted *away* from their homeland. Why? It didn't make sense to me. Months passed. Every so often, I'd make my way back to the computer, just to have another look. Each time, the same questions filtered through my mind: Who were these children? How did they end up on those planes?

Orphans play a peculiar role in our consciousness. The idea of a child without parents defies the natural order, evoking a pity so deep it feels instinctive, like some remnant of our pre-conscious past. Perhaps it's the pathos of the image that explains why so many myths and legends include children raised by wolves, or floating down rivers in woven baskets, or wandering lost through haunted woods. Our desire to help such children takes on a meaning that goes well beyond the individuals themselves. By saving them, we're saving ourselves and saving our species.

And yet, we have always treated children badly, too. Throughout history, children have borne the brunt of war, and illness, and poverty. Nearly three thousand years ago, the Spartans created a brutal army of ruthless young men by forcing little boys to survive in the streets. During the seventeenth and eighteenth centuries, young boys served as "powder monkeys," carrying explosives to gunners on board ships. Even in times of peace, children have filled out the ranks of farm workers and laborers throughout the world. It wasn't until the mid-nineteenth century, around the time that Charles Dickens introduced both Pip and Oliver Twist, that society began actively addressing the gap between our expectations of how we *should* treat children and the reality of their suffering. In 1851, the Massachusetts legislature introduced the Adoption of Children Act, the first legal mandate requiring that adoption decisions promote the welfare of the child, not the desires of adults. Over the next few decades, American society came to regard adoption as a viable means of ensuring the well-being of children who had no families to care for them.

By the twentieth century, this commitment to our own orphans expanded to include helping foreign children made vulnerable by war. After the Holocaust, the U.S. government accepted as immigrants thousands of displaced children. Though the attempts were haphazard and often unsuccessful, some effort was made to find these children's families before placing them for adoption. Following Fidel Castro's revolution in Cuba, a program known as "Operation Pedro Pan" evacuated thousands of Cuban children, in small groups and on commercial flights, to the United States, where many were reunited with relatives. In 1970, two years after the end of the Nigerian civil war, five thousand Biafran children, who had been evacuated from the country for their safety, returned to their families and villages. "It's not your fault that you left your country," Nigeria's head of state told one group of children as they arrived, adding, "We're very, very happy to see you back here with us."

Operation Babylift followed what had, by then, become a familiar pattern: war creates orphans, and then civilized society steps in to help. If the war itself revealed our basest nature, then humanitarian interventions unveiled our best—a deeply felt desire to save the lives of defenseless kids. As an April 1975 article in *Time* magazine described Operation Babylift, which was taking place at the time, "Not since the return of the prisoners of war two years ago [has] there been a news story out of Viet

Nam with which the average American could so readily identify, one in which individuals seemed able to atone, even in the most tentative way, for the collective sins of governments." It was a feel-good effort, to be sure, but the Babylift also marked a new phase of humanitarian endeavor, and it revealed a new philosophy with regard to what it means to "save" a child. Earlier efforts had centered on reuniting families torn apart by war; adoption was a backup plan. In contrast, this mission focused completely on adoption. Evacuation organizers claimed that these children were orphans. It quickly became clear, however, that a significant number were being put into permanent homes without clear proof of their eligibility for adoption. Some children, it seemed, came from Vietnam's most vulnerable families, and they had been swept up in the panic of those last days of war and transported to new, permanent homes overseas.

Eventually, I stopped trying to ignore the story of Operation Babylift. For the past six years, I have tried, instead, to unravel the tangle of events that led, in April 1975, to the mass evacuation of those children from Vietnam, approximately 80 percent of whom ended up in the United States, while the rest were adopted by families in Canada, Australia, and Europe. Even as the airlift was taking place, controversy began to swirl over whether it was an appropriate response to the crisis facing these children. The arguments focused on many factors—the oversight of the mission, the family status of the children involved, the appalling conditions of children in wartime South Vietnam—but these debates also coalesced around a single vexing question about adoption itself: is the primary purpose of adoption to find a home for an orphan or to satisfy the needs of a family that wants a child? That question, of course, remains, to this day, at the center of the controversy over international adoption.

After the war ended, the children of the Babylift settled into their new adoptive homes and their public story receded into history. For observers who are still able to remember the events at all, the phrase "Operation Babylift" elicits vague recollections of children on airplanes and little else. But there are many people—in the United States, Europe,

Canada, Australia, and, of course, in Vietnam—who continue to ruminate over what happened back then because the events of Operation Babylift changed their lives forever. Here, I hope to tell their story.

I flew to Boston in the spring of 2005 to attend a reunion of adult adoptees sponsored by the Vietnam Adoptee Network (VAN), many of whose members had, as children, been evacuated from Saigon during Operation Babylift. The meeting took place at a Vietnamese community center in Dorchester, and, at first glance, the VAN members, stylish young professionals in leather jackets, high heels, and discreet tattoos, looked like any children of Vietnamese immigrants who had ended up settling, and prospering, in the United States. Unlike other Asian Americans of their generation, though, most VAN members grew up in white households, often in small, almost entirely Caucasian communities. Some had spent their childhoods in places like Wyoming or rural Colorado, during which time they had rarely, if ever, seen another Asian face. They had Caucasian names, too—Chris, Sarah, Robert— though some also went by names that reflected their ethnic heritage, like Kim or Minh. As I would find over the next couple of days, these young people call themselves Vietnamese *adoptees* more often than Vietnamese *Americans*, and the word *adoptee* necessarily emphasizes the gap between their ethnic heritage and the way that they were raised.

Sipping my coffee during the Saturday morning conference registration, I had to wonder: was that gap such a bad thing? Having pored over the photographs of those children on the airplanes, I couldn't ignore the miracle—I had to call it that—of what I saw in front of me. The sickly young "war orphans" who had been strapped into those jetliners had become a group of remarkably healthy-looking adults. Here was one obvious measure of Operation Babylift's achievement: these people looked great and were successful, too.

The reality of their situation was, of course, much more complex. That weekend, I listened to one VAN member after another discuss the challenges posed by their peculiar life stories. A grad student described how he and his wife dealt with the fact that he didn't know his birth date ("I insist that we celebrate for a week!" he said with a laugh). An East Coast adoptee expressed her need for a child as, in part, a desire to "know someone else in the world who looks like me." A woman with a rare disease lamented her lack of genealogic medical history. Some of these people didn't seem bothered by these gaps in their knowledge; others appeared to be grieving.

One afternoon during the conference, I walked to Dorchester's Pho #1 Restaurant with adoptee David Fisk, a shy and gentle engineer who'd flown in from southern California for the reunion. VAN had existed for about five years by then and, because most of its members had no known biological relations, they had quickly coalesced into a kind of family for each other. As we sat in the crowded noodle shop that afternoon, I sensed that David felt impatient to get back to his friends, but he was too polite to show it, resolutely sharing with me the facts he knew about his past. He believed he was the son of a Vietnamese mother and an African American GI father, and his light brown skin and curly black hair made him look more like a black American than a person from Vietnam. Unlike most of the Babylift adoptees, he was old enough to remember his birth parents, too. In fact, he had memories of both his life in Vietnam and his evacuation to the United States.

Despite the memories, the holes in David's history were huge. He didn't know the names of his birth mother or father. He didn't know his original legal name, though he remembered being called "Hen Ly." He didn't know where he was born, or even his age (he was born sometime between 1967 and 1969, which made him anywhere from six to eight years old when he arrived in the States). He believed that he had lived in Saigon, but he couldn't know for sure. Because he arrived in the United States with almost no identifying information, he had to rely on his own thirty-year-old memories to fill out his history. Those memories had the wispy, almost supernatural quality of dreams.

Practically speaking, David's present-day life would have been better served if he had remembered specifics, like birth dates and names, but the human mind doesn't work that way. David's memories seemed absolutely random. Or, perhaps they did have a logic, but it was a logic that he could no longer understand. In one memory, he had been cut accidentally on his hand with a nail clipper and an older girl—maybe a sister?—seemed to have helped him care for the wound. "I can still see the scar," he told me, stretching his hand across the table for me to look at. I wasn't sure if he was trying to prove his point, or if he wanted to share with me this single piece of evidence that connected him to the life he'd led in Vietnam. In any case, though I carefully peered down at the smooth skin of his hand, I couldn't make out a scar there. David pulled his hand back and said, half-apologetically, "It's very light, so you can't see it now." But it was clear to me that *he* saw it.

He described other memories as well. He could remember being frightened by a Vietnamese soldier who had lost a leg, but "I didn't know there was a war going on," he told me. He remembered a little girl, who might have been a younger sister, and that she had odd scars all over her legs. He remembered a tall, black man in army fatigues, whom he believed to be his father. "I liked it when he came around," he said. David could not remember the face of his mother at all. He didn't live with her and, in retrospect, he believed she worked as a prostitute "because she was really well off." Although he rarely saw his mother, he felt that he had always been able to count on her to reappear. "I didn't feel insecure," he told me, "because I knew my mother would always come, because she always came back and visited or at least brought me to someplace else." His memories were vague, but on this point he seemed certain. "She always came back," he said.

Over the years, David had cobbled together a scenario for his early life, a story based on his own memories, some educated guesses, and the few bits of factual information he had managed to procure from his adoption agency, which had not been forthcoming. The story goes like this: His father was a black GI. His mother, a prostitute, had three children and enough money to pay other people to care for them. Eventually, she placed David and his younger sister in boarding school, but she continued to visit them. After David had spent about six months in the school, a Dutch priest arrived and took him to an orphanage filled with babies. He spent a few days there. Then, he was taken to the airport, put on a plane, and flown out of Vietnam. He ended up in South Florida with his new adoptive family, the Fisks, who lived in the town of Homestead. The *Miami Herald* and local television covered his arrival at the airport and the moment he first met his new family.

It took him about a year to learn English. Once, a Vietnamese speaker came by to translate, but, other than that, he was on his own. He couldn't remember ever being told that he had a new family now. He couldn't remember any explanations. "I just got used to the fact," he said. "I just got used to it."

There were moments during that conversation, when David spoke of his birth mother, or of his arrival in the States, or of that year spent adjusting to his new circumstances, when the various tragedies of his life became so apparent that, instead of pushing harder, I had to glance past them and move on. The scar on his hand was a scar I couldn't see, but these other scars became more visible. I was coming to realize that the reserve I had taken at first to be shyness was, more likely, inexpressible grief.

Almost an hour had passed since we'd arrived at the restaurant. We finished our coffee and then walked back up the road toward the community center hosting the reunion. It felt refreshing to be outside after sitting in the stuffy restaurant. As we walked, David told me that he didn't have any complaints about his adoptive family. He simply didn't feel close to them. These days, his attention focused on Vietnam. He had traveled there several times in recent years, spending many hours in Saigon, searching for clues to his past.

I looked at David. In a few months, I planned to leave for Vietnam to conduct research on the Babylift. "If you have some names of orphanages or anything," I told him now, "I'm happy to go by and check them out."

David shrugged. "That might be good," he replied. He looked more hesitant than pleased, though, as if he wouldn't let himself place too much hope in such efforts.

Because of David's reserve, it was hard to gauge his emotions. Other adoptees were much more expressive. The previous day, a young woman had begun to cry in one of the VAN sessions. "I just don't understand," she said, "how they decided to place people in these homes." She refrained from giving details, but her experience with her adoptive family had clearly been traumatic. At that moment, the meeting room, which was full of adoptees, their spouses, and a few guests, fell silent. The woman continued to sob. Her husband, sitting beside her, gripped her hand. Then she looked up again. "I mean," she cried, "when they brought us here and put us in those homes, what were they thinking?"

For all these adoptees, Operation Babylift had left psychological and emotional knots that, in many cases, were impossible to tease apart. Not all were unhappy with their lives, but the experience had complicated their sense of who they were in the world. I would later speak with Bert Ballard, who arrived in the Babylift as a tiny infant. He said that he encourages his fellow adoptees to take responsibility for their lives rather than hold onto anger over what happened back then. "This is the life we were given," he tells them. "Because the reality is that with the Babylift, there's lots of anger everywhere. You can't walk up and say, 'Hi, you stole my life away from me. Please apologize to me.' This is just not going to happen with an event like the Babylift."

PART ONE

CHAPTER I

Where They Came From

As victims, the Vietnamese were not exceptional. They were more a statistical, abstract concept—an aggregate—than people of flesh and blood.

MICHAEL BILTON and KEVIN SIM, *Four Hours in My Lai*

The war had lasted thirty years. It began in 1945, the year that the Allies defeated the Nazis, the year of Nagasaki and Hiroshima, the year that Franklin Roosevelt died and Harry Truman took office. In 1954, the French withdrew from Vietnam, but, after a brief, hopeful, and ultimately devastating lull, the war continued. Through Eisenhower and Kennedy, Johnson and Nixon, and into the administration of Gerald Ford, the war continued. In Korea, Algeria, and the Sudan, other wars had begun and ended. Elvis Presley became a star, Hank Aaron broke Babe Ruth's home-run record, and the United States put a man on the moon. Meanwhile, the war in Vietnam continued. In fact, the conflict in Vietnam had gone on for so long that an entire generation of Vietnamese came into the world, grew up, and began raising children of their own without ever having lived in peace.

And then, in 1975, over a period of just six weeks, the war ended.

The end began at 2 a.m. on March 10, when North Vietnamese troops attacked Ban Me Thuot in the Central Highlands of South Vietnam. Ban Me Thuot was an odd choice for a first salvo. The largest town in the region, Ban Me Thuot was nonetheless a remote outpost, sur-

rounded by mountains and jungle, wild elephants and thundering waterfalls, closer to the Cambodian border than to any major city in South
Vietnam. But the South Vietnamese had barely bothered to defend the
town, even though it lay near the intricate network of supply lines that
the North Vietnamese had built over the past three decades, the web
of routes that Americans called the Ho Chi Minh Trail. By taking Ban
Me Thuot, the North Vietnamese could consolidate their power in the
region and then expand throughout the south. Quickly and surrepti-
tiously, thirty thousand North Vietnamese troops poured into an area
defended by just four thousand South Vietnamese soldiers.

The city fell in less than two days, sending South Vietnamese forces
into complete disarray. Faced with chaos on the northwestern front and
with little chance of receiving substantial aid from the United States,
South Vietnamese president Nguyen Van Thieu made what may have
been the single worst strategic decision of the entire war: He withdrew his forces from the northern provinces, essentially abandoning
half the country. Thieu hoped to consolidate his troops farther south,
saving his forces to defend the larger cities, but civilians and military
personnel in the Central Highlands read the decision as a sign of defeat.
People panicked, gathering a few belongings and leaving their homes.
Soldiers abandoned their posts and fled as well. Even some of Thieu's
most trusted generals simply walked away. Within days, Highway 7,
a narrow, barely usable mountain pass, had filled with half a million
people surging toward the coast. Soon after, the Highland towns of
Pleiku and Kontum fell as well, widening the swath of the exodus already in progress.

What had begun in the highland towns as an effort by worried families to get out of harm's way became, over the miles and days, the end
of many of those families. Only a quarter of the people who left for the
coastal cities ever got there. Some turned back, and many others died
along the way. Richard Blystone, reporting for the Associated Press,
told of how things fell apart on the long march to the coast: "Two children arrive alone. Their father put them aboard a helicopter thinking
their pregnant mother was on board. But she was not. . . . A school-

teacher says his family walked through the jungle to avoid North Vietnamese shellfire and thought their luck had changed when they were able to climb aboard a truck. But later they realized that their five-year-old child was missing in the scramble."

The *Saigon Post* published a series of dispatches from the Vietnamese journalist Nguyen Tu, who was walking amid the throngs of desperate civilians. "It's a pity to look at those people who could not afford to ride on cars or trucks or whatever vehicles [were] available," Tu wrote. "They are the miserable ones who can only use their feet, and they are the largest bunch—women, children, elders walking as rapidly as they could, but not having even a drop of water to squelch their thirst."

On March 16, Tu described the sky over Pleiku as "scintillating with thousands of glittering stars. Are they a secret code urging us to hurry up?"

Events in the Central Highlands sent a wave of panic through Saigon, and many of its citizens began making serious preparations to flee Vietnam. For an Australian woman named Rosemary Taylor, the new developments presented a much more complicated challenge than simply getting a single individual, or even a family, out of the country. As the in-country director of Friends For All Children (FFAC), a U.S.-based adoption agency located in the South Vietnamese capital, she had hundreds of children to worry about.

Taylor, a young woman with lush, dark hair and a warm smile, lived alone in a small room on the eight-acre grounds of Phu My, a sprawling shelter for the poor in Saigon. Though she may have looked out of place in this location, Taylor had spent the past eight years here, devoting her life to finding adoptive families for displaced children overseas. In 1968, her first full year of arranging adoptions, she sent a hundred and fifty children abroad. By 1975, she was running four nurseries in Saigon, all now collectively sponsored by FFAC, and had arranged overseas adoptions for thousands of children, which made her the most accomplished foreign adoption administrator in Vietnam.

In early 1975, a total of 134 orphanages were operating in South

Vietnam, and they collectively cared for just under twenty thousand children. Many of Taylor's wards began their lives in rural villages. They usually entered the adoption system unexpectedly. An orphanage worker might go outside and discover a blanket-wrapped newborn squalling near the front gate. A vendor from the market might bring in a child she'd found left among the stalls that morning. Hospital staff, too, brought in babies whose mothers had given birth and disappeared. The orphanages took in plenty of war orphans, children whose parents had died in the fighting, as well. The small rural facilities, whether run by the government, charities, or religious orders, were uniformly poor and simple places. They had too many children to care for and lacked money and basic supplies. They did what they could on very little, with varying success. Death rates ranged from high to extraordinarily high.

By 1975, Vietnam's orphanages had become notorious and, for many Western observers, a steady source of dismay. The United States sent millions and millions of dollars to Vietnam. Why had so little of it been used to help these children? Earlier in the decade, the American journalist Judith Coburn made several visits to Go Vap Orphanage, the largest institution in Saigon, and her account provides a vivid description of what life was like there. "As soon as you entered the tiny, fenced-in concrete courtyard, you were swamped by hordes of children of all ages, hurtling into your arms, hugging your legs, and plucking at your sleeve," Coburn wrote later, in the *Village Voice*. "The 273 children there at that time slept in four rooms so crowded with beds that the children near the walls could not get out without crawling over scores of other children. Life was confined to these rooms or the outdoor courtyard, a 25-foot concrete square. There was a small, roofed-over area of the courtyard where the children ate or huddled when it rained."

Conditions in the provincial orphanages were less horrific than those at Go Vap, but it was only a difference of degree. Though smaller, and therefore accommodating fewer children, they were equally overwhelmed and equally incapable of adequately caring for those who regularly appeared at their doors. A wide range of organizations ran and funded these orphanages, including local charitable groups, the South

Vietnamese government, Buddhist communities, and various Catholic orders. Among these organizations, ideas about goals and responsibilities varied widely. Generally speaking, the Buddhist, charitable, and government-run orphanages were dedicated to rearing the children themselves, despite the constraints. Many of the Catholic-run orphanages, however, had come to believe that the best hope for their children lay in overseas adoption. The Vietnamese nuns who ran these orphanages would probably have agreed with the ideas of Rosemary Taylor, herself a devout Catholic, who saw the religion as a force for good in Asia. "Christianity certainly believed," Taylor would later write, "that it was right to free men from the menaces of hostile Gods and an enslavement to fate, and uphold the unique preciousness of each human being." Typically, the sisters would release a group of children, who would then stay in the foreign-run orphanages until the adoption paperwork was complete and they were healthy enough to travel abroad.

Because the foreign-run agencies received financial support from overseas, they had resources that went well beyond what most Vietnamese-run facilities could manage. Rosemary Taylor, for one, had developed an extensive and effective program in Saigon. "The children at Allambie [nursery] are divided into families of six or eight," explained one FFAC newsletter. "Each family has its own room and the same child-care workers assigned. The night-duty 'mother' sleeps in the room with the children. If you drop by at bedtime you will find 'mother' bringing in a tray with cups of milk for her pajama-clad children." Not surprisingly, Taylor's nurseries, and those of other foreign-run organizations, succeeded in drastically reducing death rates and improving the health and well-being of their charges before they left Vietnam for their new homes abroad.

By the spring of 1975, foreign adoption had become a well-known alternative to the misery that individual children faced in Vietnam. As welfare policy, however, it did very little. According to the South Vietnamese government's own statistics, the nation had 879,000 "orphans," a classification that included not just children of parents who had died, but any child without parents to raise them. Throughout the war years, the South Vietnamese government and international community—including, most notably, the United States—had proven themselves incapable of addressing that crisis in any meaningful way. The main reason that most of these orphans remained off the streets was not because of adoption. Rather, they benefitted from an informal fostering network through which relatives and neighbors took individual children into their homes. In one sign of the interconnectedness of Vietnamese society, in fact, some 20 percent of South Vietnamese families had an orphan living with them. To the extent that anyone was addressing the orphan problem in South Vietnam, it was the Vietnamese themselves, village by village and family by family.

Rosemary Taylor, then, was not stopping the cycle of war and poverty that had devastated the lives of so many South Vietnamese; none of the foreign agencies could achieve this impossible task. They could, however, help the children within their own orbit. In the spring of 1975, as South Vietnam moved closer and closer to the brink of collapse, the adoption agencies set into motion a plan for complete evacuation. Most of their children were already slated for adoption overseas anyway, so they decided to get the kids out soon rather than face the possibility that they'd never get out at all.

Taylor had previously sent an average of two dozen children overseas every month. Now, working with the files that lay in stacks all over her tiny room at Phu My, she was preparing the adoption documentation for hundreds of her wards to leave the country as soon as possible. Among the orphanages that Taylor managed in Saigon at that moment, she had six hundred children in her care. And she was determined to get every single one of them out of Vietnam.

Less than a week after the North Vietnamese army began its attack on Ban Me Thuot, Cherie Clark was on the road from Saigon into the Mekong Delta, traveling through contested territory to pick up children still living in provincial orphanages. The military debacle in the Central Highlands had sent a chill through South Vietnam, and Clark, an Indiana-born nurse who ran a Saigon orphanage sponsored by the

American group Friends of the Children of Viet Nam (FCVN), wanted to evacuate as many children from the provinces as possible. Like Rosemary Taylor, her counterpart at FFAC, Clark and her colleagues regularly brought children to the relative safety of Saigon before finalizing their adoptions. Now, they were speeding up the entire process.

In mid-March, the Mekong Delta was seeing continuous low-level fighting, battles that were loud enough to be heard every evening in Saigon but which did not yet approach the violence taking place in the Central Highlands. Highways remained open, though sporadically, and merchants continued ferrying goods on the roads and waterways that ran from the countryside to the city. Oddly, despite the increasing momentum of the war, Saigon's markets still bustled, as crowded and copious as ever. Up north, half a million refugees were struggling along the road from Ban Me Thuot to the coast, but merchants in Saigon were still hawking pineapples and papayas, fresh shrimp, coconuts, and heaping kilos of rice.

Clark rode with two Vietnamese colleagues, Thuy and Sy, who knew the routes well. Generally, they made these trips to deliver supplies to provincial orphanages, returning to Saigon with a few children to place for adoption. With the situation in Vietnam growing increasingly dire, however, today's visit took on new urgency. This might well be their last foray into the Delta. Merely traversing these routes at all meant taking a risk, but the Catholic nuns who ran the provincial orphanages were adamant. A Communist takeover seemed imminent, and they cabled Clark to hurry down to evacuate as many children as possible.

If South Vietnam's capital was able to retain a sense of normalcy, the countryside was not. The three FCVN colleagues saw tanks and weapons, jeeps and convoys, and many weary soldiers. They also saw the effects of battle. In the town of Vinh Long, they stopped at a military hospital full of wounded and dying men. "Flies were everywhere," Clark later recalled. "The stench was terrible—the reek of blood, dirt, feces, and death cloyed the air. Some men lay quietly weeping, awaiting the inevitable, while others moaned in pain, longing in vain for someone to come to their aid."

They moved on, anxious to reach the city of Can Tho before night-fall, when a civilian vehicle would face even greater risk. Once they arrived, however, the nuns at the Can Tho orphanage had a new request. Could they travel farther south the next day and pick up more children in the coastal town of Bac Lieu? Clark hesitated. Bac Lieu lay fifty miles down a provincial road that the South Vietnamese military only lightly defended. Any vehicle traveling in that direction put itself in grave danger.

Clark agreed to go. "We had to help the children," she later said, giving the explanation that had become a kind of mantra for the Americans and foreigners of other nationalities who, like Clark, ran orphanages in Vietnam. From the outside, Clark's dedication seems admirable, though somewhat curious. After all, she had a husband and children of her own back in Saigon. For many observers, in fact, Clark's willingness to put herself in danger makes little sense. The journalist Chris Hedges, who has himself covered conflicts all over the world, wrote a book that explains this impulse, *War Is a Force That Gives Us Meaning.* In it, he writes that war has an almost intoxicating attraction for certain people. "Even with its destruction and carnage," he points out, "it can give us what we long for in life. It can give us purpose, meaning, a reason for living." Cherie Clark, who would turn thirty in 1975, perhaps sought that kind of purpose. Though she had grown up in the American heartland, she had developed a restless curiosity about the world that had never been sated by the short visits she and her husband took within the United States. When, in the fall of 1972, she became aware of the plight of Vietnam's mixed-race children, the offspring of local women and U.S. GIs known as *con lai*, she decided to adopt. By the time Clark and her husband, Tom, an engineer for IBM, moved to Vietnam to run FCVN a year and a half later, they were parents of seven—four biological kids and three adopted from Vietnam. They moved the entire family there with them.

Like Rosemary Taylor, Cherie Clark had no professional training in international adoption. In 1975, however, few would have questioned their lack of credentials. Adoption professionals were not expected to

have any kind of specialized training, though the field was slowly beginning to move in that direction. "[In] the United States, adoption . . . in-
volves some of the most sensitive, fragile, and complicated aspects of all
human services," the adoption researchers Marshall D. Schechter and
Doris Bertocci have pointed out, adding that adoption, more than any
other area of social services, traditionally relied on laypeople. Day in and
day out, and in conditions that left no time for careful consideration,
Clark and the other adoption administrators working in Vietnam were
making decisions that would alter the lives of hundreds and hundreds
of children permanently.

Cherie Clark may not have had training or experience, but she did
have passion. She and her family got along well inside FCVN's Saigon
compound, despite the fact that they were living in a war zone. Once,
Clark's four-year-old daughter, Beth, was kidnapped from the premises.
The child might have disappeared for good had not a quick-thinking
group of FCVN employees and neighbors raced after the kidnapper to
save her. After that incident, Clark hired a security guard to patrol the
compound, but she "cried thinking how close we had come to losing
Beth forever. For days after, I was terrified to leave the children alone,
even for a minute."

The plight of the Vietnamese children continued to gnaw at her,
though, and the need to do something for those children led her back
to Can Tho and, now, the next morning, down the frightening road
to Bac Lieu. Clark, Thuy, and Sy set off on the drive, anxious to give
themselves enough time to make it there and back before sunset. The
three remained silent during the entire journey down to the coast. Any
sudden noise or movement on the road could signal an attack. When
they finally arrived, they rushed to unload their supplies, unwilling to
pause long enough to drink the cups of tea offered by the orphanage's
nuns. With barely a word, they arranged ten infants in the back of the
FCVN van, and then Clark and her colleagues drove away.

On the road back from Bac Lieu, a group of South Vietnamese soldiers forced the van to pull over. A battle was in progress a few miles
away, they explained, and it was too dangerous for the vehicle to con-

tinue. For a long time, the group waited in the hot sun by the side of the road. Low-flying planes passed nearby, heading to battle. The three staff members did what they could to help the babies, who, because they were already weak and malnourished, were at heightened risk of dehydration. Finally, the soldiers allowed them to continue. They arrived back in Can Tho just as the sun was setting. The next morning, they loaded the van with the ten Bac Lieu babies and an additional twenty from Can Tho, and then they started back toward Saigon. On the way, firefights forced the van, with its thirty infants inside, to stop again and again. One of the weakest children died along the way.

In South Vietnam, people called it *radio miệng*—"mouth radio"—the constant stream of news and gossip that raced through towns and cities, swirled into open windows, whipped down alleyways, and wafted among the noodle stalls that popped up along the sidewalks each evening at dusk. In late March 1975, a lot of that news centered on the fate of the con lai. In Danang alone, there were hundreds, if not thousands, of them, and most stood out in a crowd—the dark-skinned, stocky kid, the blond child, the girl with the Afro, the boy with blue eyes. Their mere existence served as a lingering reminder of the U.S. presence. As the North Vietnamese forces moved south, so did rumors of what would happen to these children when the Communists arrived.

According to the mouth radio, Communists hated the con lai and they would kill these children when they took over the country. They wouldn't do it simply, either. They would slit open the belly of a con lai, pull out the liver, and eat it. People knew that you couldn't always rely on mouth radio, but, in this case, the rumors were convincingly consistent throughout the South.

A tremor of fear swept through the community of con lai mothers. In Danang, they were a club of sorts, the kind of club you weren't exactly *glad* to be a part of but relied on nonetheless. Back in the United States, many people had an image of the Vietnamese women who had slept with American GIs: slender, vampy, sultry, and almond-eyed, the mystery of Asia wrapped in tight miniskirts. The mothers in Danang were more motley and pedestrian than that. Some had worked as prostitutes, but many had filled out the ranks of cooks, laundresses, and janitors who had staffed the military bases during the height of U.S. involvement there. They were poor women, many of them mothers and widows already, for whom a liaison with a soldier had offered a short spell of camaraderie, or financial security, or love, before they found themselves alone again, except now they had one more mouth to feed.

Kim and Han were two such women. They had worked together in a laundry on a U.S. base in the 1960s. Both were married women whose husbands had disappeared. Kim's had done so mysteriously, just after the South Vietnamese forces drafted him into the service. On the morning he was scheduled to appear for duty, he vanished. The authorities, assuming he had joined the enemy, jailed Kim to ferret out information. Kim knew nothing, but, still she remained in prison for a month while they beat her to get at the truth. When her captors finally released her, she went home to find her three children wandering, as she perceived it, "like dogs" on the streets.

The disappearance of Han's husband was more mundane. The couple had eight children together, and one day, he simply abandoned them, moving to the town of Quang Ngai with another woman. Han remained in Danang with all the children and no way to support them.

The chance to work for the U.S. military came, then, as a salvation for both of these women. Kim began as a laundress at the Navy hospital, then moved to the cafeteria, where she oversaw a team of cooks who provided meals for high-ranking American officers. It was fairly easy work that paid well. One American in particular, an officer she called "Sky," treated her especially nicely. He saw the misery in her life and tried to help her by easing her workload, building her a house, and giving her money for her children's clothing and school. On Sundays, he took the whole family out to a restaurant. Kim repaid Sky's kindness in the only way she knew how. By the time she gave birth to their daughter, whom she named Hiep, Sky had already returned to the United States and left them all behind.

Han met the man she called Huet at the military base as well. Just as

Sky had done with Kim, Huet took to Han's children almost as avidly as he took to Han herself. He gave her the money to build the family a house and paid for school and food. His efforts weren't merely financial, either. Huet, a Navy man who had no wife or family of his own, became a kind of father figure for Han's kids, taking them to school and picking them up, tutoring them in their studies. Han's neighbors called him "the Old American" because, having been born in 1927, he was almost a generation older than most GIs. The Old American proved to be more stable and reliable than the younger guys, too.

Unlike Sky, who left Vietnam before his child was born, Huet stuck around. He was there when Han gave birth to their daughter, Ho Thi Ngoc Anh, in May 1968, and for years afterward he remained a part of the family. In fact, he didn't leave them until 1973, when the United States pulled out of Vietnam following the Paris Peace Accords. By then, more than six years had passed since he and Han first met. Ngoc Anh was five, a sweet blond child who looked like her father. Han noticed, though, that he didn't express any greater affection for Ngoc Anh than for any of the other kids. When he said good-bye, he said good-bye to all of them.

By March 1975, it had been a long time since any letters had arrived from Huet. The Communist victory loomed, and, realizing that any association with the enemy would endanger her family, Han collected all his letters and burned them. As the days passed, she became more and more scared. One by one, the northern towns of South Vietnam fell to the Communists. Any stranger on the street, she worried, might see Ngoc Anh and hurt her, simply because her father had been an American. For a while, Han hid Ngoc Anh in the house, but she couldn't keep a growing girl indoors forever. At night, she would cover Ngoc Anh's hair in a scarf, and together they would walk the streets in darkness, just to get a bit of fresh air. Han was desperate. What would she do when the Communists arrived?

She had one option. In the center of Danang, some foreigners ran an office that, people said, would take in children like Ngoc Anh and send them overseas for adoption. Han didn't know anything about the organization or even its formal name. Locals just called it *Mẹ Quốc Tế*

—International Mother—and they shared among themselves the address: 5 Ba Dinh Street. In the panicky atmosphere of Danang during those days of late March, the phrase "Mẹ Quốc Tế: 5 Ba Dinh Street" passed among the mothers of con lai like a secret password that could save their children's lives. Ngoc Anh could have a new set of parents, a nice home, an education. Most importantly, she could survive.

Days passed, but Han could not bring herself to take Ngoc Anh to 5 Ba Dinh Street. She loved her daughter too much. How could she give up the girl forever? To the north, south, and west, cities and villages fell to the Communists. With half a million displaced persons in the city, Danang felt like a refugee camp. People lay on the sidewalks and in ditches; families camped by the side of the road. They looked sick, hungry, full of despair. Han could hear bombs dropping outside the city. Still, she hesitated.

Meanwhile, Han's friend Kim was frantic over what to do with her own little girl. The South Vietnamese media, far from providing objective reporting, was quick to pass along any allegations of Communist brutality, whether proven or not: local officials murdered, homes and churches burned, refugees shot while trying to flee to safety. In Kim's mind, there didn't seem to be any question that her daughter would be killed. While Han continued to waver, Kim acted. Early in the morning of March 15, she took Hiep across the Han River, which separated their home in the Son Tra district from central Danang. The building that housed Mẹ Quốc Tế looked like any other pretty French-era villa on that quiet, shady street, except that a line of frightened women with their children stretched out the door.

Inside, a crowd of people pressed toward a desk where an American woman sat scribbling into a notebook. As each mother reached her desk, the American asked a few questions and then jotted down the answers in her book: child's name and age; mother's name. The atmosphere was too harried for discussion or counseling of any kind. Kim simply presented Hiep's birth certificate and answered questions while the American woman took notes in her book.

Despite all these preparations, Kim continued to believe she could find some way to stay with her daughter. Finally, after she'd completed the procedures, she approached one of the American officials and made a proposition. "Let me go with her," she said.

The official looked at Kim. It might have been possible if she'd come earlier, he said, but now they were leaving in an hour.

Kim began to cry. Beside her, Hiep was crying as well. Kim trailed the man around the room, begging now: "Let me go with her!"

The official seemed unmoved. "You can't," he replied.

Kim and Hiep walked off together and sat down. Hiep was only seven years old. What if she forgot her mother's name and everything about her past? Quickly, Kim wrote down both of their names on a piece of paper, then strung the paper onto a cord and placed it around Hiep's neck. She whispered to the girl, "I'm sending you to America. If you go, you'll have a happy life. You can go to school."

Hiep shook her head stubbornly. She refused to leave her mother. Kim pressed on. "You'll go by plane and you'll be adopted and you'll work and then you'll have money and you can come back."

The child was sobbing now. Kim grew sterner. "If you stay here, the Communists will kill you and waste your life," she said. "You're young. You can go to school. I gave birth to you and now I'm letting you go because if you stay here, you will die."

An hour later, the children were piled onto a bus and driven to the airport. Kim followed the bus from behind, watching for a last glimpse of her daughter. After the plane departed, she went home. She was sick for days.

The news that Kim had relinquished Hiep had a profound effect on Han. She had heard of other women taking their children to Mẹ Quốc Tế, but when she thought of her own daughter, she had always resisted. Now that Kim's child had left, though, Han wavered. The two little girls had played together their entire lives. As con lai, they shared a bond that was as deep as the bond shared by sisters. With Hiep gone, Han had more trouble justifying her decision to keep Ngoc Anh in Vietnam.

A few days after Hiep had gone, Han sent her oldest son into central Danang to learn the procedures that one had to follow to send a child overseas. He came back with disturbing news. The Communist siege was imminent, and Mẹ Quốc Tế had shut down, evacuating all its staff and children south to the capital.

The boy, though, had returned with an address. It was still possible to send Ngoc Anh overseas, he said, but they would have to take her to Saigon themselves. Over the next few days, Han set a plan in motion, selling their possessions and preparing to take her entire family out of the city. She sold the wooden beds, the flimsy table where they ate their meals, their bowls and chopsticks, pots and pans. She even sold her house, the small but solid home that Huet had helped her build for her family—it seemed so long ago now. None of that mattered, she told herself. She needed money.

About the same time that Han was trying to decide what to do about her daughter in Danang, President Gerald Ford convened a session of the National Security Council in the Cabinet Room of the White House. It was the gray, chilly Friday afternoon of March 28, 1975. Easter was two days away, and the president had gone to an early morning Good Friday worship service at St. John's Episcopal Church near the White House.

That morning, the front page of the *New York Times* carried as its top story an assessment of the situation in Danang. "The North Vietnamese advance surged southward yesterday along the central coastal plain of South Vietnam," the reporter, Bernard Weinraub, had written. "Behind it, virtually all of the northern part of South Vietnam had been engulfed, with only the enclave of Danang, South Vietnam's second largest city, remaining in the hands of Saigon Government forces."

A grim group of a dozen or so men met with the president that afternoon. In addition to the president and Vice-President Nelson Rockefeller, the assembly included Secretary of State Henry Kissinger, CIA Director William Colby, and Chief of Staff Donald Rumsfeld. The current debate in Washington pitted administration officials eager to support the Saigon government against members of Congress who were determined to cut off aid. Publicly, at least, the Ford administration

continued to assert that there was still some hope of saving South Vietnam, but to do so the United States needed to continue its financial
support for at least another few years. Two days earlier, in fact, Kissinger
had argued at a news conference that, if the United States did not keep
sending money and supplies to Vietnam, it would "deliberately destroy
an ally by withholding aid from it in its moment of extremity."

In private, though, the president and his advisors seemed resigned to
the idea that that ally might have destroyed itself already. After a fruitless debate over whom to fault for the current military fiasco (Colby
said it was Vietnamese president Nguyen Van Thieu; Kissinger said
"the refugees clogged the road and the troops didn't know how to move
anyway"), Ford turned to his CIA director and put it simply: "You are
not optimistic about Danang being held?"

Colby was blunt. Even with the support of South Vietnamese Marines, he said, "It should fall within two weeks."

"What about the evacuation of civilians?" the president asked.

From their places around the Cabinet Room's mahogany table, the
administration officials could look out over the tranquility of the Rose
Garden in the late afternoon light. Vietnam, after all, was nine thousand miles away. But the CIA director's depiction of Danang made the
catastrophe completely vivid. "There have been terrible mob scenes,"
he told them, "both at the airport where they stormed loading aircraft
and at the port where they jammed aboard ships. Some of the military
have even shot their way on to the ships. A small number [have] been
loaded, but law and order has broken down completely and it is almost
impossible."

Such was the atmosphere in Danang when Han and her family made
their way down to the Han River. Her oldest daughter had stayed behind, but she still had eight children to keep safe. Ngoc Anh had spent
the last few weeks in hiding, and for her, the journey from her house
presented many peculiar fascinations: sunlight, traffic, diesel fumes and
heat, the calls of street vendors, who were still, despite the crisis, making
a bit of money selling bread and rice and fish. The water's edge, though,
was a scene of chaos. Normally a busy center of trade by sea, the Danang

waterfront had now become, for many Vietnamese, their only hope of escape. Anxious crowds swarmed the shore, trying to find a way to the refugee ships moored past the mouth of the river in the Bay of Danang. Because the Paris Peace Accords had prohibited the U.S. military from entering Vietnamese waters, the U.S. Military Sealift Command had dispatched merchant marine vessels to evacuate the refugees. Three days earlier, six barges had traveled north from the southern city of Vung Tau. A day after that, ten more ships joined the effort. Vessels that had hauled millions of tons of military cargo into the country over the past decade now faced the task of evacuating tens of thousands of refugees to relative safety farther south. In the shallows, refugees stood hoping for a ride, their trousers rolled to their knees, clutching children and the few bags and parcels they had managed to carry with them. Cramped fishing boats, sampans, barges, and tugs moved back and forth between the river and the bay, ferrying people to the ships offshore.

Once they made it out to where the ships were moored, the refugees had to find a way to board these enormous vessels, several of which measured over five hundred feet in length. Some people managed to come up the gangways. Others climbed ropes. Sometimes, the ship's crew lowered the boom and used cargo nets to haul up the passengers, who hung clustered together like so many fish. The least fortunate did not make the transfer at all, so dangerous was the task of disembarking one boat and boarding another, much larger one amid the thrashing waves of the South China Sea. People fell between vessels and disappeared. Parents lost their grip on their children and saw them drop to the waves below. Elderly people lost their footing and slipped. Out of the pandemonium came the anguished sounds of screaming and wailing.

Han had eight children with her, and they had truly become refugees now. She carried little besides the money she had earned from selling their possessions, a sack of manioc root, and some crackers to keep from starving. Their fellow passengers took particular pity on them, though, so unusual was the sight of a woman traveling alone with so many children. Somehow, the entire family found a space together in one of the dank cargo holds of the ship.

For a day, the children huddled around their mother. Outfitted for normal duty, the merchant marine vessels could carry as much as ten thousand tons of cargo in their sectionalized holds. For this mission, they had space for thousands of passengers, but they lacked the supplies and infrastructure necessary to transport so many people, great numbers of whom were old or sick and weak. They carried no food or toilets for anyone besides their own crew, and too little water. On top of that, the crews, which were civilians due to the mandates of the Peace Accords, had no way to control the hundreds of deserters from the South Vietnamese army who had boarded with the other refugees. Many of those men were well armed.

Han's children spent the voyage hot and thirsty, crying or sleeping, nibbling on the crackers their mother rationed. In a sense, they were among the lucky ones because they had only fled from Danang. Thousands of the refugees aboard the ship were the survivors of the massive exodus from the Central Highlands. These people had been on the road for weeks already. Many had walked hundreds of miles, carrying children and suitcases. By the time they made it to Danang, many were exhausted and ill. Without any form of medical care on board the ship, passengers began to die. The bodies lay there in the hold, the dead beside the living.

Han and her children sat. They didn't move. Looking up the stairs toward the sunlight, they could see other refugees massed on the deck above, but they couldn't go up for fresh air. The military deserters roamed the vessel, terrorizing the passengers. Not far from Han and her family, these men strung a dead body upside down from the rafters and tied a sack around its head. "If you're not quiet, this will happen to you," they announced to the passengers. They raised their rifles and shot at the body as if they were holding target practice. If someone spoke too loudly or cried, the armed men would yell, "Keep it down or we'll shoot you." Ngoc Anh clung to her mother. Han focused on her children and keeping them alive. She held them close. She didn't know where the ship was going or how long it would take to get there. She only knew she had to make it to Saigon.

CHAPTER 2

All Americans Go Home Now

When we think of fighting wars, children rarely come to mind.

P. W. SINGER

A few months after I attended the Vietnam Adoptee Network (VAN) reunion in Massachusetts in the spring of 2005, I was sitting in a hotel lobby in Saigon, waiting for my new research assistant, Thuy, to pull up outside on her motorbike. Over e-mail, I had hired Thuy (whose name is pronounced "Twee") to translate, schedule appointments, and ferry me around town. It was a dark September afternoon, threatening rain, and the street was, despite the ominous clouds, full of roaring motorbikes, honking trucks, and street vendors walking slowly along the sidewalk looking for customers to buy the sweet puddings or baguettes or lottery tickets they had for sale.

After the war ended in 1975, the new Vietnamese government changed the city's name from Saigon to Ho Chi Minh City, but, even thirty years later, Vietnamese still often use the former name. At this moment, the old term seemed right to me. All morning, I'd been reading David Butler's *Fall of Saigon*, which evokes the sadness, anger, and apprehension that spread across this city in March and April of 1975 as the Communist offensive moved ever closer. One evening, he wrote, a young boy pedaled past on a bicycle, "looked at me and waved his arm in a great sweep. In the dusk, I could just make out the precocious zeal in his face. 'Go home,' the boy cried. 'All Americans go home now, go home.' "

Looking out the floor-to-ceiling windows in my hotel lobby, it was clear that the city had now welcomed back the Americans, as well as the French, the Swedes, the British, the Australians, the Japanese—the list went on and on. Three decades after the end of the war, the city was now a hectic, hopeful place of skyscrapers, shopping centers, and even KFC. In fact, the only thing I had seen all day that reminded me of the war were the rusty American-era hangars that still sat beside the runway at the airport.

By the time Thuy pulled up, a slight rain had begun to fall. I pulled on my poncho before I even stepped outside. "Hello," I said, walking across the sidewalk toward her.

She got off her motorbike and we shook hands. "Yes. Hello, Ms. Dana," she said. She was wearing a rain poncho as big as a *hijab*, so it was only possible to see her face. She seemed to be in her late twenties, thirty at most. A pair of glasses covered her eyes, which were, in any case, almost completely inexpressive.

The two of us had been exchanging e-mails for the past few weeks. In searching for an assistant, I had narrowed my requirements to three duties: translation, scheduling, and driving. I needed a translator because, though I speak Vietnamese, I had trouble understanding the Southern Vietnamese accent, which also made it difficult to arrange meetings on the phone. I also couldn't drive a motorbike. Through a friend of a friend, I had found Thuy. "Nice to meet you, finally," I told her.

"Yes," she replied, and, though this response struck me as fairly unenthusiastic, her smile seemed kind enough. "Shall we go?" Thuy had succeeded in locating a woman whose name and phone number I'd gotten from a contact in the States. Now, we had 15 minutes to get to her house, and that wasn't a lot of time in a big city on a rainy day. I climbed onto the back of her motorbike and we drove away.

Within a minute or two, it was pouring. Water sprayed from between the wheels of the motorbikes and rushed in torrents along the edge of the road. Horns blared. The roar of the rain sounded like one more gigantic engine forcing itself through the city. With one hand, I held onto the edge of my seat. With the other, I tried to keep the hood of my poncho over my bicycle helmet. It was impossible to stay dry in a mess like that. Through it all, Thuy wove the motorbike steadily through the city. It was not yet two in the afternoon, but the sky was gray as dusk.

We were on our way to meet "Tuyet"—I've changed certain names to protect people's privacy—who had worked for Rosemary Taylor's agency in Saigon during the war. In all, Taylor and her foreign colleagues maintained operations in the city that included four nurseries and employed, by 1975, a staff of four hundred people. The first nursery, established in 1968, was called To Am, a Vietnamese term meaning "warm nest." Three years later, in 1971, the group opened a home for older children, Allambie, an Australian aboriginal term that meant "rest a while." In 1972, Taylor and her colleagues opened "Newhaven" for babies and toddlers. Finally, in 1973, the group established Hy Vong ("hope" in Vietnamese), which operated as an intensive-care nursery. Tuyet, as we would learn, worked at Newhaven between 1972 and the end of the war in 1975.

When we arrived, Tuyet, who was waiting for us in the doorway, began to laugh. "You must be wet all over!" she called as we pulled up, chiding us for being out in such a downpour. She was in her sixties, diminutive, bright-eyed, and exuberant. Thuy and I both tried to argue that the rain didn't bother us, but Tuyet was right.

After a few minutes, we finally settled down at a long table in Tuyet's front room, a cluttered space of magazines, books, souvenir candy tins, stacks of official-looking documents, half-empty cups of tea, and the little assemblages of fresh fruit, prayer papers, and incense that the Vietnamese use in offerings to their ancestors. Tuyet poured us each a steaming cup of tea.

Before coming to Vietnam, I had read as many accounts of Operation Babylift as I could find. Several foreigners, including Rosemary Taylor, had published memoirs, but the Vietnamese in these stories—

caregivers, birth parents, even the children—played secondary roles. As soon as Tuyet began to talk, the nursery, a gracious villa, came to life. Now I could imagine, in the grand salons, rows of cribs and baby baskets holding dozens of infants, some wheezing from the effects of asthma and other bronchial diseases. The sounds of crying, laughter, coughing, and babbling floated up and down the stairs, combined with the smells of diapers and urine, soapy laundry, boiling vegetables, and steaming rice.

"Watching four children is not easy!" Tuyet reminded us. On many of her shifts, she had been responsible for four toddlers at the same time. I thought of Rosemary Taylor's descriptions of the sweet "room mothers" who brought the children their cups of milk before bed. It wasn't until now, though, that I could really picture it. "There were times when I'd take them out to play," Tuyet said, "and they'd dirty their diapers and I'd have to go right back in and change them. As soon as this one finished pooping, that one would poop. As soon as this one finished peeing, then that one would pee!"

I stared at her. "Did you ever feel that it was too much to manage?"

She threw her head back. "It was always too much!" she said, laughing. "But it was really fun."

As we talked, I was startled at how clearly Tuyet could remember individual children, even after thirty years.

"Of course, I remember," she said, then added, as if to explain, "They called me 'Mom.'"

At that moment, Tuyet got up, hurried across the room, and found a scrapbook. She came back and opened it for me, pointing to various children who had been in her care. In recent years, she told me, some of the adoptees had returned to Vietnam and visited her. "Look at this boy." It was a photo of a naked child, his stomach hugely distended, his arms and legs thin as sticks, his skin covered with boils. He looked like an infant, but he was actually much older. Before she brought out the scrapbook, it was easy enough to picture the orphanage as merely a happy place, full of laughing, wiggly children. The photo reminded me of the grimness of the situation.

Tuyet ran her finger across the face of the child in the photo. "He was in Newhaven," she said quietly, adding that the medical staff had squeezed open his boils and found nothing but pus, a sign of infection. Then, she suddenly turned her attention to a photograph right next to that one, a picture of a smiling child. "This is him after a few months. Doesn't he look healthy?"

He did look healthy, and I was impressed by the obvious success of his care. My eyes drifted back to the "before" photo, though. "Were you worried that he might die?" I asked.

She shook her head. "No, because he looked strong," she said. "Although he was covered with boils, his face was still bright. It didn't have the sluggishness of a child who was near death." I took another look at the boy's face. She was right. The horror of his body obscured his expression, but, looking closer, I could see it. He did look alert.

"He's in Iraq now," Tuyet said, her tone so nonchalant that she could have been telling me he'd just run out to the store to pick up eggs. "He's never been back to Vietnam, because he's in the army."

The idea—the irony—of this Vietnamese war victim ending up a soldier in Iraq was more than I could absorb at that moment. And, to be honest, I was still distracted by the proposition that you could judge a child's health by the expression on his face. I looked at Thuy for assistance. "Could you ask Tuyet to explain more clearly how she could foresee that a baby wouldn't die?"

Thuy asked Tuyet and, for a moment, they discussed the issue in Vietnamese.

"I was sure he wouldn't die," Tuyet finally responded.

I looked at Thuy for help on this one, but her face was blank. She didn't seem any more invested in the question than Tuyet was. "Did he look intelligent?" I pressed on.

Tuyet sighed patiently. "You know when a child could die," she said, picking up the scrapbook again and paging through it until she found a picture of another ill child. "Here, for example—this little one died. The eyes aren't clear." She continued through the book, pointing at other pictures. "That one died. This one also died. I buried this one. I buried this one in a cemetery that has been completely destroyed now. I went in a car to bury him."

Eventually, I brought up the subject of adoption. The fact was that Tuyet's job lay in helping children become healthy enough to leave their homeland forever. "When the children went away, did you feel that they would have better care overseas?" I asked.

Tuyet nodded. "I was glad when they left," she replied, "because they would have adoptive parents to raise them." The look in her eyes was firm and certain, revealing a practicality that, over the next few months, I would see again among the women, like Tuyet, who had cared for these children in the orphanages. They seemed convinced that life abroad was better for these kids, because life in Vietnam was just too hopeless.

But still, Tuyet, who had no children of her own, suffered when they went away. On the days of their departure, she told me, she refused to hold them. If she had held them, she worried that she wouldn't let them go. "Oh, God," she said. "I stood watching them leave and I cried."

CHAPTER 3

A Sea of Human Need

*There is a mandate struggling to register itself. Events in Vietnam have
loosed the mighty river of American decency, a spontaneous flood of desire to put
the government in the service of an unambiguously good cause, like helping the
homeless, the tempest-tossed, the wretched refuse of Vietnam's teeming shores.*

Columnist GEORGE F. WILL, April 10, 1975

While Han and her children had rushed to get themselves out of Danang during those last few days of March, Ed Daly, the owner of the cargo firm World Airways, rushed in. Or, more precisely, he rushed in so that he could bring as many refugees—specifically women and children— out of the city as possible. Later, people who knew Daly, or had merely read about him, would debate what might have motivated the man to risk his life in such an effort. Was he a big-hearted humanitarian who, seeing that people were suffering in Danang, committed his money and airline to the effort to save them? Was he a thrill-seeker looking for a last adventure before the war ended? Was he a savvy businessman who realized the public relations value of saving refugees and having those efforts recorded on TV? Whatever his reasons, the gun-toting, cigar-chomping Daly, a fifty-two-year-old California-based native-born Irishman, had long been one of the most prominent—and colorful— foreigners working in Vietnam. He had made millions from the U.S.

27

government by ferrying military supplies and troops into and around
Southeast Asia. In late March, the United States offered him a contract
to ferry twenty planeloads of refugees from Danang. Within a few days,
however, the authorities had come to consider the flights too risky and
cut off the contract. Daly understood their concerns. His own staff had
had to use Mace to maintain order among the panicked refugees on the
ground in Danang. But the airline executive, determined to continue
with the evacuation, decided to attempt the flights anyway.

Early on the morning of March 29, two of Daly's World Airways
727s took off from Saigon and headed north toward Danang. Daly himself flew in the lead jet, accompanied by three flight attendants and a few
members of his staff. The jets also carried a contingent of reporters that
included representatives from CBS News, United Press International,
and the British media. Despite the obvious dangers, Daly didn't bring
along any guards to maintain security. He did, though, carry a gun.

The two-hour flight north went smoothly, and when the first jet approached the runway, those on board were surprised to look down on
a virtually empty airfield. The plane touched down, braking as it raced
along the tarmac. Just then, people began to appear on the ground. For
a moment, those on board could see only a few individuals moving toward the airplane. Then, they saw more. Dozens, then hundreds, then,
thousands and thousands emerged from bunkers and headed across the
airfield toward the plane. They came on foot, in trucks and military
jeeps, personnel carriers and tanks. They rode bikes and motorbikes.
Many of the vehicles were full of soldiers—former South Vietnamese
military men who had deserted their positions when the war began to
go awry—but whole families were out there, too. Women with babies.
Old people. The wounded on crutches, hobbling along the tarmac. All
of Danang, the entire mass of humanity, seemed to be rushing toward
the airplane. Some began to shoot at it, too.

Daly and his crew devised a plan. He and Joe Hrezo, World Airways'
station chief at Clark Air Force Base in the Philippines, would go out the
back stairway, line people up on the tarmac, and then board the plane
from the rear. But the idea that things would proceed in an orderly man-

ner proved to be wildly optimistic. Within seconds, the plan fell apart. As the stairs descended, the throng on the ground clambered over it, fighting each other to get inside the plane. The mob surrounded Daly, mauling him and ripping his clothes. The Irishman fired into the air, trying to bring the scene to order. Then he ran out of bullets and swung the gun threateningly, hoping that the show of it might intimidate the crowd. When he saw one man pull a woman off the railing, then step on top of her to get himself on board, Daly slammed the man's head with the butt of his gun. The whizzing of bullets mixed with the roar of thousands of people pressing toward the aircraft. Daly and his crew had flown to Danang to evacuate the most vulnerable victims of war— women and children. Instead, they had to fight off South Vietnamese soldiers determined to get on board themselves. Jan Wollett, Daly's chief flight attendant, later described the scene to the journalist Larry Engelmann:

> [a] family of five was running a few feet from me, reaching out for help to get on board. It was a mother and a father and two little children and a baby in the mother's arms. I could see the fear in all of their faces as they ran and reached out for me. I reached back to grab the mother's hand, but before I could get it, a man running behind them shot all five of them and they fell and were trampled by the crowd. The last I saw of them they were disappearing under people's feet. There were just several loud shots and they were gone—all five of them. And the man who shot them stepped on them to get closer to the air stair. He ran them down and jumped onto the air stair and ran up into the aircraft.

The crowd would soon overwhelm the entire plane. The pilot, realizing that his crew was now in danger, began to taxi for takeoff, even though the rear stair remained down, with Ed Daly on it. As the plane gained speed, Daly and his colleagues pushed themselves up the stairs and made it to safety just as the plane took off. Others weren't so lucky. One man clung to the bottom stairs as the plane gained altitude. At about six hundred feet, he lost his grip and fell. Daly and Hrezo wrestled the stairs closed, extricating another man whose body was stuck in the apparatus. Then they pulled off their belts and buckled them around the damaged stairway to keep it shut.

In the 727's few minutes on the ground, hundreds of people had fought their way on board. Up to seven now jammed into each of the three-seat rows. Down below, others had stowed themselves in the aircraft's cargo pits and wheel wells. It didn't take much for the pilots to surmise that people had lodged themselves in the landing gear. Indeed, a body had become wedged there, keeping the wheels from locking in place. In the end, the damaged 727, which had a maximum carrying capacity of 133 people, departed for Saigon with 358 people on it, almost every one of them an adult male. Also on board were the countless weapons carried on by these former soldiers of the South Vietnamese military. Hand grenades rolled up and down the aisle as the aircraft banked and turned.

Jan Wollett tried to calm the people who had managed to get on the plane. As she moved down the aisle, she noticed "a horrible look" on many faces. "Finally," she thought, "they realized what they had just done." These former soldiers had just killed their own compatriots to save themselves. Desperate, the men peppered Wollett and the other flight attendants with a single question: "Will another plane come?" they asked. The flight attendants lied. Yes, they said. Other planes would come.

Ed Daly was a businessman, and in business one defines success by the accomplishment of concrete goals—fly to Danang, evacuate women and children, bring them safely to Saigon. Daly's flight had failed in one central aspect of its mission—the part about women and children. Yet businesspeople also learn to put setbacks in a more positive light. Years later, in describing the events of March 29, 1975, World Airways' corporate literature proclaimed that "Daly, on his own, flew [World Airways] 727s to Da Nang to rescue women and children. . . . The 'Last Flight From Danang' garnered worldwide media attention as Daly and World crew fought off thousands of would-be passengers seeking refuge on the aircraft, dodged bullets and grenades, and ultimately carried more than 300 people to safety in Saigon."

How many of those passengers were actually women or children? In the sad final tally, only eleven.

After some beers, dinner with her boss, and a round of interviews with international reporters, flight attendant Jan Wollett went to bed. Her colleague Joe Hrezo, feeling grateful to be alive, went out to a bar and "found a girlfriend." And Ed Daly got back to work.

That morning, Daly had been awake before dawn. Then he'd flown to Danang, fended off the horde of panicked former soldiers, flown back to Saigon on a damaged plane, and faced a mob of reporters when he got there. He still had his gun with him, too, and when the throng of journalists annoyed him, he banged it on a table and announced, as Hrezo later remembered, "I want to have your attention here or somebody's going to get shot." Some reporters grew peeved by Daly's bluster and left in a huff, but most stayed to listen. By the next day, the story of Daly's flight from Danang would be spread across the front page of morning papers all over the world.

The interviews finished late in the evening. At that point, the airline executive might have finally gone to bed. But then he received a request for one more meeting. FFAC, the agency that sponsored the largest number of adoptions from Vietnam, had heard news of the flight to Danang. Would Mr. Daly be willing to meet with them?

Wende Grant, Rosemary Taylor's colleague who ran the agency's Colorado headquarters, was pleased by Daly's response. Not only would he meet with her, but he suggested that she come right over. Grant immediately agreed. Over the past few days, FFAC's administrators had been searching for a way to evacuate all six hundred of the children in their orphanages from Vietnam. It was a complicated prospect, and for it to succeed, three things had to fall into place at the exact same time: they needed exit permits from the South Vietnamese authorities, entry authorizations from countries overseas, and transportation.

Grant hoped that Daly could help with the third requirement—

airplanes. She considered Daly's flight to Danang a failure—after all, he'd "rescued" a planeload of South Vietnamese military deserters—but she felt convinced of his concern for children. Hoping that such concern would translate into transportation for their kids, Grant and her colleague Elaine Moir ignored the city's curfew and hurried over to Daly's suite at the Caravelle Hotel.

In wartime Saigon, the Caravelle enjoyed the kind of landmark status reserved for establishments like the Waldorf in New York and the Ritz in Paris. The hotel, which opened in 1959, offered its guests such luxuries as an exclusive rooftop bar, vintage wines from France, and, perhaps most appreciated, air conditioning. At one time or another, the embassies of Australia and New Zealand had operated from this address, and the news agencies NBC, CBS, and ABC had all located their headquarters here.

For Grant and Moir, stepping into the opulent lobby of the Caravelle must have felt like stepping out of the war and into peace. Inside the hotel, the tumult of the outside world became muted. True, the establishment had not managed to evade the war altogether. In fact, a bomb blasted through the hotel's fifth floor in 1964. Now, as the fighting moved closer to the streets of Saigon, patrons of the rooftop bar reputedly could witness the flash and roar of firefights without getting up from their tables. But, still, the serene corridors of the Caravelle offered a luxurious contrast to the grinding poverty that Grant and Moir faced every day as they worked with Rosemary Taylor to keep FFAC's nurseries running in Saigon.

Although Grant still lived in Colorado, she made regular trips to Vietnam, and only two weeks before, she had evacuated several dozen Cambodian orphans from Phnom Penh, including a pair of twins she planned to adopt herself. The experience had unsettled her, not merely because of the personal danger she faced going into Cambodia's capital during fierce fighting, but also because she had witnessed the agony of Cambodian parents who understood that, when the Khmer Rouge overtook the city, both they and their children would die.

"A young Cambodian physician in the Ministry of [the] Interior was responsible for signing the [orphan] children's joint passport and exit authorization," Grant later wrote. "As he spoke with [Grant's colleague] Dolly Charet in French, I saw that his body was twitching uncontrollably; Dolly explained later that the man knew he would be killed. He was worried about being able to fulfill his duties until the end and wanted to be sure someone would care for his infant son. He had asked Dolly if she would adopt the child if he could get him out of the country."

Neither Charet nor Grant was willing to take the man's son. Their mission was to rescue orphans, not children who had parents to care for them. Still, Grant recognized the moral implications of FFAC's policy. "We were trying to get people to put forth extra effort to save forty-three orphans," she acknowledged, "knowing there were tens of thousands, including their own children, who would not be saved." Over the next few weeks, as the war in Vietnam came to its crashing end, this clear distinction—orphan or not?—would become, for many who ran adoption agencies, more blurred.

When Grant arrived at Ed Daly's suite that evening, then, they had a number of things in common. Both carried the emotional scars of a recent brutal experience of war. They were both foreigners in Vietnam. Both had risked their own lives to save others. And both were savvy, clear-sighted, and capable people. Still, they didn't understand each other very well.

The meeting got off to an awkward start. The small group of foreign women who ran FFAC had developed a reputation around Saigon as both zealously committed and intensely driven. They went about their work with a fervor that, since the Communist offensive began a few weeks earlier, had developed into an all-consuming passion to get their children out of Vietnam. Unlike the diplomats, military advisors, and businesspeople who could flit around behind the scenes and somehow make things happen, FFAC was poor and powerless, operating from a well of single-minded desperation. When its foreign volunteers weren't working feverishly to accomplish their goals, they engaged in a constant discussion among themselves over how much time they had left to complete their evacuation.

The airline executive, on the other hand, didn't seem to be in *any* hurry. Ed Daly was a raconteur, and the drama he felt like recounting was the adventure of his flight to Danang that morning. With Grant and Moir as his audience, Daly went over the details two, three, even four times. Precious seconds ticked by. The women heard yet again about the mob of people, the crush on the airstair, and the sudden, precipitous takeoff with Daly pulling himself back into the cabin, step by treacherous step. The serene atmosphere of the Caravelle could barely contain Ed Daly's nearly frantic excitement.

Somehow, finally, Grant managed to make her request. Her needs were, after all, quite simple. FFAC had six hundred children to evacuate from Vietnam. Would Daly fly them out?

Ed Daly said he would.

He promised her a 747, too. The wide-bodied jumbo jet was the largest passenger aircraft in the sky.

At 2:30 a.m., Grant and Moir stepped from the gleaming lobby of the Caravelle and back into the anxious streets of Saigon. They were bewildered by the speed with which Daly had agreed to their request. But they also felt hopeful.

The titles of the two largest foreign-run adoption agencies in Vietnam sounded confoundingly similar: Friends For All Children (FFAC) and Friends of the Children of Vietnam (FCVN). Besides the easy-to-confuse names, the two agencies operated in comparable ways. Both were based in Colorado, volunteer-run, and dependent on donations. Both maintained nurseries in Saigon, received most of their children from poor Catholic-run orphanages in the provinces, and relied on extensive, unofficial networks of contacts to keep their operations going. Unlike the large charities that came to sponsor adoptions from Vietnam late in the war—Catholic Relief Services, the Holt Adoption Program, and World Vision, for example—neither FFAC nor FCVN served under the umbrella of a long-established international organization. They had both emerged in direct response to the war in Vietnam.

The two agencies were related, let's say, but they barely spoke to each other. And Rosemary Taylor had, at different times, run the Saigon operations of both.

Taylor had come to South Vietnam in 1967 when the Australian Council of Churches offered her a position as an educational social worker. She arrived in Saigon with a wide-ranging, if somewhat scattered, resume that included working as a psychiatric research assistant in England, volunteering at a Jesuit Mission school in Alaska, and teaching chemistry and algebra to Canadian twelfth-graders. In Vietnam, she immediately demonstrated an independent spirit and impatience with injustice that would mark her entire career there. Only a few weeks after her arrival, she wrote an angry letter to her superiors back in Australia, blasting the behavior of her boss in Saigon as a "parody" of Christianity. "I'm not exaggerating," Taylor wrote. "Would you believe that in this time of war when everything is upside down, when the servants themselves sleep in the garage and eat off packing-cases in our backyard . . . the Director and his wife [complain] because our cook never serves 'hors-d'oeuvre.'"

Before too long, Taylor found herself out of a job. She was new to Vietnam, tortured by dysentery, unemployed, and alone in a country at war. At that moment, most people would have packed up and gone home. But Rosemary Taylor had the sort of character that could regard her present measly circumstances with cool objectivity. From her point of view, her situation offered a simple choice: leave now or commit herself entirely to this country. "It would be illogical—absurd, even—to choose to remain in such uncomfortable circumstances without a strong conviction that one's presence was useful," Taylor decided, demonstrating a quality that would set her apart from so many foreigners in this country. She could handle with equanimity and cool reason the kinds of stressful situations that would completely derail many others, even those with greater knowledge and experience than she had.

In the end, Taylor decided to stay. "I was aware that I must have appeared somewhat of an 'adventuress,' or at best an amateur, to the personnel of more established organizations," she later admitted. "But somehow it didn't occur to me to give up. There was a sea of human need around me; I knew I had the resources to respond, though how to do so had yet to become clear."

Over the next few months, Taylor's own mission would begin to make itself clear. She began to live in a small room in the compound of the Catholic-run Phu My shelter for the poor, and she quickly took up the task of helping her destitute fellow residents. Through her contacts within the expatriate community, she managed to procure food and supplies. U.S. soldiers spent their days off organizing parties and picnics for the children in Phu My's orphanage, and Taylor came to believe that the soldiers' avid enthusiasm emerged from the fact that they saw these activities as "the only way that they could justify their presence in Vietnam."

As the months passed, however, Taylor became convinced that the orphanage system was merely a temporary solution to an intractable problem. It pained her to see so many children wasting away in institutions. Then, in late 1967, she met an aid worker for Terre des Hommes, a Swiss organization that concentrated its efforts on relief work and also arranged occasional adoptions with families overseas. Taylor soon began assisting with the adoptions herself. By the end of the year, Taylor had taken over the responsibility of coordinating them.

Rosemary Taylor, who later became the most forceful and impassioned advocate for international adoption in Vietnam, began her own education on the subject during these early days at Phu My. She had "begun to appreciate the dimensions of the problem of abandoned and orphan children," Taylor wrote, adding,

> [N]othing in my previous experience or reading had prepared me for this. I was coming into contact with hundreds of newborn babies with no identity and no prospects. There were healthy and handicapped babies; the fully Vietnamese and the mixed-race, the legitimate and the illegitimate. Poverty, illegitimacy, birth defects, and the fact that the children were never 'wanted' would account for most of the abandonments, but there were also a few orphaned through the death of the mother, or abandoned by a wealthier family because of an inauspicious birth date.

Taylor had clearly found her calling. What began as the sporadic departure of three or four children leaving Vietnam at a time had, five years later in 1972, turned into a diaspora. By then, Taylor had placed over a thousand Vietnamese children with families overseas. She was, by the end of that year, running an extensive operation that included three nurseries in Saigon and a staff of one hundred Vietnamese who, along with a small group of foreign volunteers, were caring for hundreds of children. Taylor had also become a prominent authority on adoption policy, one to whom U.S. officials looked for guidance as they tried to map out legislation.

By now, Taylor also had vital support in her efforts. A friend from Australia, Margaret Moses, had joined Taylor in Vietnam and, together, the two women articulated the philosophy behind their mission. In the face of governments that often seemed to willfully ignore the plight of children in war zones, Moses had proposed what she called "an idea as old as time," namely, that governments who could not protect the lives of their children should "abdicate responsibility" to volunteers whose only responsibility "would be to let the children live, and to send them to where they could." In a sense, then, Taylor, Moses, and their foreign colleagues in Vietnam had become those volunteers.

Besides helping Taylor to promote the intellectual underpinning for their work in Vietnam, Moses offered an emotional warmth to the Vietnamese staff that the more reserved Taylor couldn't provide. Jobs in the nurseries demanded grueling labor and Rosemary Taylor, as the director, had high expectations for everyone who worked there. "It was difficult, particularly in [the] early years," she wrote, "to find local staff who were willing to implement our ideas of child care; they could not easily accept that mere orphan children deserved such consideration while their own children or siblings had even less." At one point, citing such differences in attitude, Taylor dismissed half of her Vietnamese staff and replaced them with new employees who were more sympathetic to her group's mission.

Even those caregivers who managed to retain their employment sometimes found themselves at their physical and emotional limits, and they worried about how their boss would judge them. One member of the Vietnamese staff, who deeply respected Taylor, nonetheless described the anxiety that she and other locals felt about doing something wrong. Taylor's nurseries prioritized the care of the children over everything else, an ideology somewhat at odds with Vietnamese culture, which considered children to be a part of the family but not necessarily its most precious element. "We had to be very careful," the staffer explained. "For example, if you ate a child's porridge, you'd be fired. If you took even a napkin or clothes from a child, you'd be fired. You had to take care of them very carefully. . . . [Rosemary] didn't say much; she didn't shout at anyone, but everyone was scared of her. She looked serious and she was powerful."

Given the awe, and in some cases fear, that many on staff felt toward Taylor, Margaret Moses provided a welcome warmth. The two women, in fact, played quite different though very compatible roles in their organization. One former American staffer believed that Rosemary Taylor was "ultimately a very shy person" who didn't mix well with others, while Margaret Moses "would put you under her wing so that you would understand what was going on." The American colleague described Moses as "very outspoken, very down-to-earth, very astute and aware. And always yearning for something."

For better or worse, Margaret Moses seemed to need human contact in a way that the more reclusive Taylor did not. Another foreign volunteer suspected that Moses suffered from severe loneliness and remembered her calling herself a "failed nun." This colleague came to think that Taylor and Moses had committed themselves to their work in Vietnam for very different reasons. While Rosemary Taylor was fighting "for justice," Margaret Moses might have been trying "to save her soul." The means were similar, but the goals were very different.

In the summer of 1973, Rosemary Taylor made a formal association with the Friends of the Children of Vietnam (FCVN). For the past few years, the agency had sent Taylor's nurseries money and supplies from its Denver headquarters and found potential adoptive families for her children. Now the relationship became official. Taylor began to work closely with Wende Grant, who was in charge of FCVN's adoption activities in Denver.

Unfortunately, FCVN's U.S. office was becoming factionalized over bitter disagreements about resources. In October 1973, the agency split into two parts. As Grant perceived the agreement, the original FCVN would focus on support services for Vietnamese children, while the new group, run by Grant and Taylor, would call itself Friends For All Children (FFAC) and would concentrate on adoptions. It quickly became clear, however, that the original FCVN did not, after all, intend to stop arranging adoptions. Instead, FCVN hired its own staff and the two groups became competitors. The only thing both sides seemed able to agree upon was the fact that the name of the new organization, FFAC, which had been selected with the idea of retaining connections between two "sister" programs, now created near-constant confusion over which group was which. By that time, however, it was too late for either group to change its name.

In March 1974, FCVN sent to Vietnam its first staff person, Ross Meador, a good-humored, energetic, and apparently quite gutsy 19-year-old from California. A month later, Cherie Clark and her family arrived and, together, they began to turn a rented villa into a children's center. Now Saigon had two Colorado-based agencies organizing adoptions from Vietnam. By the time the Communist offensive began in March 1975, the two groups were competing for seats on airplanes that could take their children out of Vietnam.

Wende Grant had been unsure if she could trust the fast-talking Ed Daly. Within hours, those worries proved correct. The morning after she met him was Easter Sunday, March 30, and already the offer had changed. Now, instead of the promised jumbo jet, Daly decided to fly out two sets of children on two different planes, one for those destined for Australia or Europe, and the second for those headed to Canada or the United States. Then, his plan changed again. Daly would provide one plane and fly three hundred children. Then, he could offer nothing. By the morning of Wednesday, April 2, four days after their first meeting, a new plan had emerged: Daly had a DC-8 ready to evacuate, as Taylor and Grant later remembered it, "600 children—not one less —who were to be boarded in half-an-hour for the most dramatic, action-packed television coverage." Taylor and Grant, completely exasperated with Daly now, refused his offer. In their view, "[the] conditions were physically impossible. We could never board so many children in such a short time, and we could not provide adequate escorts for 600 children."

Given the difficulty of meeting Daly's conditions, Taylor and Grant were probably just being cautious, but another player acting in the shadows probably helped nudge the FFAC administrators away from Daly's plane. Over the past few days, the World Airways president's relations with the U.S. government had completely deteriorated. Surely, his rash and unauthorized flight to Danang had caused some to question his motives. And the news that he'd called Graham Martin, the U.S. ambassador to Vietnam, "nothing but a used-car salesman"—to his face—didn't help, either. The U.S. government did not want Daly involved in any aspect of the evacuation of children from Vietnam. U.S. officials were finally ready to set in motion their own plan to get them out.

It was April 1, and Alex Stalcup, chief resident in the department of pediatrics at the University of California, San Francisco (UCSF), thought that the chair of his department, Mel Grumbach, was pulling an April Fool's Day prank on him. Grumbach had stopped Stalcup in a UCSF hallway and said, "I got a call from people over at the Presidio. They've got some sick orphans." The story that Grumbach went on to tell sounded too strange to believe: hundreds, perhaps thousands, of orphans from Vietnam would be arriving on planes in the coming days and taken to the U.S. army post at the Presidio, in San Francisco. Most of the children were in bad shape physically. All would need medical attention.

As the two talked, Stalcup realized Grumbach wasn't joking. The young pediatrician knew, of course, about the deteriorating situation in Southeast Asia, and the possibility that the government of South Vietnam would soon collapse completely. In the face of the chaos that had begun to envelop that country, the idea that planeloads of refugee children would suddenly arrive on U.S. shores didn't seem too far-fetched. A meeting was about to take place at the Presidio, Grumbach explained. "Would you go over and check it out?"

Stalcup drove over to the Presidio. First established by the U.S. Army in the 1840s, the post at the Presidio spread across some of the most beautiful land in San Francisco, a hill sloping down toward the bay and the Golden Gate Bridge that spanned it. When Stalcup arrived, he walked into a meeting crowded with people. Many represented the nongovernmental organizations that ran various orphanages in Vietnam. Others came from the military post. And a few worked for Ed Daly's World Airways, which was based in Oakland, across the bay. At the center of the mass of people stood a young woman, Charlotte Behrendt, whom Stalcup came to learn was Ed Daly's daughter.

Behrendt explained that a World Airways jet full of children would arrive at the Oakland airport within a day or two at most. She needed food, beds, and medical attention for them. They had all been placed for adoption, but they needed somewhere to stay until they could be united with their new families. Oh, and they were sick, too. Hepatitis, measles, chicken pox: these children suffered from the kinds of diseases that were beginning to disappear from the daily rounds of pediatricians in the United States.

By the time the meeting concluded, Stalcup, a twenty-nine-year-old Californian with two young children of his own, had been elected medical director of a new organization, SPOVO, an acronym that stood for Support for the Orphans of Vietnam.

Cherie Clark didn't know about any of this yet. The Saigon director of FCVN had arrived in Vietnam only eleven months before, and she felt like she was playing a constant game of catch-up. In name, her organization had operated in the country for years already. But, like a high-tech tank without an engine, the agency's momentum had stalled when Rosemary Taylor stopped working with it. Essentially, Clark, Ross Meador, and their colleagues had had to cobble a new agency out of nothing. While Taylor's FFAC now ran four nurseries with a local staff of hundreds and fifteen foreign volunteers, Clark had very few American colleagues and a small Vietnamese staff to help her run FCVN's program. In the months since she'd arrived in Saigon, disarray in the city and bad luck had forced the agency to move its headquarters twice, most recently only five months before. By early April, FCVN was running two facilities—one in Saigon itself and one that housed older children in Thu Duc, on the outskirts of town. The agency also maintained an extensive foster-care system, putting FCVN children with local families until their adoption paperwork could be completed and they could travel abroad. All together, FCVN had hundreds of children in its care and, like Taylor and Grant, Cherie Clark was now trying to evacuate every one of those children from Vietnam.

FCVN had, over the past few months, managed to achieve a lot. But Clark often felt that she did not receive accurate information from U.S. authorities in Saigon. For days, she had been trying to wrangle visas for her wards to enter the United States. Throughout that time, U.S. officials denied her requests to expedite these visas. Over and over, they told her that, despite the crisis overtaking South Vietnam, all visas still had to go through the normal channels, which took months. Clark—like everyone else in Saigon at that time—knew she didn't have months, and she begged officials to ease up on their policies.

What Cherie Clark couldn't know, of course, was that her plea cut to the very core of the debate then raging among high-level U.S. diplomats. With the collapse of South Vietnam imminent, many of these officials argued that the time had come to begin a mass evacuation, which would include children slated for adoption. Others, however, most notably U.S. ambassador Graham Martin himself—Ed Daly's "used-car salesman"—believed that beginning an evacuation now would set off a panic in Saigon, exacerbating the chaos and violence. A decision to expedite visas for adoptive children would amount to a tacit agreement to put the large-scale evacuation into play. While the debate raged, U.S. officials continued to pretend that they were conducting business as usual.

On the morning of April 2, Cherie Clark and her husband, Tom, got back into FCVN's van and tried again to find a way to evacuate their children. Like everyone in Saigon, she was hearing rumors that an evacuation would soon begin. Without knowing what was taking place behind the scenes, however, she could not understand why U.S. officials would continue to deny it. Every minute of delay, she felt, put her children in greater danger. For hours, the Clarks crisscrossed the city to meet with officials who they hoped might help them. Once again, the effort seemed futile and the couple had to drive back to the FCVN headquarters in despair.

As the van pulled through the gates leading to the large French-era villa they had rented on Tran Ky Xuong Street in the Gia Dinh district of Saigon, the agency's social worker, Thuy, ran outside waving a piece of paper in her hand. It was a copy of a letter to South Vietnam's prime minister, Tran Thien Khiem, from the country's deputy prime minister, Dr. Phan Quang Dan. Clark recognized immediately that the contents were "extraordinary" because, for the first time, they offered a clear plan for getting her children out of Vietnam. The letter, in translation, read:

Dear Mr. Prime Minister,

At the present time, approximately 1,400 orphans have been brought to Saigon, and are being cared for by international welfare agencies prior to being taken to foreign countries where they will be placed with permanent adoptive parents. At present, operations of the Ministry of Social Welfare and Hamlet Building and the Inter-ministerial War Victims Relief Committee have been severely hampered by some complicated situations, among which requiring immediate resolution are the problems. The orphans cited above which must be handled in conjunction with many other important difficulties that we are faced with. Moreover, the whole question of collective emigration of this number of orphans mentioned above is further exciting world opinion, particularly in the United States, much to the benefit of the Republic of Vietnam.

Right now, there are two 727's belonging to World Airways that have been waiting all night at the Tan Son Nhut airport, prepared to transport free of charge the emigrating orphans. Mr. Daly, the President of the above mentioned airlines, is an international figure. The American Ambassador has also interceded with me to permit the orphans to leave the country together. He stressed, in addition to this emigration issue, how a million refugees and war victims fleeing the areas taken over by the communists would help to turn American public opinion regarding Vietnam, particularly the orphans arriving in the United States, given extensive TV and press coverage with narrated reports from witnesses of the situation, would have considerable influence.

If you agree, Mr. Prime Minister, to approve the emigration of the orphans mentioned above, the Ministry of Social Welfare and Hamlet Building will coordinate with USAID to carefully monitor and control the international welfare agencies' implementation of this operation.

The letter, including the signatures of both the deputy and prime ministers, was marked, "Approved." A second letter accompanied Dan's, this one from another South Vietnamese official, who advised Clark to bring to the office of social welfare a list of all the FCVN children she wished to transport overseas. Within a week, the contents of Dan's letter—and particularly its hope to "turn American public opinion" —would be blasted across the pages of U.S. newspapers amid accusations that U.S. and South Vietnamese officials were evacuating children as a political maneuver to gain international sympathy for South Vietnam.

Clark didn't know such things, and she probably wouldn't have cared. She was focused on getting her children out of the country. Now, she and her husband rushed to the office of the U.S. Agency for International Development (USAID) to confirm the news.

Over the course of her time in Saigon, Clark had come to know many of the U.S. officials who worked on adoption matters. Now, one of them at USAID, Robert King, told her that, indeed, the South Vietnamese government had approved the evacuation of the children, and that the U.S. government would, finally, expedite visas as well.

Clark couldn't believe it. "Just like that?" She asked. "Nothing else?"

Actually, King told her, there was something else. She would have to find a plane.

No problem, Clark responded. She had the letter from the prime minister saying that Ed Daly had two planes on the ground right then, waiting for children to board.

King dismissed that idea in an instant. The seats on Ed Daly's flight were taken, he said. Rosemary Taylor had claimed them for her own children, who would be flying out that very day.

For the rest of the meeting with King, Clark maintained her composure. Inside, though, she was seething. King had confirmed what she had suspected all along: some kind of hierarchy existed among the adoption agencies in Vietnam. Rosemary Taylor enjoyed access to critical information from the U.S. government, while Clark did not.

As it turned out, the USAID officials lacked the most up-to-date information as well. Within a few hours, Clark, who had by now grown desperate, received a phone call with some news. FFAC had ended up rejecting the seats on Daly's plane. The Clarks and Ross Meador immediately rushed over to Tan Son Nhut Airport to approach Daly for a ride.

They found the airline executive in a crowded, smoke-filled airport cafeteria, surrounded by journalists and his own staff. He was furious, having only recently heard of Rosemary Taylor's refusal of his offer of a plane. Now, he sat ranting about Taylor's agency and the U.S. government.

When the Clarks and Meador entered the room, Daly, a bearish, red-faced man in a rumpled hat, stared at them suspiciously. Cherie Clark immediately noticed what he held in his hands: a bottle of Johnnie Walker in one and a handgun in the other.

She stepped forward and introduced herself. She started to explain that she ran an orphanage in Saigon and that she had two hundred children she wanted to get out of the country.

Daly cut her off. "I'm not talking to any fucking women!" he roared.

Clark backed off. Her husband and Meador moved forward in her place, gingerly laying out what they were trying to do. When Daly heard about the agency's situation, and the fact that they had hundreds of children they needed to get out of Vietnam, his stance softened. The Clarks and Meador couldn't have known it, but Daly's pride must have been at stake at that moment. He had the night before boasted to the international press that he would take up to fifteen hundred children out of Vietnam on two separate jets. Scoffing at the notion that he needed government permission for such flights, he'd told the Associated Press, "Let 'em stop us." Now, with Taylor's withdrawal of her kids, the greatest danger Daly faced might have been acute embarrassment. In that light, Cherie Clark's arrival presented a new option. Daly said he would take Clark's kids, but his plane would be taking off in two hours.

At that time, most of FCVN's children lived in foster homes scattered throughout the city. They had no possibility of rounding up all those kids in two hours. To make matters even worse, a large number of the infants suffered from malnutrition and other serious diseases. To put them on an airplane so hastily could endanger their lives. And Clark wondered if perhaps Daly himself was too unstable to trust. These three factors combined to push her toward a decision. As much as she wanted her children to take the seats on that plane, Cherie Clark said no.

Clark returned to FCVN's villa that afternoon more despondent than ever. All the efforts of the day had brought her no closer to getting her children out of Vietnam.

And then, at about eight o'clock that night, the roar of jeeps racing into the driveway suddenly shattered the quiet of the neighborhood. Uniformed men got out and rushed inside, hurriedly explaining that they were airport immigration officials, police, and some of Ed Daly's World Airways staff. Final clearances had come through from the South Vietnamese government. If Clark could get her children ready in an hour, Daly's planes would take them out of Vietnam.

Now, with one more chance and no other options, Cherie and Tom Clark came up with a plan. It was true that they couldn't get their sick infants in from the foster homes on such short notice, but they might be able to bring in their older children from FCVN's small facility that Meador ran in Thu Duc, just outside of town. Tom Clark jumped into a van and drove out to Thu Duc, thirty minutes away, while Cherie remained at the central facility, organizing food and supplies for the flight overseas. As soon as he reached Thu Duc, Tom found Meador and explained what had happened. Together, they rallied together the children and staff. They had to hurry. Every one of these children would be leaving Vietnam that night. With the news, the children went wild with excitement. They were school-age kids, old enough to understand their situation and the fact that they were scheduled to be adopted by families overseas. Some had even met their future parents, who had come to Vietnam to visit. Over the past few days, the children had heard the near-constant rumors about evacuations, and the rumors had left them agitated and too excited to settle down. Now, the moment had arrived.

Within minutes, Clark and Meador squeezed a few dozen children into FCVN's two vans and raced back to the headquarters in Saigon. There, the Clarks added more children from the main villa. In all, some fifty-two children and four adults made the final short ride to the airport. Cherie Clark followed the vans in one of the police vehicles, which by then was piled high with supplies. The caravan, lights blaring and horns honking, raced through the dark city.

Ed Daly met the group at the airport, once again surrounded by reporters. Cameras began to flash. If he was disappointed by the meager number of kids—the airline executive had certainly not succeeded in airlifting fifteen hundred children from Vietnam—he didn't show it. To Clark, Daly seemed exhilarated by the drama and attention. The monster of the afternoon was now playing the role of the dashing hero, standing on the running board of a jeep as it raced across the tarmac toward a jet with the familiar red-and-white World Airways insignia on its tail. As Daly must have recognized, the scene made for glorious television.

The children seemed confused by all the commotion, but with Daly prodding them on, they climbed aboard his airplane. Cherie Clark followed them up the stairs. To her surprise, Daly had equipped the aircraft well. Although the cabin had no seats, a web of safety netting covered the floor and, on top of that, Daly's crew had piled enough blankets and pillows to make the floor of the plane look like an enormous rumpled bed. Clark realized she hadn't needed to bother with supplies. World Airways staff had stocked the jet with food, milk, diapers, even Coca-Cola.

At that moment, though, despite the relief that she felt over the comforts of the aircraft, Clark was anxious. "[We] didn't know where the plane was headed," she realized. "I didn't even know how long it would take for the children to reach their final destination in America. There was nobody to look after them; nobody even knew their names."

Hurriedly, Clark and her husband conferred. Together, they decided that Tom and one of the nuns on the FCVN staff would remain on board and accompany the children to the United States. Neither of these adults had a passport, clothing, or a visa to leave Vietnam, but they decided to go nonetheless. At that moment, their priority lay in making sure the children would have familiar adult faces on the journey with them.

Nervously, Clark said good-bye to her husband and the children. She even gave the gruff Daly a final impulsive hug, which, for a moment, seemed to humanize the man. Then she hurried down the stairs and stood with her colleagues on the tarmac, staring up at the jet, its engines already beginning to hum. From here, they could make out the tiny faces of the children staring down at them through the windows of the plane. Some of the children seemed to be waving good-bye.

Suddenly, an immigration officer emerged from the airplane holding two teenage boys by the neck, one under each arm. He pulled them roughly down the stairs. "These boys aren't leaving," he announced to Clark. "They are old enough to be fighting for their country and they shouldn't be running off to America."

Ed Daly raced down the steps after them. He pulled a couple of notes from a wad of hundred-dollar bills in his pocket, then offered them to the officer while Clark pleaded for him to let the boys go. One of the boys had two brothers on board, she explained. It would be cruel to split up a family. The official remained unmoved. Even the offer of money—such a commonplace incentive in the Saigon of that day—didn't weaken the officer's stance. Clark continued to beg, but Daly, without another word, turned and strode back up to the airplane. The door slammed shut behind him, leaving Clark, the official, and the teenagers on the tarmac.

Daly had to hurry. Tan Son Nhut Airport lay under the constant threat of enemy bombardment, and the flight crew had heard reports of an imminent assault on the airport. Suddenly, the runway lights went out. On the flight deck, the crew could see only the vaguest outlines of the airfield bathed by dim moonlight. Had someone just signaled an attack? Ken Healy, one of the pilots, decided to take a chance. Slowly, the aircraft began to move down the runway, gaining speed. The cockpit came alive at that moment with demands from the air traffic control tower. "Don't take off! Don't take off!" an official yelled. "You have no clearance."

"Just watch me," Healy replied.

Inside the plane, the children lay on the floor, their eyes widening with surprise at the strange new sensation of a hundred-plus-ton aircraft lifting into the air. Tom Clark, Ed Daly, and the other adults on board braced themselves as the plane left the runway. On the ground, Cherie Clark watched the big jet slowly disappear into the sky.

The first planeload of children had left Vietnam.

PART TWO

CHAPTER 4

If You Are Out There, We Love You and We Are Looking for You

In a small apartment near downtown Saigon, the 23-year-old widow
of a soldier, with two small children, trembled and bit her lip.
"Where is there to go after Saigon?" she asked.

New York Times reporter BERNARD WEINRAUB, April 3, 1975

After the war, both Cherie Clark and Rosemary Taylor published memoirs about their experiences evacuating children from Vietnam. In these
accounts, birth mothers handed over their children and then disappeared from the story completely. Infants appeared, as if by sleight of
hand, in alleyways and under trees, left alone in hospitals, or wailing by
the trash heap behind some provincial clinic. Cherie Clark wrote that,
toward the end of the war, "some mothers literally threw their babies
over our compound fence, and we would find them lying in the courtyard." The image is horribly evocative, but it did nothing to explain how
these women had come to believe that they had to resort to such drastic
means to get their children out of Vietnam.

On a Web site called Vietnambabylift.org, I discovered a "Looking
For . . ." page, which served as a bulletin board for birth families and
adoptees trying to find one another. These e-mails never contained
many details—usually a birth date or a birth name, and sometimes the

name of an orphanage where a child had been relinquished. Some posters mentioned birthmarks or scars that might help to identify their family members. But, really, these people pressed forward with no more than desire, heartbreak, and a couple of facts.

One of the great controversies about Operation Babylift revolved around the orphan status of these children. The foreign adoption agency administrators tended to claim that the children they sent overseas had no parents, had been abandoned by their parents, or had been willingly relinquished by their parents so that they could travel to new adoptive families overseas. Some of the postings I read on the Internet, however, told a different story. In this version, poor parents used local orphanages as temporary foster homes, leaving their children in these shelters while they earned money, or recovered from illness, or went off to fight in the military. Adoption agency administrators claimed to know precisely which children in their nurseries were abandoned (and thus eligible for adoption), and which had parents and were boarding only temporarily. And yet, the Web site postings describe situations that were far more ambiguous. One woman wrote:

"Dear Ma'am, My name is Do Thanh Tinh. . . . I am writing to you to respectfully your assistance in finding any information about my missing daughter. I have not been able to find my daughter for many years. My daughter was taken from Tien Tra ward, Hau Duc district, Quang Tin province (Quang Nam Province now), Viet Nam in 1975, during the Viet Nam Babylift to the United States. My daughter's name: Do Thi Chau (Nickname: Do Thi Qua). Anyone who worked in adoption agency can contact me."

And here was another one: "Hello, my name is Tuan Nguyen and I am searching for my baby sister My Thi Nguyen. I have very little information of what happened to her. When she was 18–24 months old my mother was faced with hardship and was not able to raise us. I was raised by my grandmother and My was sent to Tan Mai Orphanage at Bien Hoa. When my mother found out that the Viet Cong was about to invaded Saigon, she immediately went to the orphanage to find my sister to bring her home. By the time she got there, the nuns told her that one of the [Roman Catholic] Fathers took all the children to France. We do not know if she was a part of 'Operation Babylift.' My sister is Amerasian (mother is Vietnamese and father is American). Her birth certificate shows her name as Nguyen Thi My. If you are out there, we love you and we are looking for you."

And this, from a Catholic nun in the Mekong Delta: "I would like to look for my like brother whose name is Minh Nguyen, was born on October 10th 1971, in Mai Linh, Quang Tri, Viet Nam. He is now about 34 years old. His father is Dan Nguyen (called Ho). His mother is Cach Thi Le. He got polio when he was three year old (he couldn't walk). So my mother sent him into Nuoc Ngot Orphanage in Hue where many foreigners as well as doctors came to examine and cure orphans. Thanks to the intermediary of this orphanage an American couple supported him, brought him to America to cure his legs and promised they would bring him back to my family when he was well again. During the histories event in 1975, my family moved to the South Viet Nam and we lost his track from then on. My dear brother, where are you now?"

In her book, Rosemary Taylor had declared that "the babies were unwanted from the start." The Web postings didn't indicate which agencies had carried these particular children out of Vietnam, and Taylor's own agency may have had nothing to do with any of them. Still, Taylor's statement was beginning to look less like an assessment of fact than a very strongly held opinion. Clearly, some of the children *were* wanted. Deeply wanted, even after thirty years had passed.

I contacted a brother and sister in Saigon, who had written one of these "Looking For . . ." appeals on behalf of a friend, a birth mother who now lived in a remote province of central Vietnam. She was old, sick, and depressed, desperate for news of the daughter she had given up so many years ago. One evening, the two siblings came by my hotel in Saigon. They were middle-aged professionals, well-educated, and excellent English speakers. Their own lives had not been affected by the Babylift, but because they could function in the world of e-mails and Web sites, they had become detectives, using modern technology to try to find the daughter of a poor acquaintance in a rural province.

They told me that the birth mother, Le, had named her daughter Thu. The little girl's father abandoned them just after the baby's birth and, for the next seven years, Le raised the child alone. Then, in the spring of 1975, the Communists began their advance on Saigon. Le feared the Communists, like so many South Vietnamese at that time, and she came to believe that her daughter would have a better life in the United States. Le worked in the storeroom of the Seventh Day Adventist Hospital, a well-established international medical facility in Saigon, and through her job, she had contact with foreigners.

In some ways, this connection to foreigners became her curse. If you don't have an opportunity, you never have to make a difficult choice. Le had an opportunity, and so she struggled over whether to send her daughter overseas. Finally, toward the end of April, only days before Saigon fell, she made her decision. She put her daughter into an orphanage associated with the hospital. The little girl cried, arguing with her mother that she didn't want to leave. She clung to her, sobbing, but Le insisted. She pulled herself away from the child and left her, then ducked into a nearby room and watched the girl, trying to keep an eye on her as long as she could. That night, the orphanage directors evacuated the entire facility. All the children were taken to the airport, put on a plane, and flown out of Vietnam.

Le watched the plane take off. Right at that moment, as the aircraft carrying her daughter began its slow rise into the air, she realized she'd made a mistake.

Le's friends looked at me. "She has spent the rest of her life," the sister said, "regretting that decision."

CHAPTER 5

Lost in the Shuffle

*COMINGS AND GOINGS: As those now famous 57 Vietnamese orphans were
on their way to Oakland, courtesy of Ed Daly, an Air Force C5A was taking off from
Travis Air Force Base, bound for Saigon with 17 Howitzers and 75 recoilless rifles . . .
Add bitter ironies of a bitter week: Vietnamese officials refusing to allow some 500 other
orphans to leave Saigon aboard Daly's DC-8 because "the way that plane is fitted out
makes it unsafe for the babies." They're safer on the ground in South Vietnam???*

San Francisco Chronicle columnist HERB CAEN, April 4, 1975

"A weary group of 52 Vietnamese orphans arrived at Oakland International Airport last night 17 hours after the pilot of their jet transport made a daring ascent from Saigon airport," reported a front-page article in the *San Francisco Chronicle* on April 3, after Ed Daly landed in California with that first group of children. Dr. Alex Stalcup was on the ground waiting with a medical staff and enough "laps," as the arrival team called the adult volunteers, for every child.

The night was clear but breezy, and it was important to get the children out of the airport and settled as soon as possible. When the plane landed, Stalcup's staff immediately went into triage mode. The scene was completely different from the disorganized rush to board the plane that the children had experienced in Saigon. Now, ground crews set up ramps at both ends of the World Airways jet and the medical officials climbed aboard. They entered from the back of the plane and quickly moved forward through the cabin. A member of the medical staff would approach each child and conduct a brief physical examination, then attempt to identify the child by going through any accompanying papers or by collecting information from the flight attendants and adult volunteers who had escorted the flight.

All across the United States now, stories about the crisis in Southeast Asia filled the newspapers, but Alex Stalcup distanced himself from what was taking place over there. Over the chaotic weeks to come, he wouldn't have time to think about war, or politics, or even to question the reasons for the sudden arrival of all these children into the United States. He had a more pressing concern: avoiding a medical disaster. From Stalcup's point of view, "whatever the philosophy behind [the evacuation], this was a bunch of infants and young children with the potential to be very sick. In large numbers. Each child was a black box [who] came with no medical records."

Actually, although many of the children Stalcup would care for over the next few weeks arrived with nothing, others had flimsy sheaves of paper describing medical history or current medications. Sometimes, these records became misplaced in flight, however, or attached to the wrong child. Often, infants arrived in cardboard boxes, with all their identifying information attached to the side. If any unexpected "event" occurred in that box—and vomiting, diarrhea, and sudden, messy sprays of urine were normal events even for healthy babies—the documents could be damaged or even ruined. As Stalcup's wife, Janice, who volunteered with the Babylift effort, put it, "Some of [the children] had pretty good records and some of them, you know, you're thinking, 'Oh my God, this is the only thing that ties this kid to its past and it's in, you know, six zillion pieces.'"

To attempt to keep track of the children, Stalcup's staff gave each arriving flight a letter designation and each child received a number to go with it. The fifth child taken off of plane "D," then, would be designated "D-5." Any children transferred to the hospital were labeled "SK" (sick kid). It was a very basic method of identification, but Stalcup and his colleagues hoped that by using it they could keep track of each child.

For that first flight, it didn't take more than an hour to move through the airplane and complete the initial triage procedures. Stalcup loaded four of the children into ambulances and sent them directly to the hospital. The rest left on the caravan of buses making the twenty-mile drive across the San Francisco Bay Bridge and through the glimmering city. By 12:30 a.m. on April 3, the caravan pulled into the Presidio.

Harmon Hall, the Presidio's thirty-three-thousand-square-foot Army Reserve facility, had been transformed over the previous few days into a receiving center for hundreds, if not thousands, of unaccompanied Vietnamese children for whom the Bay Area would be the first point of entry into the United States. Rows of mattresses covered the floor of the gymnasium-like main hall. As the children came inside, each was passed to a new "lap," given a sponge bath, a snack, and a quick medical examination. Finally, the volunteers tried to get the children to go to sleep, but they were too excited to settle down.

Most of these children had been Cherie Clark's wards in the villa that FCVN rented in Thu Duc, outside of Saigon. The villa had been spacious and full of light, but barbed wire surrounded it and the inhabitants had no way of protecting themselves from the constant fighting going on around them. These were children who had grown used to hiding under tables at the sounds of bombs. This huge, bright room full of soldiers and volunteers represented an amazing, and no doubt confusing, change of venue for them.

If the children were excited, the adults were as well. Volunteers had come from all over the Bay Area, and the staff at the army post had mobilized for the effort as no one could remember. The sixteen-hundred-acre Presidio might have been one of the most geographically spectacular army installations in the world, but it was a sleepy post, the kind of place where a stolen purse or broken headlight could make the pages of the paper, the *Star Presidian*. As an army installation, the Presidio's responsibilities were administrative, mostly concerned with supporting various government tenants, from the Letterman Medical Center to the 6th Region of the Army Counterintelligence Command, which occupied the buildings spread out across its hills. Col. Robert

Kane, the genial post commander, liked to describe himself as "a hotel-keeper on a grand scale."

In short, the arrival of children from Vietnam provided the most direct connection to the war in Vietnam that the Presidio had ever experienced, and the post staff enthusiastically mobilized for the challenge. Over the past few days, engineering crews had installed new sinks and emergency lighting systems. Communications specialists had set up four new telephone lines (as the weeks passed, this number would prove to be seriously inadequate; a total of thirty-three new phone lines came into service before the operation concluded).

The preparations had depended on the combined efforts of many, including army soldiers, Red Cross workers, medical staff from the University of California at San Francisco and the army's Letterman Hospital, and hundreds of civilian volunteers. The Red Cross provided food from the post commissary, diapers from Walgreens, and nearly $2,500 worth of children's clothing, purchased at Sears. Expenses, as it turned out, were not a problem. One day, Walter Shorenstein, the prominent San Francisco philanthropist, would write Alex Stalcup a check for $1 million.

Eventually, the army filed a complete report on the Babylift operation. In true military style, it could account for everything from the number and dimensions of the signs on the infants' washroom (six 17" by 22" signs, each boasting 4" letters) to the difference between normal and overtime wages for one Shirley L. Small, a post supervisor GS 9/10, whose rates went from $8.03 to $10.19 per hour during the operation.

But there was one figure that even the most particular army accountants could not pin down. Cherie Clark claimed to have taken fifty-two of her children to the airport in Saigon. A few children, not from FCVN, were also on the plane and two of Clark's children, the pair of teenage brothers, were not allowed to board. When Ed Daly's jet touched down in Oakland twenty-five hours later, the *San Francisco Chronicle* reported that fifty-two children had arrived. When the army released its final report at the end of June that year, it listed the number of children on that first flight as fifty-nine. And the Red Cross, in its own report, said that there were fifty-seven.

It's doubtful that anyone, other than Shirley Small herself, would quibble over the accuracy in the report on her wages. But what did it mean to get the number of children wrong? Had more children been placed on board the plane at the last minute? Had other children disappeared? When you're talking about these kinds of numbers, a single mistake meant that one human being, or maybe more, had somehow gotten lost in the shuffle. As it would turn out, over the next few weeks, such discrepancies would occur again and again.

In Connecticut, Syd and Norm Gelbwaks were waiting on news of the daughter they hoped to adopt. They had heard the stories of atrocities coming out of Vietnam. Mixed-race girls were being raped and killed because they weren't "pure" Vietnamese. And the war itself upset them. Over the years, Syd had read a lot of history about the conflict in Vietnam, and she had come to believe that the United States was responsible for many of the problems there. When a group called Mothers Against the War marched in Washington, D.C., Syd—herself the mother of three—joined them. Her husband, an engineer, never actively participated in the protests. But, quietly, he supported her.

The Gelbwaks, both of whom were in their thirties, had been trying to have a fourth child. Again and again, though, Syd's pregnancies had ended in miscarriage, which led to their decision to adopt. Unlike so many prospective adoptive parents, they didn't want an infant. They wanted an older child, one relatively close in age to their boys—who would be eleven, thirteen, and fourteen by the time the child arrived—and, this time, they wanted a daughter. The boys responded with excitement to the idea that they would soon have a little sister. Norm's parents, orthodox Jews, were less enthusiastic when they heard that a Vietnamese orphan would soon join the family. To calm their fears, Syd and Norm promised that the child would go through a conversion ceremony. The little girl from Vietnam, they assured his parents, would become a Jew.

Although the couple was working with a local agency, it was the Holt Adoption Program, the country's most prominent international adoption organization, that would bring their daughter from Vietnam. Holt had only recently begun its program in Vietnam, but Syd and Norm heard good things about it and felt confident about the process. By early April 1975, though, stories of Operation Babylift began appearing in the newspapers. Vietnamese children were starting to arrive, but the Gelbwaks family had yet to receive a referral, which meant they had no name, no age, no picture, nothing. Clearly, the government of South Vietnam was about to collapse. Again and again, Syd called and wrote the agency. "When," she asked, "will my daughter arrive?"

"Don't worry," the staffers would say. "She'll be here next week."

But "next week" stretched into the next and the one after that. Syd had long ago written in her journal these hopeful words: "It will be soon that we get our daughter."

Activity in Rosemary Taylor's Saigon nurseries turned feverish as Vietnamese caregivers and foreign volunteers rushed to get the children out of Vietnam. Keeping track of so many children, many of them infants, had never been easy. Most of Taylor's wards arrived without names, identities, or history, the kind of fundamental information that helps to differentiate one person from another. To deal with this lack of information, FFAC's orphanages employed a system of "nursery names" to be used during the time that that individual child stayed in their facilities. Considering the huge numbers of children—thousands of them—who moved through Taylor's nurseries over the course of eight years, the staff became inventive to find original names for each child. Some had simple Western names, like Elizabeth, Abraham, Brian, and Roy. Tran Dinh, Tien, Be, and Ngoc-Thanh went by Vietnamese names, perhaps acquired before they arrived at FFAC facilities. Other names reflected the religious or political convictions of Western staff: Thomas More, John of the Cross, and Cesar Chavez. In early 1974, one of the orphanages entered a classical phase, coming up with names whose difficult pronunciations likely struck fear in the hearts of the Vietnamese speakers who cared for these kids: Aristotle, Aeschylus, Plato, Socrates, Athena, Aristophanes, Jocasta, Agamemnon, Tiresias, Sophocles, Euripides, Marc Antony, Julius Caesar, Cleopatra, Electra, Orestes. There were strange and somewhat silly names as well. One child was called Nuoc-Mam, which means "fish sauce" in Vietnamese. Another went by "Stiff Legs." Some names were simply whimsical: Minehaha, for example, and a pair of twins called Sun and Flower.

In the nurseries, the staff came to know the children intimately. Each time a single child was moved from one location to another, however, that child faced a risk of being misidentified, particularly because most of the time they were leaving the adults who knew them best. To keep track of all these children, particularly once she began to arrange the evacuation of huge numbers of children in April, Taylor used a system of lists. Each list was organized "by country of destination, with names and birth dates of the children together with names and addresses of adoptive parents. The total information for each child was put on an index card and to this was stapled a photograph and birth certificate." The children wore identification bracelets and tags around their necks to connect them further with the documents that traveled with them. By the time they left Vietnam, some children would be wearing several ID bracelets. The categories of information on these bracelets were not always consistent, however. Many included the child's nursery name and the orphanage where they had lived. Some also contained information on the child's adoptive family, their destination country, and what kind of formula they drank. Not every child, however, wore a bracelet that contained all such information.

Despite her careful preparations, by April 4, Rosemary Taylor had still not managed to evacuate any children. Two days had passed since Cherie Clark's first group left Vietnam on Ed Daly's jet, and Taylor could finally feel some optimism about the prospects of getting her own children out of the country. The day before, the government of South Vietnam had finally authorized a *laissez passer*, which granted exit authorization to all the children in Taylor's care. But she still needed planes. She had thought, for a time, that Ed Daly's World Airways jet would hold the answer, but, in the end, it was Cherie Clark's children, not Taylor's, who ended up on that plane. Now, that first group of Clark's kids was safely at the Presidio in San Francisco while Taylor still had six hundred children in Saigon.

It had become apparent over the past few days that one of the biggest hurdles to evacuating children from Vietnam was not ideological opposition to the idea of removing them from the country, or bureaucratic ineptitude, or lack of funds—though all those factors served as impediments—but, rather, competition among the seven adoption-sponsoring agencies for space on airplanes. As Rosemary Taylor hurriedly prepared the children's dossiers in her quarters at Phu My that morning, her colleague Wende Grant sat in the Saigon office of Pan Am Airlines, trying to secure an agreement to charter a 747 that was at that moment sitting on a runway in Hong Kong. Ultimately, the Pan Am strategy also collapsed, in this case because a rival adoption agency had already chartered that plane.

And then, like the cavalry, the U.S. government came to the rescue. An official from USAID telephoned Wende Grant and offered a Galaxy C-5A cargo jet. The plane, which was landing in Saigon that morning with a load of military supplies for the beleaguered South Vietnamese government, could fly 230 children out that afternoon. Aware of the previous concerns about the safety of Ed Daly's World Airways jet, the U.S. official assured Grant that the Galaxy would be outfitted with seats and seat belts, oxygen masks, and emergency equipment—in short, he guaranteed the safety of the children on board.

Taylor and her staff didn't know that this sudden offer of help had come from the highest level of political power. Back in the United States, Americans were watching the news on television and calling their representatives in Washington to demand that the U.S. government do something about the plight of this particular group of children in Vietnam. True, the news from Vietnam was almost all bad. True, the fall of Danang a few days before had resulted in a stream of more than ninety thousand refugees moving south toward Saigon. Hundreds of thousands of Vietnamese, a huge percentage of them children, were now displaced from their homes. The roads from the northern provinces were littered with discarded military paraphernalia, abandoned cars and trucks, and the corpses of civilians who had collapsed, or been killed, while fleeing the fighting. Still, despite the extent of the humanitarian crisis then taking place throughout South Vietnam, the attention of the American public became focused on the plight of the several thousand children sitting in foreign-run orphanages, like Taylor's, most of whom had already been designated for adoption overseas. Particular anxiety focused on the fate of the Amerasian kids, the sons and daughters of American service personnel who had left Vietnam when the United States pulled out of the country. In fact, only 20 percent or so of the Babylift children were considered "racially mixed," but their situation loomed large in the minds of the American public. How would the Communists treat these children of enemy soldiers when they took over?

Perhaps most concerned were the prospective adoptive parents waiting for the arrival of their kids from Vietnam. Many of them had already been in contact with the adoption agencies for months, or even years. Some knew the names of the children they planned to adopt, had photographs and medical information, had already painted nurseries pink or blue. All they needed now was the children themselves. These parents wrote letters and got on the phone. They called their local newspapers and television stations. They petitioned their members of Congress. Before long, the plight of "Vietnam's orphans," as they were called, became a political issue. On April 3, the same day that Cherie Clark's kids arrived at the Presidio, President Gerald Ford gave a press conference at the San Diego Convention Center announcing his decision to allocate $2 million in humanitarian aid to support the evacuation of the Vietnamese "orphans." The U.S.-backed mission, which would come to be called Operation Babylift, had begun.

Christine Leivermann, a twenty-three-year-old American nurse who worked as a volunteer with Rosemary Taylor in Saigon, received the call mid-morning on April 4 that she would travel as an escort on the Galaxy flight out of Saigon. Lievermann had not been scheduled to make this journey, but last-minute reshuffling of staff put her on the roster. She would fly with the children all the way to San Francisco, then immediately fly back to Vietnam to help the agency complete its evacuation over the next few weeks. She only had a few hours to pull her things together and help get the Newhaven children ready to go.

Leivermann and her colleagues had prepared children for departure several times over the past few days, only to be told that that day's plan had fallen through. Twenty-two children from Newhaven were scheduled to take the Galaxy flight, along with children from FFAC's other orphanages, and the journey demanded a huge amount of preparation. Each child's adoption dossier had to be perfect—not merely accurate in detail, but also correctly arranged so that every set of documents clearly corresponded to a name band and identification pouch worn by that particular child. The children themselves had to be dressed, fed, and provided with enough extra clothing, food, milk, baby bottles, diapers, blankets, and, in most cases, medication to last throughout the long journey to the United States. Before departure, the babies had to be cuddled and fed. The toddlers had to hear, again, where they were going. The hardest part wasn't getting the children ready, either. It was keeping them ready. The time of the airplane's departure moved from 11 a.m. to 2 p.m. and then to 4 p.m. While the staff prepared one child, another one would wander off, or lose a shoe, or scrape a knee, making the whole process feel a bit like lining up puppies.

While the eyes of the world observed the crisis taking place in Vietnam through binoculars, Christine Leivermann witnessed the horrors in a detail that was nearly microscopic. She could smell the foul air that hung above the crib of a malnourished infant. She could see the pus in the ears of a crying toddler. She could sense the anxiety of the populace as she hurried through the streets of Saigon. And, of course, she felt it, too. The youngest of the foreign volunteers on Taylor's staff, Leivermann had spent three years working with Vietnam's most vulnerable populations, longer than practically anyone else. She had delivered food and medicine to displaced people in refugee camps. She had collected sick children from overcrowded and understaffed provincial orphanages and carried them to the relative safety of Saigon. She had feared for her own life, too, while ferrying refugees out of Cambodia. And, though she had trained as a nurse in the American heartland, she had become skilled at recognizing and treating the tropical and infectious diseases that plagued the people of this region.

Leivermann knew nothing of the intense political maneuvering then transpiring in the halls of Washington and Moscow, Hanoi and Saigon. She had no idea that President Ford had vowed to help the children. But she knew what it would mean to evacuate several hundred children on one airplane in a single day. Over the past few years, Leivermann had experienced the bedlam of escorting large groups overseas. Once, she had single-handedly transported a dozen children, nearly all under the age of two, from Vietnam to France. During that trip, the group had gotten stuck for twelve hours in India, and Leivermann had helplessly watched her toddlers "run rampant" through the airport before Air France staff finally agreed to help her. The difficulties of today's flight would be significantly greater. In the past, FFAC had transported for adoption only those children deemed physically healthy enough to make the trip. With the war about to end, however, the agency wasn't waiting for sick children to get better. "We had probably five or six different types of formula," Leivermann later remembered. "We had a number of children with cleft palates, a number of children with nutritional diseases, a number of children with failure-to-thrive." The agency had decided it was better to risk the dangers of the flight than leave these children in Vietnam. Although Christine Leivermann was a nurse with significant expertise, she realized that the task ahead of her today "was going to prove to be very challenging."

At the moment, though, concerns over logistics were not foremost in her mind. Christine Leivermann knew that the end of the war was coming, and she worried that if she got on that airplane today, she'd never make it back to Vietnam. Over the past few weeks, life in Saigon had changed dramatically. Rumors circulated wildly and the place seemed charged with an emotion she later described as "proactive grief and angst." The war itself was closing in on the city. Refugees lined the streets, begging for food, and at night one could hear explosions going off in the countryside. Even within the city itself, there was a frenetic concern about safety, with people constantly advising one another: "Oh, you don't want to go there!" And: "You can't go there right now." And: "Maybe you should go over here." Through it all, Leivermann considered the fact that she'd soon have to leave this place for good. She felt a sadness that had become pervasive among people in Vietnam at that time—Vietnamese and foreigners alike. Despite the years of war and deprivation, the continuing threat of violence, the disease, the impending victory of the Communists, Christine Leivermann had come to love Vietnam, and she felt heartsick because she wasn't ready to go yet.

By just after 2 p.m., the Newhaven staff succeeded in assembling the nearly two dozen children from that nursery who would take this flight. The children were eager but nervous, which made them disruptive and, in some cases, tearful and clingy. Soon, though, four cars arrived, and within minutes everyone had been squeezed in and whisked to Allambie, another FFAC orphanage that lay to the northwest, closer to Saigon's airport. At Allambie, they transferred to buses to take them the rest of the way.

The tension on the streets became more and more acute as the buses approached the airport. Though neither South Vietnamese nor U.S. government officials—who were afraid of causing panic—would admit it at the time, the evacuation of the city had already begun. The airport was now crowded with refugees camping on the floors and tarmac, desperately trying to obtain seats on flights. At the same time, the government could not guarantee the safety of the area. Enemy forces were so close that pilots flying in and out of the airport employed defensive tactics to avoid oncoming fire.

Once the convoy of children reached the gates, Vietnamese guards refused to let them in, forcing the buses to wait in the late afternoon sun. It was the beginning of April, generally the hottest month of the year in Saigon, and outside temperatures could easily soar into the 90s. Inside the buses, the air became even hotter, reaching levels that weren't merely uncomfortable but truly dangerous for the health of the children. It wasn't until U.S. Embassy officials intervened that the group was finally allowed into the airport. From the front gates, they drove directly out onto the tarmac toward the waiting plane.

When Leivermann and the other adults finally saw the aircraft towering over them, they were astonished. FFAC's foreign staff were experienced flyers. They regularly escorted children overseas, so they knew the types of planes that made transoceanic crossings. Because they also made frequent trips to provincial orphanages, they were familiar with the civilian and military aircraft that flew regularly within South Vietnam. The Galaxy C-5A, however, was different from anything they'd flown before. For one thing, it was the largest airplane in the world— nearly as long as a football field, in fact. "I was blown away by the size of the plane," Leivermann later remembered. Her colleague, Sister Susan McDonald, compared the cargo hold to "a gymnasium." Rosemary Taylor would report later that she was "momentarily stunned" by the dimensions of the aircraft.

First introduced by the U.S. Air Force in 1970, the Lockheed C-5A Galaxy quickly became an essential component of the U.S. military's transportation system at the time. Fully loaded, the two-level airplane could carry 270,000 pounds of cargo, including bulky combat equipment that would never have fit on other planes. It could travel vast distances as well. With a full fuel tank (fuel alone weighed more than 330,000 pounds), the plane could fly nearly 6,000 miles. With aerial refueling, its range was virtually unlimited. That morning, it had brought in a load of military supplies for the South Vietnamese government.

As the FFAC staff immediately realized, an aircraft capable of carrying military vehicles and tanks was an appalling form of transportation for a group of some 230 sickly kids. Upstairs in the troop compartment, infants could travel strapped to seats, but the older children would have to sit in the cargo hold below, which had been hastily and ineffectively retrofitted after it arrived that morning with its load for the military. The cargo hold had no seats, only a web of netting strapped across the floor for the children to sit on and, if necessary, grab onto. Ed Daly's

World Airways jet had been similarly basic, but the airline staff had made it more comfortable by covering the netting with blankets and pillows. The Galaxy had no such amenities. Trying to transport these children on such an aircraft was something like trying to carry loose eggs in the bed of a pickup truck.

"The situation was beyond words," Rosemary Taylor later wrote. "The first children were taken to the upper level which had a passenger configuration." Inside the aircraft, she remembered,

> [The] babies, sweltering and screaming, were strapped tightly, two to a seat, by the well-meaning Air Force personnel, who were helping us board the children. The babies were not supported adequately as there were not enough cushions available. I followed after, trying to prevent them from strangling themselves by slipping under the seat belts or smothering as they slid over on top of each other. My mind was numb with horror at the distress of the children, and as the Air Force worked at top speed to strap them in, I hunted up a canteen of water, found a paper cup, and went around giving each child a drop of water with my fingers since the bottles had not yet been loaded.

Taylor may, at that moment, have felt an urge to take her wards and turn around, risking the chance of never getting them out of Vietnam rather than risking their lives on that plane. But there is a kind of kinetic force that takes over when so many people are working toward a singular goal—particularly in wartime and particularly when the U.S. military gets involved. And Taylor had hundreds of other children back in her orphanages, every one of whom she wanted to evacuate. South Vietnam was crumbling. And, besides, the U.S. government had guaranteed the children's safety.

Somehow in the confusion, no one knew exactly how many children were actually being put on the plane, or how many were upstairs and how many downstairs, though later reports would estimate that about 120 infants occupied seats on the upper level and about 110 older children sprawled across the empty cargo hold below. Another fifty or so adults served as in-flight military personnel or escorts. The inability to specify an exact number of people on the plane would, during later investigations, cause confusion. At the moment, however, the adults could barely seat the children and keep them from passing out in the heat, much less embark on an organized system of registration. This was not the leisurely boarding of a civilian airplane. This was the rushed and scattered best-we-can-do scenario of a highly dangerous military operation.

It was at the airport, in the shadow of this horrible airplane, that Taylor saw that Margaret Moses, her colleague and friend, was preparing to board as well. Wende Grant had completed the roster for the flight and decided at the last minute to remain in Vietnam and send Moses instead. Taylor and Moses trusted each other so deeply, and understood each other so well, that they didn't even need to speak at this moment. Instead, Taylor "merely grimaced" because "[the] situation was beyond words and too unreal for pleasantries." Seeing Moses in a borrowed dress, carrying a beat-up old suitcase full of the children's documents, Taylor tried to focus on the positive, namely the abilities of the escorts. Seven of her most reliable staff would be on the flight. "I knew the strength of each one of our nurses," she later wrote, "most of whom were experienced escorts, and I knew they would work with superhuman courage."

On the lower deck of the plane, a tearful farewell was taking place. Pham Thi Phuong (not her real name), an eighteen-year-old caregiver in FFAC's Hy Vong intensive-care nursery, had just helped to carry the babies onto the upper deck of the plane. Now, standing in the cargo hold, Phuong began to say good-bye to one of the flight's escorts, the German nurse Birgit Blank. Working together in FFAC's orphanages, the two women had developed a strong friendship. Phuong, a practicing Catholic with a devotion to the Virgin Mary, saw in Birgit many of the same qualities of gentleness, generosity, and good humor that the girl believed the Virgin embodied. As the friendship deepened,

Birgit's family in Germany invited Phuong to emigrate there, promising to help her get an education. Birgit's mother had even sent Phuong a key to her house. The key was inexplicably embossed with the letters "Ph," and Phuong took it as a sign that fate was directing her—Phuong!—to emigrate overseas.

Many things had to happen before Birgit and Phuong could travel to Germany, however. They needed to arrange a visa. Phuong had to study German so that she'd be able to enter university there. Most immediately, Birgit had to travel to the United States with this planeload of children and then return to South Vietnam. There was no reason to believe that Birgit wouldn't manage to get back into the country, but the situation in Vietnam had grown so uncertain lately. Everyone was edgy. Phuong wasn't following the news of the war, but she could feel the strain in the air. She felt edgy, too.

The two young women stood together in the cargo hold. All around them, the children sat on the hard metal aircraft floor, some of them already gripping the netting that was supposed to replace airplane seats and safety belts.

With only a minute or two left before she'd have to get off the plane, Phuong looked at Birgit. "We've been friends for three years," she said. "When you went to Germany, I never kissed you good-bye." She began to cry. She saw Birgit as a sister, and now her sister was leaving.

Birgit burst into tears. Then she leaned over, and Phuong kissed her. "I promise that I'll come back," she said. Phuong, who had to believe her, turned and left the plane.

Christine Leivermann took her position on the top deck, where the infants would need her nursing expertise. Margaret Moses and the rest of the FFAC staff stayed in the lower-level cargo hold to take care of the older children. After loading the plane, Rosemary Taylor would stay behind to complete the preparations for evacuating the remainder of FFAC's children in coming days. Before she headed below, however, she and Leivermann offered each other good-byes, of a sort. The two had worked together for three years, but they weren't close. As the youngest

FFAC volunteer, Leivermann had never been among the inner circle of Taylor's confidantes. Like Taylor, Leivermann conveyed a quiet stoicism that kept her from revealing her feelings easily. Perhaps it was the emotion of the moment, then, that made her suddenly confide in Taylor so passionately and bluntly. "I have a very bad feeling about this," she said. She was upset about having to make this trip at all, but her biggest concern was the conditions on the airplane, and the fact that they had had to strap in infants two to a seat.

Taylor stopped and looked at Leivermann. As the founder of four nurseries, she was responsible for the well-being of hundreds of children. Her decisions could mean, quite literally, the difference between life and death. In normal times, she approached her position with a kind of all-consuming commitment and confidence that inspired respect amongst almost everyone she met. Now, though, the conditions on the airplane seemed to make Taylor hesitate. She admitted to Leivermann, "It concerns me, too." Within moments, she had disappeared down the ladder to the lower deck to continue loading the airplane.

At 4:15 p.m., the Air Force C-5A Galaxy took off from Saigon's Tan Son Nhut Airport. Despite its enormous size, the plane was designed to operate on short or inadequate runways, and it climbed fast. Because the seats on the plane's upper level were filled with infants, the adults stood, bracing themselves where they could. Leivermann had lodged herself between the first and second rows so that she could remain close to the children in her care. The cabin had no windows, which made it impossible to judge elevation or to see the city receding below them. It was possible to feel the plane level off, however, and at that point, Leivermann quickly went to work. For the next few minutes, she moved between rows, handing out baby bottles, collecting empties, and taking them to the galley to refill with sugar water. Another adult was handing out cartons of milk, and Leivermann took one.

Then, at approximately 4:30, the rear of the plane exploded.

Someone screamed, "Oh my God! My Jesus God, no!"

Eyeglasses, pens, papers, and ceiling insulation flew through the cabin. The air pressure suddenly changed, making it hard to breathe. Somehow, after a few seconds, Leivermann found that she could move. She stepped over the rubble blocking the entrance to the galley and hurried back to her section. For the briefest moment, she glanced down the stairwell. She could see nothing of the cargo hold. Instead, she saw a hole in the rear of the plane, and the ocean far below. She assumed that the plane would crash into the water and contemplated the fact that neither she nor the children could swim.

An Air Force crewman approached and put his arms around her. "Are you all right?" she later remembered him asking.

"Yes."

"Are you scared?"

"Yes."

"Will you be all right?"

"Yes."

Then he told her that the airplane's cargo door had blown off and that the plane would "probably land all right because it's happened before and the planes usually landed okay."

At that moment, other crewmembers were fumbling with radios and wiring. The explosion had cut off contact with the flight deck, but they could feel by the motion of the plane that the pilots were struggling to maintain control. Oxygen masks fell from the ceiling, but Leivermann quickly discovered that not all of them worked. In some cases, the entire unit fell out when she pulled on it. Other units remained intact, but no oxygen flowed through them. In any case, the wiring on the masks was much too short to reach the tiny babies strapped in the seats. At first, she tried to hold each child up to reach a mask, but then she realized that some of the infants were in greater need than others. In fact, a few children were already losing consciousness. One had become cyanotic, its skin turning blue from lack of oxygen. She began to help the most distressed infants first.

While Leivermann struggled with the children, the Air Force crew tried to rescue one of its own, a serviceman who had gotten stuck in the stairwell and was being pulled by the vacuum pressure toward the hole in the lower section of the plane. With massive effort, the men succeeded in pulling their crewmate back upstairs. Leivermann again glanced down below. She could see nothing of the cargo hold, or the hundred-plus children and their escorts who had been seated down there. She saw only the sea.

The noise in the plane was deafening, something Leivermann later compared to the sound of a train approaching through a tunnel. The passengers could feel that the pilots had turned the plane around, and now it was descending. Finally, one of the crewmembers signaled that they had reached an altitude at which they no longer needed oxygen. Leivermann and the other adults dropped the oxygen masks they had been using on the infants and began moving through the rows of seats, trying to pad the area around the children in any way they could. The air turned warmer and bits of paper fluttered through the cabin. Peering down the stairwell, the passengers could now see rice paddies, rivers, and villages below.

The friendly crewman approached Leivermann again. "Are you okay?" he yelled.

She answered, "Yes."

It was clear that they were about to land. Leivermann noticed the little identification pouches hanging around the children's necks. Hurriedly, she pulled the pouches off, deciding that it was better to lose the children's documentation than to risk them choking to death during the landing. Then she braced herself.

Just after 5 p.m., the Galaxy crashed into a rice field, one mile short of the airport runway to which the pilots had tried to return.

The plane bounced once, then came down again, sliding across the ground, shearing apart and leaving burning debris behind it. Crouched between two rows of seats, Leivermann felt an intense surge of heat as flames shot up the stairwell, followed by a torrent of mud, water, and weeds. The gigantic aircraft ground and scraped as it broke apart. Within the cabin, a life raft inflated, flipping some of the seats, babies still strapped inside them. Ceiling panels dangled and fell to the floor, burying other children. Christine Leivermann felt a wave of panic then. Children were dying, she realized, and she couldn't save them all.

Then she stood up and, without even brushing the mud off her face, began to try.

At its highest point, a Galaxy C-5A airplane stood as tall as a six-story building. Christine Leivermann had been on the upper deck when it crashed. Now, opening the exit door, she looked outside and realized that she was only eight feet off the ground.

Somewhere, this information registered in her mind, leading her to wonder about all the people—Margaret Moses, Birgit Blank, the other FFAC staff, and, of course, all the children—who had been seated below. Now, though, she didn't stop to think. She leaped to the ground, her eyes on a small body lying face down in the wet field. Quickly, she turned the child over to keep it—she couldn't tell if "it" was a boy or girl—from asphyxiating in the muddy water. Then she and the other adult survivors began to evacuate the plane, passing the children between them, one by one. The rescue helicopters seemed to take forever to arrive, though they may in fact have made it to the site in minutes. The rescue teams loaded the survivors onto the helicopters and lifted off for Saigon.

It wasn't long before Jay Ruoff, whose USAID had arranged the flight for FFAC, called Wende Grant with news of the disaster. "The plane has crashed," he told her. "It went down just outside Tan Son Nhut [Airport]." An hour had not even passed since the C-5A lifted off. Wende Grant had not had time to stop worrying about exit authorizations and passports. Now, Ruoff suggested that she hurry to the hospital. "[There] are some survivors," he said.

Grant found Christine Leivermann at the Seventh-Day Adventist Hospital. If Christine wasn't injured, Grant told herself, perhaps many of the children and their adult escorts had survived as well. Grant asked Leivermann what had happened. "The whole God-damned back end of the plane blew out," Leivermann answered. "That's what happened."

By the time Rosemary Taylor and Sister Susan McDonald arrived a few minutes later, Wende Grant knew more. The fact that Leivermann had survived was, after all, one of the few pieces of good news they would hear that evening. "Over half are dead," Grant reported. Margaret Moses was dead. Birgit Blank was dead. Lee Makk. Dolly Bui. Sister Ursula. The list went on. As night fell, they were able to accumulate the grim statistics. Seventy-eight children had died, among them the ones known as Desmond, Big Cuong, C. S. Lewis, Helen Rosalie, and tiny Thy, completely blind, who had been found abandoned in a dispensary in Pleiku. Of the seven FFAC staff on that plane, only Christine Leivermann survived.

Pham Thi Phuong stood and sobbed in the street. She cried all the way home. Throughout that night, she sat on the balcony and cried, thinking of her friend Birgit. Eventually, Phuong's mother asked dryly, "When I die, will you cry this much for me?"

In the coming months and years, there would be detailed inquiries and lawsuits. As Christine Leivermann had heard onboard the aircraft before the crash, the Lockheed-built Galaxy C-5A had a history of design problems. Rosemary Taylor later discovered that, at the time of the disaster, the military and Lockheed were in discussions about ways to mitigate these issues. A report published by the military's Pacific Command simply stated that "during climbout at altitude above 23,000 feet, the aft bulkhead door blew out through the clam shell doors and struck the tail." The debris ruptured hydraulic lines, compromising the pilot's ability to fly the plane. Though there was early talk of sabotage, that possibility was quickly dismissed by the military, which seemed to have been aware that it was loading children onto a plane with a history of problems.

In all the confusion surrounding the disaster, no one seemed sure about how or where to bury the dead children. By May 9, over a month after the crash, the U.S. military's Central Identification Laboratory (CIL) and the U.S. Army Mortuary, both in Thailand, reported that they had received no confirmation about the disposition of the children's remains. The centers had tentatively identified forty-five bodies using wristbands or name tags. Another thirty-one children had not been identified at all. According to the military report, the remains were eventually cremated at a Buddhist *wat* and buried in a Catholic cemetery in Thailand. U.S. military personnel who worked at the identification lab and in the mortuary contributed money to pay for a headstone.

Beginning in the summer of 1975, FFAC became involved in a series of lawsuits aimed at Lockheed. One suit, filed by the families of adults who had died on the plane, was settled within a year. The cases involving the children, both the survivors and the dead, lasted over a decade, however. As Rosemary Taylor explained it, "We felt strongly that Lockheed should not escape liability for any fault it had in the plane crash just because the victims were orphans." Taylor and her colleagues believed that the surviving children should receive money to help them with the educational and medical expenses that would result from their injuries. As for the children who had died, FFAC hoped that compensation for the loss of these children's lives would be used for charitable purposes. To that end, the agency established the Margaret Moses Memorial Foundation, hoping to use any funds to support the needs of orphaned and handicapped children in developing countries.

Ultimately, after eleven years of litigation, Lockheed did offer compensation for almost all the injured and dead. In the case of the deceased children, however, the judge decided to award the money to the prospective adoptive families rather than to charity. The awards were more than $85,000 for each child (no money was awarded on behalf of the sixteen children who had not yet been assigned). Some went to families who had known and cared for the children they had planned to adopt. Other families, however, had not yet even received their adoptees' names before those children died. All the families received the same amount of money and, despite the fact that the judge strongly urged them to donate their punitive damage awards to charity, few sent any money to the foundation established by FFAC. Rosemary Taylor's memoir, which appeared a few years after the final decisions, revealed her bitterness about the outcome of the trial:

At the time of writing about a third of families have sent donations ranging from 0.6 per cent to about 30 per cent of their re-
spective awards. Several families wrote to thank us for working on
their behalf for eleven years to gain this money for them. One of
them cheerfully described the European travel her family could
now afford. The majority of the recipients simply accepted the
award and as yet have not even bothered to respond.

· · ·

In the hours and days following the Galaxy crash, the processing centers
in the United States began to send more and more Babylift children to
their new homes. Most prospective parents continued to wait, however,
unable to turn their eyes from their television sets.

In Wakefield, Rhode Island, prospective adoptive mother Kathy
Lawrence became hysterical when she heard news of the disaster. She
and her husband, Wesley, had already received an adoption referral
from Cherie Clark's agency, FCVN. But the reports about the plane
crash were slow to reveal which agency had sponsored the children
on that plane. Prospective adoptive families across the United States,
Canada, Australia, and Europe faced the sudden new anxiety that
their children had perished. Only slowly did the information emerge
that the Galaxy had been carrying children from Rosemary Taylor's
agency, FFAC. Even with that confirmation, the similarity of the two
agency names—FFAC and FCVN—meant that many FCVN families
would continue to have sleepless nights. In Wakefield, Kathy Lawrence
couldn't drag herself away from the television, so worried was she that
her baby girl had died. The Lawrences knew no one else adopting a
baby from Vietnam, but it seemed that the tragedy had transfixed their
entire community. She thought of the day of John F. Kennedy's assassination. It seemed to her that the Galaxy crash riveted the nation in
much the same way.

In Cumming, Georgia, Colleen Ballard connected the plane crash
with her own infertility. "Oh my gosh," she thought. "Here are so many

kids dead and I can't have any." She and her husband, Jerry, had been trying to conceive for six years. Months before, they had filed the paperwork to adopt a child from Vietnam. Now, the image of all those dead children felt like tragedy piled upon tragedy. She wanted a child of her own. She wanted to become a mother. And now, on the television, she saw all those motherless children, dead.

In Washington, D.C., Lisa Brodyaga felt revulsion. An antiwar activist and lawyer, Brodyaga had believed from the beginning that the Babylift was a racist attempt to remove children from Vietnam simply because the country was poor. "Who gave you the right to be God?" she had thought. Once the Galaxy crashed, her anger turned to horror. In her eyes, the effort to evacuate so many children on an ill-equipped cargo jet looked like "they had just crammed all these kids into the belly of the plane and taken off with them like they were so many boxes of soap." Brodyaga had herself begun the process of adopting a child. As she watched the aftermath of the Galaxy tragedy, however, she had no idea that that child would be coming from Vietnam.

CHAPTER 6

Standing on Two Legs

Many people cannot help sighing as to whether or not in future these Vietnamese orphans will still remember that they are Vietnamese and that their fatherland is Viet Nam, the land where they were born.

Commentary on Operation Babylift in the South Vietnamese newspaper *Trang Den*, translated in the English-language *Saigon Post*, April 12, 1975

The Ben Cat River is one of several narrow waterways that meander through Ho Chi Minh City. Out in Go Vap district, the river serves as a dividing line between urban and rural. The urban side is rough-and-tumble, dirty, and loud, with buildings that look like they've been slapped together using salvaged metal and recycled nails. Just across the river—a one-minute ride on a little ferry—lies the rural district of An Phu Dong, which is mostly rice fields and palm trees, wild bougainvillea, coconuts, and scrappy farm dogs. It was in these rice fields of An Phu Dong that the Galaxy crashed, about a mile short of Tan Son Nhut Airport, to which it had tried, unsuccessfully, to return.

Late one afternoon, Thuy and I went to visit old Mrs. Tram, who lived on the urban side of the river, close enough to have heard, thirty years ago, the sound of the Galaxy going down on the other side. "The plane couldn't fly, so it crashed," she told us. "It looked like it really wanted to fly. . . . It made a whirring sound. It exploded into pieces and crashed, you know, on my brother's land."

"Your brother?" I asked. I hadn't expected that.

"He grew sugarcane and apricot trees and the plane crash destroyed everything. They never received any compensation. The sky collapsed, and so they got no compensation."

Mrs. Tram was eighty and kooky. Thuy and I struggled to keep up with her ideas, which zigzagged between past and present as if everything happened at the exact same time. I couldn't blame Mrs. Tram's personality entirely. Failing memory was, of course, an inherent drawback to my doing research on events that took place thirty years earlier. Everybody I'd spoken with had to struggle to remember details. But Mrs. Tram's memory was particularly idiosyncratic.

"Did your brother have any children?" I asked. I thought that maybe I could speak with them.

"Who? They all died. They were fat and they had high blood pressure."

She had blood pressure worries, too. At eighty, she had ended up with a body shaped like a baby's: an enormous torso and tiny arms and legs that couldn't hold her up. Unable to walk, she had to push herself across the room on her hands. She was frustrated and jealous of people who could move around easily. "Other people will take three steps to go downstairs to get outside. I only take one. What I mean is"—here her expression turned to a smirk—"I just fall down." She was half-blind as well, because, during the war, a Viet Cong (VC) soldier had, maybe accidentally, poked her in the eye with a bamboo pole. In her mind, she connected the present-day government with the Viet Cong that had damaged her eye, and she told us that when a bureaucrat came by to collect fees for her house she responded, "You already put out my eye. Now do you want me to dig your father's grave, too?"

All of this was very hard to translate. Mrs. Tram's language was so rough and, well, *picturesque*, that Thuy, who could be shy and prudish, looked like she was barely hanging on. Sometimes she would look at me in exasperation and whisper, "I can't translate that." Mrs. Tram had such a thick Southern accent and used so much local slang that I could barely understand any of what she said. I wasn't sure if Thuy didn't know the

English translations for these words or if she was just too embarrassed to use them. Later, when I translated the transcript of the interview with my Vietnamese-language teacher in Hanoi, I realized that Mrs. Tram had used so many novel forms of "shit" and "fuck" that I didn't know how to translate them, either.

The old woman also didn't like the interview process. She didn't mind talking. In fact, she loved talking. But she didn't like that she had to pause sometimes so that Thuy could translate her words into English. "Oh, you talk forever," she muttered.

Little by little, though, we were able to piece her story together. Mrs. Tram's husband was a neighborhood official who also, on the side, helped out the Viet Cong. In that part of Saigon, and throughout much of South Vietnam, people regularly shifted their allegiances as a means of survival. As Mrs. Tram pointed out, "We had to stand on two legs" —meaning, work for both sides—"or else they would have killed us."

As soon as people in the area heard the plane crash, Mrs. Tram's husband rushed to the ferry landing and crossed to the other side to help. He saw the children lying dead on the ground, the plane cut in two. "I'm too afraid of ghosts, so I didn't go," the old woman told us. "He said the children were cut in pieces. He said that some were still alive."

Vietnamese referred to the cargo jet that crashed as "the baby plane" or "the orphan plane." All the local people I'd met who lived in Saigon at the time could remember the disaster, but few knew who those babies were, or where the plane was going, or why it was leaving Vietnam. They were rooted to *this* place and didn't have a clear sense of anything that was, to them, merely passing through. The foreigners, on the other hand, often seemed to float above everything, like mariners unable or unwilling to duck their heads, even momentarily, beneath the surface. Several local people told me, for example, that the plane had crashed on a Viet Cong camp, killing a group of young soldiers hiding there. The An Phu Dong district, where the plane came down, was so famous as a contested area that a popular song had been written about it. "Here in An Phu Dong," the chorus goes, "the soldiers are always strong and brave . . . the people are proud of their country." I never saw any mention of the Viet Cong deaths in any published accounts of the crash, but that didn't mean these soldiers hadn't died then. Many deaths went unreported in those days, and the story of the Viet Cong soldiers seemed to be common knowledge among the people in the area. In fact, I heard, there were two small altars to the dead at the crash site, one for the people who'd been *on* the plane and another for the people who'd been *under* it.

On Mrs. Tram's front porch sat two three-seat sets of metal airplane chairs, which her husband had scavenged from the Galaxy after it crashed. I had first heard about Mrs. Tram, in fact, from former orphanage staff who weren't happy that her husband had taken these relics from the plane and put them on his porch. The chairs did, in fact, seem like a macabre souvenir. Indeed, I heard that there had been offers by someone—perhaps Rosemary Taylor herself?—to buy the chairs, but Mrs. Tram refused to sell them.

Sitting with her on the front porch of her house, the controversial seats looked like a pair of uncomfortable metal sofas. "How did your husband get them home?" I asked. They were constructed of a now-battered gray steel, and, with their wide armrests and hinged bottoms, looked both cumbersome and heavy.

"At first, he pulled them through the rice fields with fishing line," she said. "Then he used rope. The water in the rice fields came up to his belly." Once he got out of the rice fields, he pulled on the rope from the front while his brothers pushed from behind. Eventually, when they reached the river, they carried the chairs across on a boat. In all, the distance was a mile, at least. In other words, it was an exhausting job. After he got home, hundreds of people, mostly refugees camped out near the local pagoda with nothing better to do, gathered around to see what he'd brought back.

I asked the obvious question. "Why did he bother?"

"He said that they were worth a lot of money," Mrs. Tram explained. Metalsmiths could recycle the steel and make bicycles, extremely valuable commodities in a poor community like this one.

If he was a scavenger, though, why didn't he choose something smaller, easier to transport, more valuable? "Why did he pick the seats?" I asked.

"People did take money, but my husband thought soldiers would arrest you for that. No one would arrest you for taking these seats."

The seats, then, were worth the effort. But then days and weeks passed and the family never sold them. "People said that they're the seats of dead people and I'm really afraid of ghosts," the old woman told me. In fact, the Galaxy crash haunted the entire family. "My husband had nightmares," Mrs. Tram said, "about all those children who died so miserably." Days and weeks turned into months and years. The seats remained on the porch. Eventually, they became an unplanned, haphazard memorial to the people who died that day.

It was getting late. Mrs. Tram claimed that she wasn't tired, but you can't keep an eighty-year-old talking all night. I had one last question: "Did you and your husband know why the orphans were leaving Vietnam?" I asked.

She shrugged. "That year they took a lot of children to America. They said they were going to be adopted in America, but that's not really why. That's not true." She didn't have any alternate theories as to why the children had been taken away, but she certainly didn't believe this one. "It's not natural to take children like that," she told us, "and they did it so many times."

In Hanoi, I studied Vietnamese through the Hanoi University of Foreign Studies. Another American in the program, an MBA student named Steve George, was a Vietnamese adoptee who grew up in Wyoming. Steve had decided to spend a semester in Vietnam to learn about his heritage and check out business opportunities in the country. Besides studying the language, he liked to tool around on his rented motorbike, work out at a local gym, and, on vacations, travel to the south to see what information he could dig up about his birth family.

Steve was not evacuated during Operation Babylift. His parents adopted him as an infant a year earlier, in 1974, through Rosemary Taylor's agency, FFAC. He was of mixed race and knew nothing about his biological parents. Once, sitting in a café on Ly Thai To Street in Hanoi, Steve talked with me about his possible ethnicity. He had darker skin than most Vietnamese, but he didn't look African American. He had the kind of hard-to-pinpoint "non-white" look that actors like Ben Kingsley have parlayed into roles as ethnically diverse as Iranian, Indian, and Jew.

"Actually, growing up, my nickname was 'the Mad Mexican' because a lot of people think that I'm Mexican," he told me. "Some of my friends say, 'You could be in Mexico next year, looking for your birth father.' Because I really don't know who I am."

When he visited Cambodia, people thought Steve was a native son. His broad nose and full lips did suggest the *apsara* dancers one sees on the temples of Angkor, and he started thinking, 'Wow, I could be Cambodian, too.'"

Although he knew almost nothing about his past, Steve had had some luck in his search for information. Like David Fisk, he had a scar story. While the scar on David's hand remained an almost invisible and very personal reminder of what he'd lost, Steve's scar had helped him make contact with his past and, to some extent, recover it.

When Steve had made his second visit back to Vietnam a few years earlier, he met Pham Thi Phuong, who had worked at Rosemary Taylor's Hy Vong orphanage, the same orphanage where Steve had lived as a baby. Phuong was the first person Steve met who had a direct connection to the adoption agency that had brought him out of Vietnam. The two had a meal together and Phuong and her husband showed him some sites in Saigon. Then, as they were planning to say good-bye, they pulled out pencils and paper to exchange contact information. It was at that moment that Phuong, who had only known him as "Steve," saw that his last name was George. "You're George?" she asked.

Steve said, "Yeah." Perhaps it was simply coincidence, but his nursery name in the Hy Vong orphanage had been "George," which was also the surname of the family that adopted him.

"You're *George?*" She was getting excited now. Steve nodded. He had no idea what she was getting at. Steve had brought along a Vietnamese friend who could translate for him. Suddenly, she started speaking frantically in Vietnamese. Steve only knew a few words of the language at that time, but he heard one that he recognized: *bụng*, or "stomach," which was something you needed to know if you wanted to say that you were hungry. Why did she keep saying "stomach"? He stood anxiously waiting while the two Vietnamese conversed.

Finally, Steve's friend turned to him. "She knows you," he said. "She took care of you because her sister-in-law burned you on the stomach." Phuong's sister-in-law, another caregiver, had accidentally scalded the baby's belly with water that was too hot, causing a serious burn on the infant's delicate skin.

"Are you George?" Phuong asked.

Steve looked at her. He had traveled to Vietnam two times already and, though he liked the country, he had felt no more affinity for the place than he would for any other pretty tropical destination. Now, for the first time, he felt something stir. He lifted his T-shirt and revealed a scar that ran across his belly. All his life, he had wondered where it came from. Now he knew.

Their relationship changed instantly after that, and Steve's relationship with Vietnam changed instantly as well. Now, for the first time, he began to seriously consider the idea that he might have family in this place. Little by little, he'd begun making calls and meeting people who might offer clues about his past. He showed me his birth certificate and a photograph of himself as a baby. "There could be a very, very small chance that someone could be looking for me," he told me. "But if I don't try, I'd regret it. I'm not the type of person that I want to have regrets like that."

CHAPTER 7

Good Intentions

*Our mission of mercy will continue. The survivors will be flown here when
they are physically able. Other waiting orphans will make the journey.*

President GERALD FORD, April 4, 1975

"It is nice to see you Americans taking home souvenirs of our country
as you leave—china elephants and orphans," a bitter South Vietnamese
army lieutenant told *New York Times* reporter Malcolm Browne a few
hours after the Galaxy crash. "Too bad some of them broke today, but
we have plenty more."

The army officer expressed an anger toward the U.S. government
that was steadily increasing in South Vietnam. "You got what you
needed from our country," he said, "and now it is time for you to leave,
letting us pay the final bill."

While many in the United States had, at least until the Galaxy crash,
regarded the Babylift as a positive thing, many in Vietnam worried that
the focus on the orphans would distract attention from the far-more-
extensive problem of displaced Vietnamese adults and families. "The
Communists have an excellent record in looking after children," one
American observer in Saigon told the reporter. "Orphans here under
the Communists would probably be better off than under the present
Saigon Government. The real tragedy is the leaving behind of adults
who may face reprisals or death for having worked for the Americans."

In the United States, however, concern over the plight of the children had reached nearly epic proportions. Just before the Galaxy disaster, an editorial in the *San Francisco Chronicle* had commended President Ford for authorizing $2 million in U.S. government funds to fly two thousand children out of Vietnam: "It is the President's obvious intent to spare no expense or trouble where the welfare of these helpless victims of war are concerned, and the nation will applaud him for it." The newspaper editorial, it seemed, mirrored a national fascination about these children that was growing more intense by the day. At the Red Cross offices in San Francisco, for example, as soon as word went out about the Babylift, the switchboards "lit up" with calls from people interested in adopting children.

Truly, Americans were looking for catharsis after the psychological trauma of a disastrous war, and the children of Operation Babylift seemed capable of providing it. USAID, which was organizing the airlift, had set up a toll-free hotline in Washington, D.C., to deal with the public response to the crisis in Vietnam. According to the call center's logs, twenty-seven hundred calls came in on April 3, the day that the World Airways jet carrying the first load of children arrived in California. On April 4, the day the Galaxy crashed, the center answered nearly five thousand calls, and in the following days, the telephone company would report to the call center that the lines were so overburdened that as many as three thousand calls an hour were not getting through. According to phone company records, seven hundred thousand long distance calls came through the capital on a normal day, but on April 4, some 1.8 million calls reached the city. It seemed that people heard the news about the Galaxy crash and immediately telephoned their government agencies and members of Congress, perhaps because they didn't know what else to do.

Several days later, watching the outpouring of concern for these children, Lucien Pye, a political scientist at the Massachusetts Institute of Technology, mused to the *New York Times*, "What strikes me is this amazing psychological phenomenon, this outburst. . . . We're trying to prove that we are not really abandoning these people. The guilt feeling is very deep, cutting across hawk and dove alike. We want to know we're still good, we're still decent. . . . Who is the orphan? . . . The children, or Vietnam?"

And the children continued to arrive. Within twenty-four hours after the Galaxy crash, FFAC loaded 324 of them, including most of the survivors from the day before, onto a Pan Am flight bound for the United States. Rosemary Taylor couldn't help but note that, this time, the plane "was configured throughout for transporting children." She described the "special supplies aboard; cardboard cartons to box the babies safely, milk, diapers, plastic bags and blankets." The Pan Am flight had many of the very amenities that Ed Daly had provided on his original World Airways flight—the flight that, only days before, Rosemary Taylor had declined to accept, perhaps because of safety concerns expressed by U.S. officials. Now, Taylor and her colleagues had to confront the fact that "there would have been adequate space for all our children had we not attempted to use the C-5A the previous day, but it took the tragedy of the day before to convince Pan Am that we needed them." That, Taylor explained, and the $150,000 that an American supporter of FFAC had committed to defray the $230,000 total cost of the flight.

FFAC had lost so many of its adult volunteers in the crash that nearly every remaining non-Vietnamese staff member had to accompany this new flight out of Saigon. Only four foreign staff, among them Rosemary Taylor, would remain in the country. All the rest, including Wende Grant, would staff the Pan Am flight. Christine Leivermann had barely had time to change out of her torn and muddy clothes after the disaster. Now, Rosemary Taylor watched as Leivermann boarded the new flight "without any fuss . . . as if yesterday had never been."

Wende Grant later described the experience of traveling on a plane filled with 324 children, most of them infants. She called the initial leg of the flight, to Tokyo, "a marathon" of feeding children and changing diapers. "Low-sided cardboard boxes were under each seat, stowed like carry-on luggage. A tiny baby was in each box. Some larger boxes, too high to slide under a seat, were wedged between seats. These held larger babies. After takeoff we pulled boxes from beneath seats as if opening dresser drawers. Crawling on the seats, we examined the contents of each drawer, holding, feeding, and changing the little inhabitant before returning him or her to the folds of the red Pan Am blanket that lined each box. Soon we were confused as to which child had been fed, which had been sleeping when checked and so passed over. An empty box could mean that a stewardess was carrying that baby up and down the aisles to still his crying. Had she fed him at the same time?"

In Vietnam, the FFAC staff had learned to care for huge numbers of children with very few resources, so this flight was perhaps not as overwhelming for them as it would have been for almost anyone else. But they were also accustomed to having full authority over the children in their care. It came as a shock, then, to arrive in Japan and realize that the U.S. government had decided to manage the operation and that FFAC had lost its autonomy.

As soon as the plane landed in Japan, a group of U.S. military medical staff boarded and began to examine the children. Grant confronted them, contending that "these were our children and if we needed medical help, we would request it." The doctors ignored her, then announced that they wanted to hospitalize twenty children in Japan. Grant was furious, and she also believed that the doctors were focusing on children with superficial ailments while failing to notice the peril of others. A number of dehydrated babies in respiratory distress were at that moment waiting "in the back section [of the airplane] for the departure of our military medical specialists so that Christie [Leivermann] could put them on IVs."

Grant threatened to hold up the flight and demand that all 324 children be hospitalized. Finally, the military pediatricians agreed to take only the two "worst cases," which, to Grant's surprise, were a child with a boil on the head ("It could break inwardly and cause brain damage," said the doctor.) and another whose eyes had crusted closed because of conjunctivitis ("[It] could cause blindness."). In comparison to the very ill babies in the rear of the plane, the doctors' form of triage seemed, to

Grant, nearly laughable. She thought of the challenges FFAC had faced over the last eight years: "The nurses fighting for the lives of children discarded at birth. Hy Vong full of babies who couldn't survive, with Birgit standing over them, using talent and abilities born of desperation and determination and keeping so many alive. Now Birgit was dead. And Margaret, who managed so many impossible situations—gone."

Eventually, after Grant secured promises that those two "worst cases" would be brought to the United States as soon as they recovered, the flight was again allowed to depart. Now, a staff of Red Cross volunteer nurses had come aboard. They began to relieve the FFAC staff, who were exhausted.

Leivermann continued working, though. Within five minutes of leaving Japan, she decided to start an IV on another child who had become very ill. As she began to set up the apparatus, one of the new Red Cross volunteers confronted her. "Who are you to be starting an IV? Are you a doctor?" the woman asked. Later, Leivermann wished she had claimed that she was, but instead she explained that she was a nurse and, yes, she did know how to start an IV. It seemed odd to be arguing now over procedures that she had been performing routinely in Vietnam for years.

About halfway through the flight, a Red Cross nurse began moving through the cabin trying to fill out a U.S. Immigration and Naturalization Service (INS) I-94 form for each child, which would enable them to enter the country without visas or passports. Although FFAC followed the standard procedures for international adoption, the process occasionally galled Wende Grant. Once, when she was filling out the paperwork for a child that she herself planned to adopt, she commented to Rosemary Taylor, "It is almost too much that we must satisfy state, national, and foreign requirements when all we want is our babies." Her annoyance over all the regulations didn't change once she became FFAC director, either. About one particular day in 1973, she later recounted, "[W]hile the authorities were concerning themselves over names, titles, and licenses, eleven more abandoned scraps of humanity arrived at To Am [nursery], from Providence Orphanage in the [Mekong] Delta."

Now, as their jet moved closer to the continental United States, Grant and her colleagues explained FFAC's identification systems to the volunteer nurse and spent a few moments helping the woman document some of the children according to the information on their ID bracelets. It wasn't long, however, before Grant and the others drifted back to feeding and holding the babies, leaving the overburdened nurse to "[crawl] over and around the boxes [of children], transcribing the information on to the I-94 forms" by herself. From the sidelines, Grant observed the volunteer struggling through her task. "Had she been able to mark, indelibly, the forehead of each child thus processed, the plan may have had a modicum of success. As it was, babies were removed from the boxes to be fed just before the nurse reached them, and returned when she had already passed their row. Babies already registered were moved a row farther back where they would be duly registered again as the nurse worked her way systematically towards the tail section of the plane." Clearly, it was an impossible job for any single person to manage. Days later, when the children were ready to be released from the Presidio to their new adoptive families, the INS asked FFAC to match each child to the I-94 form that had been completed on their behalf. Not surprisingly, many of the I-94 forms were incorrect. Grant merely noted drily that the need to match the forms to the children "was to add immeasurably to the confusion over the identities of the children."

But those problems came later. At the moment, on board the plane, Christine Leivermann and another Red Cross volunteer, a retired nurse, were engaged in the more pressing struggles of life and death. Hours earlier, the volunteer had approached Leivermann with a simple question: "What can I do to help?"

Quickly, the young nurse had led the older one to a large group of infants with severe cleft palates. At first, the Red Cross volunteer balked at the challenge. It's a difficult task to get milk into the mouth of even one child with a cleft palate. Leivermann was asking her to feed ten. "But she did it," Leivermann later recalled. "I think everybody wanted to make it work. Everybody. From the flight attendants down. Everybody wanted to make it work."

• • •

At about 10 p.m. on Saturday, April 5, Wende Grant's plane, Pan Am Clipper Flight 1742, touched down at San Francisco International Airport. On the ground watching it land were hundreds of Red Cross volunteers, a mob of reporters, armed security officials, and the president of the United States.

Gerald Ford and his wife, Betty, had flown in an hour earlier from their vacation home in Rancho Mirage, California. The two, who had planned to meet the Galaxy C-5A the day before, had changed their schedule to meet the replacement flight. For the past hour now, the president had been cheerfully greeting volunteers, medical staff, and local officials while they waited for the jet to arrive from Asia.

As the president made his rounds, Betty Ford visited on the buses with Red Cross volunteers who would be serving as "laps" for the 324 children on board the plane. Dr. Alex Stalcup, busy with his duties as medical director of the Presidio's reception center, made a point to find the First Lady and say hello. Though Mrs. Ford might not have known it, Stalcup had recently been involved in a very heated debate concerning her health. A few days earlier, the White House had called him to let him know that the president and Mrs. Ford planned to welcome the first planeload of children when they arrived in California.

"She can't get on the plane," Stalcup had replied. Though he didn't mention it, he worried that the presence of the Fords would turn the arrival of the children into a political event. But he had a different reason for denying Mrs. Ford entry to the airplane. The First Lady was currently undergoing chemotherapy for cancer, and she would be susceptible to diseases carried by the children, particularly chicken pox, or varicella. "I'm not going to be responsible for someone with no immune system getting varicella," he explained.

At first, the White House staff argued with him, but Stalcup remained firm. "I'm the boss," he said.

"Well, who are you?"

The twenty-nine-year-old Stalcup hesitated. It wouldn't sound like much to the staff of the president of the United States, but he had nothing else to say. "I'm a chief resident in pediatrics!" he told them.

Surprisingly, the White House relented. The First Lady, whom the young doctor found to be "very gracious," would not step onto the children's plane that night.

Now, President Ford, his wife, and hundreds of others watched as the plane taxied up the runway. Floodlights lit the tarmac, bathing the jet in a yellow glow. It stopped. For a time, nothing happened. In the roped-off media area, a crowd of reporters jostled for view. The "laps" on the Red Cross buses waited for their call. All along the roofs of the airport, armed guards stood sentry, protecting the commander-in-chief. Down on the tarmac, a group of VIPs stood waiting in the chilly air.

Finally, an airport ground crew wheeled a set of mobile stairs out to the rear door of the plane, then another to the front. Several ambulances crossed the tarmac and stopped at the foot of the stairs. The plane's door opened, and the medical team, led by Stalcup, raced aboard. For a few minutes, the crowd on the ground saw nothing more. Then, they watched as Christine Leivermann and another volunteer stepped off the plane. In their arms, the two women carried infants hooked to IVs. Carefully, they made their way down the stairs and settled the children into ambulances. Then they walked back up to the plane and began carrying more critically ill children down to the vehicles below.

Inside the plane, Alex Stalcup and his staff were performing triage. He had seen instantly that it had been "a particularly gruesome flight. Babies were in shoeboxes. Babies were in legal boxes. [There were] a lot of infants, very sick kids. Some were in overhead compartments. . . . And there were stacks of dirty diapers and exhausted personnel that had been up for, like, the entire time from Saigon. And it smelled bad. It was ugly on the plane. People just standing looking shell-shocked. So, I was interested in getting these really sick kids out."

At that moment, the president of the United States stepped through the front door. Stalcup had begun triaging from the back of the plane. Now he met Ford in the middle. Stalcup saw that the president was upset. For the past hour, Ford had been thanking volunteers and greeting local officials. The crash of the Galaxy the previous day had shaken the country, sending angry reverberations and recriminations across the front pages of the newspapers and through the halls of Congress. At last, a plane full of children had arrived safely. It was great news. Here inside the cabin, however, the president had to face the real human consequences of what was happening in Vietnam. Over the past few days, while vacationing in Rancho Mirage, he had managed to intersperse his presidential duties with rounds of golf, but the crisis in Vietnam never drifted far from his attention. Only that morning, Ford had discussed the situation with Secretary of State Henry Kissinger and Army Chief of Staff Gen. Frederick Weyand. It was one thing, though, to talk about the war in the luxurious atmosphere of a vacation home near Palm Springs. It was quite another to enter the stale and overburdened cabin of a 747 jetliner and find hundreds of sick and weary children, some of whom, having survived a plane crash the day before, still had burn marks, cuts, and even shrapnel wounds on their bodies.

The president looked at Stalcup. "Alex, am I in the way?" he asked.

It struck the young doctor at that moment that the president had not come here merely for political reasons. In fact, Gerald Ford looked close to tears. Stalcup picked up a baby girl, put her into the president's arms, and told him, "This one's yours."

The president grasped the baby, then turned and walked back up the aisle. By the time he appeared in the doorway of the plane, he had managed to smile. The news cameras began to flash, catching his every step. Gerald Ford carried the baby down from the plane and toward one of the buses.

Back inside the dank cabin, Wende Grant and her colleagues, who had suffered through the Galaxy crash and then immediately boarded the Pan Am flight to escort hundreds of children across the ocean, were beginning to break down. Some simply collapsed into seats and started to cry. Others focused on the question of how to reach friends and relatives in the United States to report that they were alive. Stalcup, moving through to examine the children, sensed "a lot of emotional tension and grieving around the plane."

Slowly, the medical staff completed the triage process, the protocols that they had developed for removing the remaining children from the airplane in an orderly manner. Each volunteer "lap" entered the plane through the rear door, picked up a child, and exited down the front stairs either carrying that child or holding it by the hand. Soon, a line of hundreds of volunteers snaked through the plane and then filed back down to the tarmac and walked toward the waiting Red Cross buses.

Alex Stalcup was pleased by the disembarkation. Wende Grant was not. As director of the agency responsible for evacuating all these children from Vietnam, she felt her authority over what was happening on board the plane evaporate. FFAC had chartered the jet privately. Now she had to watch as "complete strangers boarded, picked up a child each, and departed." No one asked her permission or even approached her for information on the children's status. To Grant, it seemed that "the rest of the children and escorts had to wait until President Ford came on board" before they could deplane. Worse, when Grant tried to find out what was happening to the children, she was told to sit down. In the end, when she and several colleagues from the adoption agency realized that "[our] children were no longer our business and we were not with them," Grant broke down. The nightmare of the last few days had become too much to bear. After a while, the women found a ride and started for the Presidio.

T. T. Nhu did not want to help out at the Presidio. The twenty-eight-year-old native of Hue, in central Vietnam, had grown up in New York City, then met and married a young American lawyer named Thomas Miller in Vietnam. Though the couple now lived in Berkeley, just across the bay from San Francisco, they had recently returned from Saigon. Both of them had opposed the war in Vietnam since the beginning and had worked to ameliorate the destruction through their efforts there. By April 1975, they were utterly fed up and had lost all faith in the U.S. government. Nhu had no interest in getting involved with Operation Babylift, which she saw as an "abduction."

But she made the trip over to the Presidio anyway. Ever since that first World Airways flight left Vietnam on April 2 carrying Cherie Clark's children, Bay Area radio stations had been broadcasting appeals for Vietnamese speakers to help translate for the new arrivals. Two Vietnamese friends of Nhu, Tran Khanh Tuyet and Muoi McConnell, had decided to volunteer and so, though still reluctant, she agreed to join them. When the three young women arrived at Harmon Hall, the Orphan Airlift administration gratefully welcomed them. Soon, they had put on aprons bearing a large "I" for Interpreter, and they were making their way through the cavernous facility. The place was packed with people. Newborns lay on mattresses scattered in rows up and down the floor. Adult volunteers stood cuddling babies in their arms, handing out snacks to the older children, or changing diapers. In the washrooms, infants were being bathed in some of the dozens of busboy tubs that local restaurants had supplied to the effort. Through it all, toddlers and older children played in the aisles between the mattresses or raced through the building on donated trikes.

In Cherie Clark's account of the evacuation, she stated that the older children in her facilities had not only understood that they were being adopted, but, in many cases, had already met their future adoptive families, who had visited them in Vietnam. On the night of their evacuation on Ed Daly's World Airways jet, Clark described the children as "ecstatic" that they were finally on their way to their new lives overseas.

What quickly became obvious to Nhu and her friends at Harmon Hall, however, was the fact that not all the airlift children understood quite so clearly what was happening. Now that they had found adults with whom they could communicate in their own language, some of the children began to pepper the interpreters with questions that indicated that they didn't know what was going on. "Where am I?" they asked. "Where am I going?" Nhu tried to explain to the children that they had arrived in San Francisco, California, in *America*. She explained the purpose of the airlift. She told the children that they would soon be settled with new adoptive families in this country.

Some of the children, though, shook their heads. They weren't orphans, they told her. They had families in Vietnam. Mothers or fathers or grandparents, sisters or brothers. They were very confused, and they yearned for familiar faces. Apparently, in the hectic rush to evacuate the orphanages, some children—it was impossible know how many—had been put on the airplanes too hastily. These children didn't want to be adopted. Now, they asked, "When can I go home?"

Nhu wasn't surprised that some of the children weren't orphans. As principal researcher on an NBC documentary about mixed-race children and international adoption, she had learned firsthand about the fluidity of family situations in Vietnam. Orphanages often served as childcare centers, safe places where parents could leave sons and daughters temporarily if they found that, because of the war or for other reasons, they couldn't care for them. But the fact that these parents had left their children in orphanages didn't mean, in Nhu's opinion, that they had relinquished their rights to their kids permanently. The young Vietnamese interpreter did not have direct experience with the adoption agencies that had brought these particular children out of Vietnam, and she didn't know the circumstances under which these children had ended up with these organizations, but she did know that many of the children in Vietnam's orphanages did not need new families. They had families already, scattered throughout the country. The end of the war, she had always hoped, would mean that these families could finally reunite.

Nhu didn't know what to do. In other parts of Harmon Hall, her friends Tuyet and Muoi were making the same discovery that she had. A huge international evacuation had already been set in motion, and these young Vietnamese women had no power to slow it down.

The children looked up at Nhu, waiting. "Write down everything you can remember about your families," she said. "Names. Addresses. Anything you know." Then she told the children to keep the information safe so that they wouldn't forget it. They would need it someday, if they were ever able to go home.

As medical director of the Presidio's receiving center, Alex Stalcup issued reports on the health condition of the children as they arrived. Throughout those first few weeks of April, more and more arrived. After the Pan Am flight loaded with some three hundred children landed in California, Stalcup told the *New York Times* that the situation on board was "the most incredible scene of deprivation and illness I've ever seen." Stalcup's medical team saw children suffering from pneumonia, dehydration, diarrhea, chicken pox, and other diseases. They sent forty-seven children from that flight directly to the hospital. He told the newspaper that some of the children were "unquestionably near death when they landed," but they seemed to be improving with treatment.

On April 8, in Washington, Sen. Edward Kennedy noted Stalcup's assessment in a tense exchange with Daniel Parker, the administrator of USAID. Kennedy, the chair of the Senate Judiciary Subcommittee to Investigate Problems Connected with Refugees and Escapees, had invited Parker to testify at a hearing on the Babylift and the refugee situation in Vietnam. The children now arriving in the United States, Kennedy pointed out, had been living in orphanages supported by USAID funds. "How do you explain their poor condition?" he asked.

For a time, the USAID official responded to the question by describing the challenges posed by the airlift flights. "I do not think the condition on arrival of orphans making the flight of some 10,000 or 12,000 miles is necessarily an indication of the condition in which they left. This is a rigorous flight," Parker said. "It is a flight halfway around the world."

In his nearly thirteen years in the Senate, Kennedy had become a vocal advocate for the poor and, as head of the Senate subcommittee on refugees, he was doing his best to shed light on the situation of the poor in Vietnam. To find out about the plight of the Babylift children firsthand, he would, during the weeks of the evacuation, make a private visit to the Presidio. According to Col. Robert Kane, the post commander, Kennedy seemed earnest in his interest, which wasn't the case for all the politicians who arrived. Kane later remembered that Sen. Henry Jackson, who was then contemplating a presidential bid, had shown up with "a large entourage." One of Jackson's aides asked if the senator could hold a child so that photographers outside the building could take his picture. Kane responded, "Absolutely not. These children come from a tropical climate and most are sick." Despite the colonel's order, one of the doctors relented and Jackson got his photo with a Babylift child. Kane was furious.

Kennedy's trip to the Presidio was a different story. Before the visit, one of his aides asked that Presidio officials "smuggle" the senator onto the post to avoid media attention. On the day he visited, Kane met him outside the Presidio gate and drove him in an unmarked car to Harmon Hall. There, they proceeded to tour all the Babylift facilities. On the way out, a group of reporters spotted Kennedy and began to shout questions in his direction, but the senator refused to answer them. Kane later remembered the senator telling the press, "I just wanted to see what was happening and I congratulate the Army and Colonel Kane in doing a fine job."

Indeed, in the Senate hearing room, Senator Kennedy offered praise for the Presidio effort. It was what had taken place *before* the children arrived in California that concerned him. Responding to Daniel Parker's assertion that the children were ill because of their grueling flight across the Pacific, Kennedy snapped, "You do not get viral pneumonia, chicken pox, dehydration on an American plane in a period of thirty hours."

Now, facing USAID administrator Parker, Kennedy got to his real point: that the U.S. government had done a miserable job of caring for vulnerable children in Vietnam. He reminded the official that, the year before, Congress had appropriated $10 million for child care in that country. According to the government's statistics, only $3.9 million of that money had been spent. For comparison, the senator noted that out of $77.8 million appropriated for industrial development, $77.8 million had actually been spent. "What do you say about priorities?" Kennedy wanted to know.

Parker hedged, and for the next few minutes the two officials went back and forth over technical questions, like the use of Vietnamese piasters versus dollars and the different meanings of the words "allotted" and "obligated" in aid budgets. At one point, after Parker stated that certain figures for refugee relief had nearly doubled since the previous day, Kennedy grew incredulous. "In the last twenty-four hours, you have gone from $25.8 to $41.6 million; is that right?"

Parker bristled at the senator's tone. Though on the surface the two were disagreeing about allocations of aid, the underlying argument centered on Kennedy's growing conviction that the U.S. government had never cared enough about helping the poor in Vietnam to make sure that aid money got to them. "That implies that we made a capricious and arbitrary decision," Parker said.

"Exactly," Kennedy shot back. "That is not only an implication. That is the conclusion I have made."

In Berkeley, T. T. Nhu and her husband, Thomas Miller, became involved in efforts to force the U.S. government and the adoption agencies to evaluate the records to make sure that individual children were eligible for adoption according to international law. If possible, they believed that children should be reunited with their birth families, particularly in those circumstances in which a relative relinquished a child because of panic at the end of the war. They did not object to adoption entirely. In fact, their work in Vietnam had involved supporting foster and adoptive families. But they considered adoption a last resort, a solution one arrived at after eliminating all other options. They refused to see it as a viable answer to the more general problem of children displaced from their families during war.

On April 4, within hours of the Galaxy crash, the Millers had participated in a press conference at San Francisco's Glide Memorial Church, a famed center for civil rights and peace activism. The plane crash in Vietnam was beginning to shift the national mood on the Babylift from broad support to a more cautious concern over what was happening. Most of that concern, however, centered on the manner of the evacuation, not on whether it should have been conducted at all. In Washington, for example, Sen. William Proxmire and Sen. Les Aspin called for the Air Force to ground all C5 airplanes until the cause of the crash had been determined. They also questioned why the government would use such a plane to transport children. But they did not question the Babylift as a whole.

At the Glide event, a small group of people did just that. T. T. Nhu spoke as a representative of the International Children's Fund, which she and her husband had helped to form in response to this crisis. "We must give [the children] a chance to grow up in their own country," Nhu said. Though she recognized the well-meaning impulses of the airlift organizers, she argued that "[i]t has been symbolized by this fatal air crash what these good intentions will lead to."

Nhu and the other young Vietnamese who had served as translators at the Presidio weren't the only volunteers there who had become convinced that the Babylift was wrong. Judy Spelman, a nurse who had been helping with the effort, stressed her commitment to taking care of the children once they arrived, but also said that "[it] almost amounts to a kidnapping to take children out of their country." Spelman cited the Vietnamese tradition of boarding children in orphanages, and said that now that peace was at hand, "there was great hope of reuniting the families."

Among the speakers at the press conference was a group of Bay Area theologians that included renowned Stanford University professor Robert McAfee Brown, who compared the Babylift to a form of cultural destruction. He explained that the Vietnamese rely on a broader network of relationships than are usually seen in American families. By taking these children out of Vietnam, he said, "we are breaking into and destroying a family pattern that has been established for centuries."

Of all the speakers, the most plaintive voice was perhaps that of My Loc, a member of a group called the Union of Vietnamese in the United States, who said, "I cannot accept the U.S. government on the one hand secretly sending over weapons to continue the war and create more refugees, and on the other hand [bringing] orphans over here."

The press conference at Glide attracted some local coverage, but more often the media put the Babylift story in a more dramatic and heartwarming light. "Anguish Terrible as S. Floridians Await Viet Waifs" ran the headline of a story in the *Miami Herald*. Often, however, while the headlines provided simple, feel-good storylines, the articles revealed a more complicated situation. An April 4 article in the *San Francisco Chronicle* headlined "Orphans Ready for New Homes," for example, told of a "shy 8-year-old boy in a Snoopy tee-shirt" who said that "he left four brothers behind him in Vietnam, that he did not know his new parents, and that he wasn't able to sleep all night." Almost as a balance against this desolate image of a child suddenly displaced from his family, the article quoted the boy, who was called "David" and had no last name, as saying, "It's good to live. America is a good place."

Though the opposition to the Babylift did nothing to slow the pace of the evacuations, it did begin to arouse more heated public discussion over what was taking place. Shirley Jenkins, a professor of social research at Columbia University, told the *New York Times* that the Babylift had confused a legitimate desire to get children out of danger with the more questionable effort to place these children in new, permanent homes overseas. Jane Barton, who had worked in Vietnam for three years with the American Friends Service Committee, wondered why there had been so little discussion of repatriating these children after the war ended and conditions there became more stable, as had successfully been done with Biafran refugees following the Nigerian civil war in 1970. Dr. Howard Wriggin, of Columbia University's East Asia Institute, pointed out that the Babylift marked an "unprecedented . . . movement of children from an Asian culture to a Western one so dramatically and in such large numbers at once."

Babylift proponents responded strongly to such criticism. A spokeswoman for the Holt Adoption Program, one of the largest programs in Vietnam, repudiated the idea that the children had been thoughtlessly put on planes and flown out of their homeland: "We have a staff of 100 in Saigon who've been working with these children, preparing them. In the United States, we have screened prospective adoptive parents." As for the charge that adoption should be used only as a last resort, she said, "We know the best thing is for the mother to care for the child." The war, she argued, had made that option impossible for the parents of these particular kids.

Rosemary Taylor bristled at the criticism of the efforts of those involved in adoption programs. In her book, *Orphans of War,* she rejected nearly every argument against what had become her life's work: "The favourite cliché used against our efforts to have children adopted abroad . . . was that there was no such thing as an 'abandoned' child, since Vietnamese women loved their offspring and had a strong sense of family." Taylor asserted that, by 1975, 98 percent of the children in her care were, in fact, abandoned, and the rest, she said, came from direct relinquishment by mothers who both received counseling and were offered material support to keep their children. As for concern about the loss that children suffered by growing up far from their native culture, Taylor had no use for the notion "that a child with sallow skin and slant eyes belonged to a certain pattern of life and could only be comfortable with oriental gods." As an adoption advocate, she maintained a faith that loving families overseas would offer the best environment for children denied such basic necessities as food, good health, and love at home. "What makes anyone so smugly sure that these children would not profit from parental love and support; from a healthy diet; from adequate medical care; and from good education opportunities?" she asked.

Taylor herself might have cringed, however, if she had read an anecdote that appeared in a mid-April article in the *Village Voice*. Here, an adoption agency staffer reported that some callers to her office expressed an interest in adopting children and, apparently, nothing else. "When I asked them to donate money for food and medicine, many said they only wanted a baby," the staffer said. For these people, it seemed, adoption satisfied a need that simpler forms of charity couldn't address. "Maybe," suggested the staffer, "that's their ticket for redemption."

CHAPTER 8

Mementoes and Scars

My existence is the only memento I have of the two people who conceived me.
My body is the only evidence I have that proves they were alive and
came together on this planet.

KEVIN MINH ALLEN, Vietnamese adoptee

In early January 2006, I flew from Hanoi down to Ho Chi Minh City to see David Fisk, who had arrived from California. The two of us had been e-mailing each other ever since our conversation in the noodle shop in Dorchester, Massachusetts, the previous spring. I'd been hoping that by now I would have made some discovery about his past, but in fact I'd eliminated more possibilities than I'd raised. Now, I wanted to take him to a couple of orphanages I'd visited. Even though the chances were slim that I had found any place he would remember from his childhood, I had hopes of watching his eyes light up and hearing him say, "I lived here!"

I was curious, also, to see how spending the day with David would broaden my understanding of the adoptees' perspectives. Each person's experience growing up has been singular, of course. As I came in contact with more and more of them, I saw how their lives had diverged and become differentiated from the great mass of "waifs" who arrived on those airplanes. Not only did the adoptees' experiences differ, but they also had their own unique ways of reflecting on the complex events into which they had been swept as children. Sarah K. Lawrence, who arrived as an eight-week-old baby and grew up to become a molecular pharmacologist, described occasional teasing in grade school ("yeah, I got the typical Chinese eye thing") and, as an adult, experienced an incident of workplace harassment because she was Vietnamese. Overall, though, she expressed enormous gratitude for the Babylift, describing the evacuation itself as "a pure miracle." She felt particular affection for the foreign volunteers, most of them women, who had gone to Vietnam to help in the orphanages. "A lot of these women left their children and families at home to help babies they didn't even give birth to," she told me, "[while] at the same time dodging bullets, bombs, and explosions. That is truly amazing and I owe my life and opportunities to all those people." Lawrence believed that, were it not for the Babylift, she would have died in Vietnam. For many of the adoptees, then, historical consideration of the evacuation has become inextricably, and understandably, bound with their appreciation for their own survival.

In Ho Chi Minh City, though, things became more complicated. David Fisk, who was evacuated as an older child, couldn't necessarily feel so certain that he would have *died* had he remained in Vietnam. And, unlike Sarah K. Lawrence, he remembered his birth family and wanted to find them.

We got together early one morning at the home of Pham Thi Phuong. She was the former FFAC caregiver who had known Steve George from the time he was accidentally scalded on the belly three decades before. These days, Phuong occasionally took foreigners to visit the site of the Galaxy air crash, and she had agreed to take us. In recent years, the site had become a place of pilgrimage for returning Vietnamese adoptees and the adults who had cared for them. A group of them usually gathered on the April 4 anniversary of the disaster to hold a small memorial service to honor those who died there.

Our group consisted of six people on three motorbikes: My assistant Thuy and I, Phuong and her husband, and David and his fiancée, Kim Chi. It turned out that although David's trips to Vietnam had not yielded any solid information on his past, they had helped him with his romantic life. On one of his previous visits, he had met Kim Chi. A few days from now, they would fly back to California to be married.

It was a bright morning, warm but not stifling, and we drove northeast from Phuong's house through Go Vap district, down the road that passed the home of Mrs. Tram and her scavenged airplane seats, and onto the tiny motorbike and pedestrian ferry that crossed the Ben Cat River. If you needed to cross the river by car, you'd have to drive an hour from here to get to a bridge. On our motorbikes, though, it took only a minute to cross the river, which was no wider than an unimportant road. The little ferry, which could hold about twenty motorbikes, was painted in cheerful red-and-white stripes, had a half-roof to protect us from the sun, and bore signs that read, in Vietnamese, "Polite. Completely Safe! Civilized."

Once the ferry tied up on the other side, we took off again on our motorbikes. Immediately, the air felt fresher and the city seemed a hundred miles away. In that brief amount of time, we had crossed from urban to rural, from bustling, ramshackle neighborhoods full of honking trucks and roaring motorbikes to dusty dirt roads meandering through rice fields, with hardly a person in sight. Here and there, pretty suburban-looking villas were starting to spring up, the first hints of the development that would follow, Thuy told me, as soon as the government built a long-planned bridge. She and I were, perhaps, too busy appreciating the change in our environment, however. It took us some time to realize that we'd lost the others on the winding road.

Thuy said, "Hmm."

I wasn't worried. The two of us never talked much when we drove, but I had come to trust her completely. Our relationship had warmed considerably since our first awkward meeting on the street in front of my hotel a couple of months earlier. I could pinpoint the change to a precise moment, too. It had occurred on an earlier visit to Go Vap district, when we had gone to the notorious Go Vap Orphanage, the largest such facility in wartime Saigon. It wasn't a coincidence that so much of our time had been spent in that district. Go Vap had a large Catholic population, and many church-run orphanages were based there during the war years. The Go Vap Orphanage, in fact, had first been established in 1874 by a French Catholic order called Sisters of the Lovers of the Holy Cross, and had continued to operate, in updated facilities, until the present day. By 1975, Go Vap was the largest of the 134 orphanages in South Vietnam, a place where, as American journalist Judith Coburn had described it, "a single child's illness was an instant epidemic: 'It is all we can do to feed them and get them dressed,' the nuns told visitors, 'we have no time to play with them or love them.' The biggest problem, the senior nun told me, was the expiration of the youngest babies in their cribs. 'Many have no visible disease,' she said. 'I think it may be from simple lack of love or stimulation.' In the overcrowded nurseries at Go Vap, many babies lay in their urine and feces for hours, while the overwhelmed Vietnamese attendants rushed from crib to crib to change them."

The Go Vap Orphanage that Thuy and I had visited showed a clear improvement from the place Coburn described from thirty years before. The facility, now run by the government, continued to house hundreds of children, most of them handicapped. It seemed well run, clean, and orderly. Still, there was nothing sweet or cozy about it. The place had a grim, institutional quality more fitted to a warehouse than a home for children. Other than some decorative Santas and Winnie the Poohs tacked to the nursery walls, it contained almost none of the whimsy of childhood. In one room, a toddler stood in a crib, looking at us without expression. Most of the other children lay curled up, dozing or asleep. Down a corridor, we looked into a room full of older, handicapped children. Some couldn't see. Some were paralyzed or suffering from cerebral palsy and other diseases. One preteen boy had already begun to develop whiskers, but his body lay twisted and helpless as a baby's, his eyes blankly staring at the bars of his oversized crib.

On that visit, I had kept an eye on Thuy to make sure she was okay. I had read a great deal about the orphanages of Vietnam, so I came prepared for what we saw. Thuy, however, had no preparation, and I didn't yet know her well enough to be able to read her reactions. Following the young staffer who was guiding us around, we walked along the corridors, stopping to gaze in on the children in each room, and then moving on.

After we'd seen the entire facility, Thuy and I waited in the orphanage reception room before meeting with an administrator. Two large wooden signs hung on the wall here. One displayed the operational diagram of orphanage administrative duties. The other, like some "Give to the United Way" thermometer I'd see at home, offered a graphic representation of the amount of money that had come in to the orphanage from donations that year. I pulled some bills from my wallet and pushed them into the donation box. Then, to my surprise, Thuy did the same. When she had finished, she sat back on the sofa and looked at me. In all the obvious ways, her expression remained as detached and inexplicable as it had seemed the day I'd met her, but her eyes showed something different now. Looking at her, I saw exhaustion and sadness and, strangely, too, a look of joy. "I love this job," she said.

"You do?" Up until now, she had seemed so *uninvested* in this project. "Why?"

We had been working grueling hours together, but that was the first time we really looked into each other's eyes. "I don't want to work in tourism," she said. "I'd rather be a nurse. I'd like to work with children. But I have to make money."

From that moment, Thuy and I were investigating this story together. The change affected our working relationship in marked ways. When we first met, I would carefully explain our program for the day, and she'd silently go about making it happen. Now, we strategized, deliberating over the best way to conduct each interview, or to discover a relevant piece of information. I noticed, too, that, while in English she continued to call me Ms. Dana, when we slipped into Vietnamese, she shifted to a more intimate term. *Chị* Dana, she called me. Older Sister.

I had learned, by now, that Thuy was also fearless. The two of us spent a lot of our time driving through unknown parts of this city, half-lost, sometimes in the dark. Thuy never balked at anything. Maybe her bravery had something to do with the fact that she was unmarried and lived alone. Vietnamese considered getting married and starting a family to be one of the primary obligations of life, particularly for a woman. Living outside those expectations was, in itself, courageous.

"Let's see," she murmured now, looking around and calculating our options as we trailed along the empty dirt road. "I don't know where they've gone off to." We puttered forward until we came to a small mechanic's shop among the trees. Two men in overalls, one young and one a bit older, were walking across the gravel yard. Thuy pulled over. "Excuse me," she asked in Vietnamese. "We're looking for the site of the plane crash. Do you know where that is?"

The older man said, "You mean the orphan plane?" The crash site, apparently, had taken on importance in local lore, as, I imagine, has happened to that spot in rural Pennsylvania where one of the planes went down on September 11.

Thuy nodded.

The two men talked between themselves. Their hesitation, I sensed, was not over the location of the crash, but over the best way to tell these two outsiders how to get there.

Finally, the young man lifted his hand and pointed down the road to the right. "Keep going about another kilometer," he said. "You'll come to a dirt lane on the left, go down that about three hundred meters. It's a rice field on the right."

Thuy revved the engine and we began to drive away. "Thanks, Big Brother. Thanks, Uncle!" she shouted, reminding me, once again, how the language makes everyone into family here.

Within minutes, we arrived at the rice field. The others watched our approach nonchalantly, as if they'd always expected us. Not far away, two farmers walked through the knee-deep mud, planting rice. Phuong's husband turned into a tour director, lifting his arm and making the erratic swooping gesture of an airplane in trouble. "The plane bounced once," he told us. "It went down first about five hundred meters from here. That's where most of the people died. Then it lifted again, came down here for the second time. Right where that tree is." Out in the distance, a lone coconut tree stood at the edge of the field.

We were standing in such a solitary, peaceful place that at first I couldn't quite picture flames, smoke, the ruins of an enormous airplane. But, oddly, the rice field of thirty years ago was still a rice field, which was rather surprising considering how much change Ho Chi Minh City had experienced in recent years. It didn't take a huge leap of the imagination to see Christine Leivermann make her jump from the smoldering wreckage, turn over the child in the mud, then rush back inside to rescue more. I could imagine the helicopters appearing in the sky, making their loud and windy landing, carrying off the survivors. And I could imagine, too, the local people rushing to help, the scavengers looting, the dead bodies lying scattered on the ground. Today, the place was muddy, green, and absolutely quiet. From where we stood, we could see a couple of simple houses, a hammock swinging from the posts of a little gazebo, palm trees, the farmers, that luminous field of rice.

After the war ended, the foreigners who had been involved with the Babylift left Vietnam. Many of the Vietnamese who had worked for them emigrated overseas as well. Those who remained spent the next few decades struggling to survive, often without enough to eat. The war, their years in the nursery, even the children they had loved and cared for became a part of the past. And then, in 2000, Sister Mary Nelle Gage, who had worked with Rosemary Taylor and Wende Grant, wrote to Phuong to say that she was bringing back a group of adoptees who wanted to visit the crash site. Could Phuong find it?

By that time, twenty-five years had passed. Phuong had married and raised a family. For a long period, her husband drove a cyclo, one of the thousands of three-wheeled pedicabs that plied the streets of the city, and Phuong became a wandering vendor, selling banana leaves in different local markets. They earned very little money and never had enough to eat. Sometimes, Phuong remembered the children she had cared for in the orphanage and considered the fact that they had had more to eat than her own children had now. Then, in 1989, Rosemary Taylor returned to Vietnam and found Phuong. Taylor sent Phuong and her family $250 every year for the next five years, which made the difference between misery and a stable life. The family bought a sewing machine and started a sewing business. Finally, their situation began to stabilize.

By the time Phuong received Sister Mary Nelle's letter in 2000, she could think about things unrelated to the struggles of life. Where, she began to wonder, had the plane crashed? Could she possibly find the spot where her dear friend, Birgit Blank, had died?

As Phuong began to ask around, she found that others, too, clearly remembered the disaster. One acquaintance had lived near the site as a girl. A cousin told her that the plane had crashed near his family's sugarcane fields. By the time the Americans arrived for their visit, Phuong had found the exact spot where the plane went down. Ever since, groups from all over the world—including not only adoptees from the United States but also those who had grown up in other countries—went there as an homage to the people who died then.

We drove back toward the main road. This time, Thuy and I followed close behind the others. After a couple of minutes, we turned down a lane that ran beside a small canal and then pulled up to a cluster of simple homes surrounded by vegetable gardens and shade trees. The Galaxy had first hit the ground here before it bounced and settled, finally, in the rice field half a kilometer away.

Phuong pulled a packet of incense sticks from her bag. I noticed, by the side of the road, a strange little shrine. The base was a piece of fuselage from the Galaxy—a black metal tube, perhaps as wide as a man's arm—sticking about two feet out of the earth. On top of it, someone had built a wooden, box-shaped altar and placed a canister for incense inside it. "The woman who lived in this house set up the altar to honor all the souls who died here," Phuong said. "But she was old. She died a few months ago. Now, it's up to the family to take care of it."

I looked at the piece of fuselage, all that remained of that moment thirty years ago when the Galaxy hit the ground, killing so many people. I couldn't forget the stories of the looters who had pulled the plane apart. But I also felt moved by this family who, for the past three decades, had taken on the role of caretakers for the dead—all the dead, both foreign and Vietnamese—who lost their lives that day. Tragedy brought out the best and the worst in people.

Phuong lit the incense and passed sticks to each of us. She made the sign of the cross, then said some prayers and placed her incense in the canister, mixing Catholicism and ancestor worship in an expansive gesture that was perfectly Vietnamese. One by one, the rest of us placed burning incense into the altar as well.

"Some of the VC boys died here, too," Phuong said, reminding me of the story I'd heard from old Mrs. Tram. Here in An Phu Dong during wartime, allegiances changed as day turned to night. A government bastion became, at dusk, a Viet Cong stronghold. I considered the timing of the Galaxy crash. 4:30 p.m. Soon, the sun would set. It was the liminal time between day and night, when everything shifted. Perhaps the young soldiers were cooking their rice, setting up their camp for the night. I imagine they were happy then. Finally, after years of warfare, their forces were moving south, enjoying gorgeous success. The liberation of Saigon, they would have known, was only months, maybe even weeks, away.

And then the sickly roar of the jet. Would they have seen its shadow overhead? Would they have had a chance to run, or even think, before the orphan plane slammed into them?

Phuong said, "That's really bad luck, and unusual, to be killed by a falling airplane."

It wasn't until early afternoon that David, Kim Chi, Thuy, and I said good-bye to Phuong and her husband and began to search for David's school. Of course, he had a variety of memories of Vietnam. He could remember people and places quite vividly. A school is easier to pinpoint than a house or a person, however, and, frankly, we only had clues about his school. If we could find his school, then maybe we'd find new clues to lead us toward the unspoken goal of all our efforts—his family. On the surface, this idea seemed impossibly far-fetched, but we'd all heard stories, impossible stories, of adoptees and birth families finding each other after thirty years.

For example, I'd recently heard, secondhand, a new story about a scar. An adoptee returned to Vietnam to search for his birth mother. The young man had polio as a child, never recovered completely, and came back to Vietnam in a wheelchair. He traveled to the provincial orphanage where he'd lived as a sickly boy before his evacuation overseas.

At this point in these stories, you always hear of crowds. The returning adoptee shows up at the orphanage—maybe in Can Tho or Da Lat or Bac Lieu—and the crowds begin to gather. Dozens, hundreds. Neighbors drop what they're doing to run and see. Shopkeepers lock up their stalls to push through the door of the orphanage and watch. The neighborhood children are curious because children are always curious. But the adults have a more piercing stare. They remember the war, remember the babies in the nurseries, the cars and vans that would arrive at the orphanage, unload supplies for the nuns, and then leave with children. When these people see a returning adoptee, they're not thinking, "Who is that?" They're thinking, "Which one is that?"

So, when this young man arrived, the crowds swelled, people whispered, fingers carefully moved down the lists in record books, searching for his name. They found it. Then, they found another name alongside that one. His birth mother. Yelling and loud discussion followed. Did the young adoptee understand any of it? Probably not, but he may have had a translator. The discussion would have increased in volume until someone popped out of the crowd, ran down the road, and disappeared. Ten minutes or half an hour passed. The man waited, feeling awkward. Perhaps some Starbursts were handed out to the kids. Then, from up the road, a woman appeared, maybe fresh from the rice field or from a fishing boat in a muddy canal, tired-looking, disheveled, her hands already beginning to shake. The crowd parted. She and the young man looked at each other. Maybe five feet separated them. Two strangers stared at each other, assessing what kind of change might occur on a beloved face over thirty years.

I imagine that she moved before he did. He had traveled thousands of miles in a wheelchair, and now it was up to her to cover this final distance. She did. Then, immediately, she put her hands on his head and began searching through his hair with her fingers. Perhaps his wheelchair had convinced her, because that evidence could be enough.

Perhaps his face convinced her. Now, she searched for one more thing. Without ceremony, she dug through his hair, searching his scalp until she found the scar that she knew was on the head of her son, and then she screamed, and held him, and began to sob. Everyone would have known that she'd found it.

So, we had heard about reunions. They were unlikely, but not impossible. It was the hope that we didn't articulate to each other on that busy afternoon. Instead, we focused on the quest for David's school. No one ever mentioned his mother.

We tried the Sao Mai School first. Before stepping inside, David paused in the lane looking up at the modern building. He shook his head and said quietly, "I don't remember this."

"Come in," I suggested. Thuy and I had visited once already, and I knew that, though the front of the school was new, if you walked in through the office, passed the kitchen, and went out a back door, you would emerge into a courtyard surrounded by the old, French-era buildings with their egg-yellow walls, wrought-iron railings, and creaky wooden shutters. Perhaps when David saw that, I thought, it would stir a memory.

The nuns saw David and immediately guessed why he was here. The school had been taking in orphans and mixed-race children for generations, and it wasn't unusual for them to stop by as adults. All of us filed through the building and out the back door. The nuns watched David. Thuy, Kim Chi, and I watched him. David looked up at the pretty colonial architecture. He gazed at the roofs and the sky, at a little girl in a window looking down at us. He took his time before he voiced his conclusion, but I believe he was being polite. He knew immediately. "I just don't—" he shrugged. "I just don't remember this place. My school was more country than this. I remember a lot of trees. It was very quiet."

"Well, we have some other ideas," I said. I thought back to when I was six or seven years old. Vague, disconnected, even illogical images floated through my head. Still, they had a kind of purity. I could understand how David knew.

We stayed for a while with the nuns anyway. They were very sweet, and in the office they still had their old record books, filled with notes on children that spread back fifty years. The pages were old-fashioned spreadsheets, neatly kept but rippled with age. For each entry, someone had carefully noted vital information: child's name, parents' names, date of birth, name of the person who relinquished the child, date of relinquishment, health of the child, and information on the child's education. Each entry also included a yellowing black-and-white photo. Some of the children looked two or three years old, others as old as ten or twelve. Some were blind. Some were clearly half-black or half-Caucasian. You only had to look for a few seconds to recognize that many of Vietnam's "orphans" were not orphans at all. Over and over, in the column that indicated who had relinquished the child, the nuns had written the same word in Vietnamese: *Mẹ. Mẹ. Mẹ.* Mother. Mother. Mother. The stiff pages of the record books offered a wealth of information, then, but on the central questions, they were silent: Where had these children come from? What were their stories? What kind of poverty or misery or fear had led their mothers to give them up? And, perhaps most vexing, had these mothers intended to give up their children permanently, or had they planned to come back to get them? You couldn't tell.

Just up the lane lay the Go Vap Orphanage. David's adoption agency had told him that he spent a period of time here, but he had no idea how long. We made our way through the entrance of the complex and out into a bare, concrete-covered courtyard, which served as a combined motorbike parking lot and play area for the children. David stood for a moment, spun around, looked up toward the second floor then down along an open walkway that led between two parts of the building. Thuy, Kim Chi, and I waited and watched.

"I remember this corridor," he said.

Thuy and I glanced at each other.

He nodded. "I remember this place," he said. The orphanage was quiet at that hour of the afternoon. Some children had gone to school. Others lay napping upstairs. David's voice echoed off the concrete walls. He sounded certain, but he did not sound enthusiastic. "I didn't live here. I know that. I think I probably came here for a doctor's appoint-

ment or something." We had found something, at last, but it didn't
bring us any closer to anything significant about his life. David looked
at Kim Chi. He smiled a little, but it was a smile of resignation.

For the next few hours, we crisscrossed so many miles of the Go Vap
district that, had someone plotted our itinerary on a map, it would have
looked like scribbling. We knocked on doors. We spoke with nuns in
other churches. We asked taxi drivers and fruit sellers for directions to
a location that some old person on a street corner vaguely remembered
had served as an orphanage during the war. Still, we didn't find any other
place that David remembered.

Once, while Thuy ran to the door of a church to speak with a nun
inside, David, Kim Chi, and I waited by the side of the road, squeezed
together in the meager slice of shade offered by a storefront awning. We
had been searching all afternoon and the heat had grown less bearable
because of the dusty rush-hour traffic.

All through our quest, I had been trying to gauge David's commitment to this expedition. After all, it was his life we were searching for,
not mine, and I didn't want all this detective work to trivialize or undermine the few memories he retained. So I often asked, "Are you okay?
Should we keep going?"

And, all day, despite the trouble and the heat and the occasions when
we got lost, he'd consistently answered, "Yes."

Now he looked at Kim Chi. "Dana is persistent," he told her.

Kim Chi didn't know the word, so she pulled from her purse an
electronic dictionary that the two of them used when their language
skills faltered.

I tried to be helpful. "I think the word you want is 'stubborn,'"
I said.

All of us were stubborn, really, and, still, we failed. Over the course
of my months in Vietnam, I had developed sympathy for the people who
organized the Babylift. I never questioned their desire to do their best
for the children in their care. None of the adoption agency administrators ever claimed that, by organizing the Babylift, they were eradicat-
ing suffering in Vietnam. Instead, they had a narrower goal: to focus on

making life better for individual children. Rosemary Taylor, who had nothing to do with David's adoption, had articulated this philosophy most clearly. "While children are still statistics, they cannot be helped in more than a purely abstract way," she had argued. "But up close, the crowd dissolves and there is only one child standing before us and the only way we can alleviate the misery of the suffering millions is to comfort that one child."

But, still, I thought, here was David. *One* boy who lived in *one* place. He'd had *one* mother. Thirty years later, he wouldn't need volumes and volumes of information about his past. Why, when someone took him to the United States, hadn't they collected enough information so that, should he ever decide to return, he would know where to go? That is a kind of "help" for a child. It offers a kind of "comfort," too. Why had no one written down the name of the school or, at the very least, his real name? David didn't even have that to go on.

Later, Thuy and I shared bowls of noodles and plates of dumplings at a "food festival" near the center of the city. We arrived in the slanted brightness of late afternoon, and as we walked from kiosk to kiosk, sampling fresh summer rolls and grilled squid, the sky turned lavender, then purple, then midnight blue. I felt cooler and more relaxed than I'd felt all day. On a pond amid the trees, hundreds of lanterns floated across the water, twinkling like a constellation of visiting stars. A group of musicians sat on a stage playing mournful tunes on moon lutes and zithers. The setting was romantic and nostalgic—an idealized throwback to a Vietnam that never really existed. Thuy and I loved it.

We sat at a little table out on the grass. Thuy lifted a tangle of noodles with her chopsticks. The air smelled like garlic and mint. "Tell me about Da Lat," I said. Thuy had been born in the hill town northeast of Saigon. Da Lat, Vietnam's honeymoon capital, the summer playground of movie stars and politicians, the royal and the rich. Famous for strawberries, waterfalls, and roses.

"Right after my birth, we had to leave," she said. "You know, I was born in January of 1975, so we didn't have much time there."

"You had to evacuate?" I asked.

Thuy nodded. "What a complicated time!" she sighed.

I thought of the Spring Offensive. The North Vietnamese and Viet Cong forces took Ban Me Thuot, Pleiku, and Kontum, sending wave after wave of refugees out of the Central Highlands and east toward the coast. Of course, they took Da Lat as well.

Thuy's father served in the South Vietnamese military. He urged his wife to flee to Saigon. "My mother managed to get us to the coast. We boarded a refugee ship to take us south," I looked at Thuy. On some level, all the images I'd developed in my head of population displacements and refugee ships, as dramatic and upsetting as they were, couldn't feel much more real than a drama on TV. But Thuy had survived it.

Across the grassy lawn, the musicians had begun to strum away at an even sadder tune. A couple of children chased each other in a circle while their parents, perched on tiny stools around a wooden table, bent low to slurp their noodles. The United States had granted Thuy's family asylum in 2002, out of consideration for the time that her father had spent fighting alongside the U.S. military. By the time they received their permission, however, Thuy had turned twenty-seven and was too old to be considered a dependent traveling with her parents. The family decided to go without her and then, once they attained citizenship, sponsor her emigration. All of this explained why Thuy lived all alone in Ho Chi Minh City.

We walked along a path that led through trees hung with jewel-colored silk lanterns, pausing at a small bazaar selling silk scarves, lacquer boxes, coconut-wood chopsticks, and tins of spices. In a quiet stall, a woman sat brewing tea the old-fashioned way, in a steaming cauldron over a wood fire. "Let's try it," said Thuy. We sat down and the woman handed us small ceramic cups full of tea, its aroma fragrant and familiar. "I remember this," I said, feeling my own kind of nostalgia now. I had drunk such tea on winter days in Hanoi, when I lived there in the 1990s.

"It's trà nụ vối," Thuy said. Water rose-apple tea. "It's famous. Good for our digestion."

For a while, we didn't say a word. The loveliness of our surroundings made the disappointments of the day feel less oppressive. I held my tea to my lips and blew gently into it.

"My mother has a scar," Thuy said. "Did I tell you that?"

I shook my head.

"That boat, to Saigon, was very crowded. My mother could only find space at the edge of the boat. She was all alone. She held me, her little baby, in her arms as we sailed toward Saigon. Then the boat rocked. Suddenly. You know how that happens in the ocean?"

"Yes." I felt the boat lurch beneath my seat. "From the waves," I said.

Thuy nodded. "So she felt herself tipping. She thought I would fall from her arms. She clutched me with one arm and with the other she reached out her hand and grabbed something to hold on to, a piece of the ship. But it was a pipe, the kind of pipe that steam comes out of, and it was very, very hot." Thuy held up her hand to me and we both stared at it. "She held onto the pipe because if she didn't, she would drop me into the ocean. And even though it was very hot, and burning her skin, she didn't let go."

I looked up at Thuy's face. She was grinning broadly. "My mother still has that scar on her hand," she said. "We love that scar. That's the scar that saved my life."

"Can you still see it on her hand?" I asked. It seemed like a prize, a badge of love and courage.

"You can see it. Of course. It's so ugly!" Thuy laughed, her expression full of relief and amazement. I thought of David's scar, and Steve's scar from his burn, and the boy in the wheelchair with the scar on his head that finally, after thirty years, connected him to his mother. Thuy had told me the first happy scar story I had heard. In her story, pain led to joy. During those final days of chaos and panic and sacrifice, during those last bloody weeks of that long bloody war, Thuy had been a baby, too, and had almost been lost as well. But she had been saved. Finally, I heard a story of disaster averted.

CHAPTER 9

Ship to Parents: Severe Orphan Syndrome

To Foreigners: Young Lady owner of Restaurant still operation near Tu Do,
wants to Rent or partnership to foreigners to marry if possible.

Classified advertisement in the English-language *Saigon Post*, April 6, 1975

John Williams arrived in Seattle in the early-morning hours of April 6, 1975. As a Saigon-based staff member for the Holt Adoption Program, the largest international adoption agency in the United States, he had spent the last weeks trying to organize the evacuation of the hundreds of children in Holt's care. Williams first arrived in Saigon in 1974, hired to do work that was, in some ways, the opposite of adoption. As director of Holt's Family Assistance Program, his job had focused on offering support to families and birth parents so that they would keep their children rather than relinquish them for adoption overseas. The timing was bad, however. Within months of Williams's arrival, it became clear that Holt had to shift its focus to placing more children for adoption. By 1975, the agency had more than four hundred children for whom efforts at family preservation had failed. Those children, who were living in foster homes in Saigon, had been assigned adoptive families in the United States. Once the U.S. government offered parole visas to these children, Holt shifted its focus to getting them out of Vietnam.

In this endeavor, Williams and his colleagues experienced the same strains and uncertainties that other adoption agency administrators, like Cherie Clark and Rosemary Taylor, endured in their own efforts to evacuate. The Holt staff, however, enjoyed the backing of a large, well-established organization that had been conducting adoption placements for two decades. The agency had been founded in the 1950s, after a wealthy American couple, Bertha and Harry Holt, responded to the crisis of poverty-stricken children in Korea by deciding to adopt eight Korean children and raise them in the United States. To complete their adoptions, the Holts needed a special act of Congress, which they obtained, and then they went on to help hundreds of other American families adopt children. As devout Christians, the Holts required that their adoptive families be "saved," but followed few other standard adoption procedures, which set them at odds with the social service community. In a letter that Harry Holt wrote to prospective parents in 1955, for example, he made it clear that he regarded adoption as part of a mission for God. "We would ask all of you who are Christians to pray to God," he wrote, "that He will give us the wisdom and the strength and the power to deliver His little children from the cold and misery and darkness of Korea into the warmth and love of your homes."

Over time, Holt did evolve into a more typical agency, and even if the religious foundations of the organization remained, it came to follow the general, and secular, standards of the profession. To Vietnam, the agency brought infrastructure, experience, and money, all of which helped to provide the kind of support that some of the smaller agencies in the country lacked. And Holt had more options than those agencies as well. At the end of March 1975, the agency had turned down an offer from Ed Daly to fly children out on his World Airways jet. A few days later, the U.S. government had proposed that Holt's children fly out on the ill-fated Galaxy cargo plane, and Holt had turned down that offer as well because the agency wanted to maintain control of its evacuation. When Holt did fly out of Saigon, on April 6, it did so on a privately chartered Pan Am 747 carrying 374 children. The upper deck had been converted into a mini-hospital, staffed by doctors. In the main cabin below, nurses moved through the aisles, checking on the status of the children on board. Adult escorts had two or three children in their care, a much smaller number than the ratio on the Galaxy flight a few days earlier. Some spent the long first leg of the flight to Guam changing diapers, feeding, offering bottles, and soothing infants. Others focused on the older kids, coming up with games or simply talking with the children, helping them deal with the fears and anxieties that, for many, must have been overwhelming in this moment of finally traveling to meet their new families overseas.

Even though Holt had much broader resources than the smaller, less well-financed agencies, the evacuation remained an enormous challenge to its organizers. By this point, telecommunication between Vietnam and the United States had become completely unreliable. Before the jet arrived at the Seattle-Tacoma International Airport, the local health department had to contend with conflicting information about who was on the plane. First, they expected a planeload of children, then a flight of adults, and then, within twenty-four hours of the plane's arrival, they were told, again, to expect children. Despite these miscommunications, though, the ground staff managed to complete triage, immigration, and adoption procedures for hundreds of children, most of them infants, within a few hours. The receiving team had prepared food and housing as well but found that these resources were barely needed. Instead, Holt immediately placed its children either with their adoptive families, with short-term foster families, or onto ongoing flights to their final destinations. Months later, when Dr. Max Bader, a Seattle health department epidemiologist, described the effort in a letter to the *New England Journal of Medicine*, he took pains to differentiate the procedures at Seattle from the more chaotic situation at the Presidio. "An explanation of why San Francisco received 1,600 orphans seems desirable," he wrote. "If they had been dispersed among a few other large cities, the burden would have been more manageable." In Dr. Bader's opinion, "[The] handling of the Babylift in Seattle was surprisingly efficient due to the extensive preliminary work by the Holt Adoption Program and those social service agencies who worked with it."

John Williams spent three days in Seattle helping Holt get its children settled. Then, having had barely enough time to wash his clothes, he and a colleague boarded another plane and flew back to Vietnam. They planned either to continue Holt's operations in Saigon or, if it seemed the end was really near, prepare for a final and complete evacuation.

Although the Americans had been away only a few days, they found that the situation in Saigon had changed dramatically. On April 8, a group of three South Vietnamese fighter jets had left Bien Hoa air base for a mission aimed at Communist targets. Instead, one of the jets broke away and headed for Saigon. The pilot, later identified as Lt. Nguyen Thanh Trung, proceeded to bomb the presidential palace, and then he turned his jet in the direction of North Vietnam and disappeared. Though the attempted assassination of the president failed, the attack threw Saigon into turmoil. It seemed possible that the North Vietnamese had begun a full-scale invasion.

By the time Williams returned from the United States a day or two later, the city was calmer but, still, the China Airlines pilots made the jet descend over Saigon in an hour-long defensive maneuver, spiraling slowly down from thirty-six thousand feet to avoid ground fire. Once they'd landed, Williams and his colleague drove the short distance from the airport to Holt's headquarters. Gazing from the car, Williams could instantly see the change that had taken place in the city in the few days he'd been away. A group of South Vietnamese soldiers sitting on a fence looked, he thought, like vultures. Suddenly, one of the soldiers jumped down, grabbed a motorbike and knocked it over, kicked the driver lying on the ground, then ripped the watch off the driver's arm. The city seemed to have slipped into lawlessness.

Still, Williams couldn't know for sure that South Vietnam was collapsing. He certainly didn't trust the pronouncements that came from the U.S. government. He had lost his faith in U.S. intelligence a month earlier when a U.S. official in Danang boasted to him that South Vietnam's second-largest city was "impregnable." Danang, of course, fell less than two weeks later. The cocky U.S. official, Williams later learned, had worked for the Central Intelligence Agency.

Holt still had thirty-three children in its care. For the most part, the agency had stopped accepting new arrivals. Over the next few days and weeks, however, a few children would show up that Holt's staff simply couldn't turn away. Most of these were the Amerasian sons and daughters of U.S. GIs.

Meanwhile, Han, the mother of nine from Danang, continued her quest to get her youngest daughter—blonde-haired Ngoc Anh—out of Vietnam. Over the past few days, and with all but one of her other children along with them, Han and Ngoc Anh had made it to Vung Tau, a coastal city only forty miles from Saigon. The family was exhausted, but Han, terrified of what the Communists would do to her Amerasian daughter, refused to rest until she reached Saigon and placed Ngoc Anh with an agency willing to evacuate the child overseas.

Their journey to Vung Tau had almost ended in disaster. When they boarded the ship in Danang, Han had known only that they were headed south toward Saigon. In fact, the family had narrowly missed ending up much farther away—stranded, in fact, on Phu Quoc Island, off the Cambodian border in the Gulf of Thailand. In the South Vietnamese government's desperate attempts to address the growing humanitarian crisis, it had directed refugee ships to head to Phu Quoc, where international agencies had set up a receiving center to provide displaced people with food and shelter. Landing in Phu Quoc, though, would have made it nearly impossible to get Ngoc Anh out of Vietnam. Luckily for Han, rumors about Phu Quoc began flying among passengers on the ships headed south, and the soldiers on board, armed deserters from the South Vietnamese military, balked at the idea of ending up on an island. These men were trying to reach their own families on mainland Vietnam; they refused to allow the boats to move toward Phu Quoc. Using their weapons as a threat, they forced the ships' crews to land at Vung Tau instead.

When Han and her family finally disembarked the ship, they found themselves in what was, essentially, a resort town. Vung Tau, which the besotted French had called Cape St. Jacques, was a palm-shaded beach community that stretched along the South China Sea. During the years of the U.S. presence in Vietnam, GIs would visit Vung Tau to enjoy its beaches and nightlife in a relatively peaceful setting. Now, Han tried to herd her scared and tired children through the streets of a town nearly overwhelmed by Vietnam's most recent crisis. On the beaches, a few determined swimmers continued to play in the waves. Vacationers could still get ice cream and beer. But the refugee ships loomed offshore, disgorging tens of thousands of people every day. In that first week of April alone, some four hundred thousand people, the vast majority of them military deserters, landed in Vung Tau.

Though the voyage south had exhausted them, Han's family had been fairly lucky. Another refugee ship, the navy barge AN 2801, arrived from Hue after nine days of travel. Amid a pile of debris that included broken bicycles, suitcases, and toys, rescue workers found the bodies of fifty people, most of them women and children. Malcolm W. Browne of the *New York Times* reported that "[Hardly] a vessel of the hundreds of large and small boats that have been moving up and down the coast has avoided deaths—some from starvation, thirst, and exposure, some from shooting by renegade soldiers turned bandit, some in disputes over fragments of bread."

Though they, too, had witnessed the murder and mayhem on board, Han and her family could comfort themselves that they had survived the journey. They were worn out, but they had reached Vung Tau in strong enough shape to move on. The city's officials could offer no shelter of any kind, but—relying on an informal network that included Buddhist and Catholic volunteers and even groups of Vietnamese boy scouts and girl scouts—they provided food and drinking water to the thousands of people passing through. Finally, after subsisting on crackers during the journey south, Han managed to find a hot meal for her children on shore. Then, using some of the small amount of money she had raised through selling her belongings, she hired transportation to take the family the remaining distance to Saigon. She might have felt relief to have gotten her children off that ship, but she didn't forget her original goal in fleeing Danang. She still had to get her little girl out of Vietnam.

• • •

Kathy and Wesley Lawrence lived in a Cape Cod–style cottage in the little coastal town of Wakefield, Rhode Island. It was a starter home, the kind of place that newlyweds move into when they're planning for children. By April 1975, however, Kathy had spent three years trying to get pregnant and failing. The year before, the couple had finally turned to adoption, and they filled out the forms to adopt a child from Vietnam. That effort, too, had brought anxiety and disappointment. Ever since Operation Babylift began in early April, they had been watching the news nonstop, all the while waiting for a telephone call informing them that their baby daughter had arrived in the States. Some days, frantic for updates, Kathy phoned her agency, FCVN in Colorado, seven or eight times. The agency's director in Saigon, Cherie Clark, had managed to get a small group of children onto Ed Daly's World Airways flight to Oakland, but, still, the Lawrences had heard nothing about their little girl. Then the Galaxy crashed, sending waves of panic through the entire adoptive parent community. Each time Kathy called Colorado, she found herself sharing exchanges of worry and condolence with FCVN staff she'd never even met, people who seemed equally anxious and confused on their end of the line.

Though FCVN's Colorado staff seemed baffled, over in Vietnam, Cherie Clark was actually making progress in evacuating more of the agency's children. On April 5, the day after the Galaxy crash, she managed to get promises of seats for her children on two different military flights. The first would transport most of the center's babies and her entire American staff, who were serving as escorts. Clark herself would fly out on the second flight, with older children and her own family (her husband, Tom, who had accompanied children on Ed Daly's April 2 flight, was at that moment heading back to Vietnam to help with the further evacuation).

Once the U.S. government granted her seats on its flights, Clark found that one remaining challenge lay in satisfying new bureaucratic requirements for documenting the children in her care. The crash of the Galaxy had revealed serious problems in identifying each individual child. The records for the children on that flight, for example, had been on the plane itself, and when the plane went down, the records, including those of the children who had survived, were destroyed. To avoid the possibility of losing any more documents, the U.S. military insisted that adoption agencies produce passenger lists, in triplicate, with the Vietnamese name of every child on board. Clark, of course, didn't know the Vietnamese names of most of her children because they usually arrived without identification. In the past, FCVN, like Rosemary Taylor's FFAC, had always given its children "nursery names" to differentiate them from one another. The new U.S. military requirements meant that nursery names—the names used daily by the adults who knew and cared for the children—would no longer be accepted as a means of identification.

Now, with new flights about to take off, Clark realized that she had "only hours to come up with first, last, and middle names." Rather than risk having her children banned from the flights, she started picking names at random—hundreds of them. While their colleagues rushed through the compound filling bottles of boiled water, preparing medications, and packing extra sets of clothes for the flights, Clark and one of her Vietnamese staff members sat in front of an old typewriter, giving each child a "Minh" or a "Thuy" or a "Thanh"—any name that sounded realistic enough to make the documentation look authentic. Then they put new name tags on each child, none of which included the "nursery names" that FCVN's staff had always used.

If Saigon had not yet reached the level of panic that would engulf it in coming weeks, fear of the Communist invasion had already begun to affect the city in countless ways. On April 5, an article in the *Saigon Post* headlined "Hysteria Spreading in Town" reported that the value of the U.S. dollar had more than doubled in two weeks and that many American men were trying to marry their Vietnamese girlfriends to get them out of the country. For many South Vietnamese and foreigners, the rumors about atrocities taking place in occupied regions of South Vietnam had an air of truth, especially those concerning the fate of the Amerasian kids that U.S. soldiers had left behind. Later, after Clark arrived in the States on one of the military jets, she would tell a newspaper reporter that her agency had "been flooded with mixed-blood children because of all the reports of killings." When pressed, Clark admitted she hadn't witnessed any killings firsthand, but she said, "I've seen a thousand refugees and they say they saw it."

The rumors in the city weakened Clark's resolve to evacuate only orphans and, in some cases, Amerasian kids from the country. As days passed, Vietnamese mothers and fathers, many of them Clark's colleagues, appealed to her to take their children as well. These parents were facing a decision that, for most people, exists only in nightmares: to save their children, they would have to give them up forever. Now, the war and stress had worn them down and they had come to the conclusion that their children had suffered too much already. That day on the tarmac, Clark watched as Vietnamese parents tearfully kissed their children good-bye. Then, the U.S. military jet took several hundred more of them out of Vietnam.

Throughout those first few weeks of April, adoption mania swept across the United States. "After Defiant Pilot Leaves Saigon, 57 Orphans Arrive in U.S." proclaimed one headline in the *Miami Herald*, which made the evacuation sound like the dramatic ending to an action picture. A day later, another headline declared "Broward Officer Surprises Wife With 'Beautiful' News of Daughter." In the "Social Scene" column of the *San Francisco Chronicle* on April 9, Delia Ehrlich, who was planning a cocktail party for members of WAIF, an international adoption service, called her experience serving as a "Lap" at the Presidio "one of the most fantastic experiences I've ever had." First Lady Betty Ford echoed the impulse of many Americans when, speaking at a Los Angeles luncheon, she confessed that the photographs of crying orphans in Vietnam made her "want to adopt them."

But the furor over the program was growing as well. Some observers questioned the assumption that a Communist takeover threatened the well-being of Vietnam's children. "It is no answer to any of this to say that the Communists will carry out a bloodbath," wrote W. A. Wilson in an article in the *Vancouver Sun*. "In the first place, they seem not to have done so when they took over the northern part of the country from the French in 1954. . . . In the second, a bloodbath has been imposed on Vietnam for years. The Americans did a vast amount of bloodletting and they were never scrupulous about whose blood flowed. . . . Wars do not end without tragedies but those final tragedies are generally much smaller than the ones that occur while the fighting goes on."

In Washington, too, some members of Congress had begun to question the logic of the Babylift. At his judiciary committee hearing on the matter, Sen. Edward Kennedy pointed out that the Babylift would do almost nothing to address the catastrophe facing children in Vietnam. "[It] is a mistake to think about all Americans adopting 850,000 orphans or half orphans. That does not make sense, and it can't be done. But what is important, however, is that we look at the need for the people who are still in Vietnam and care for them there; and the orphans, the other war victims there." In short, Kennedy argued that U.S. policy needed to be changed so that the United States could offer emergency aid to areas of Vietnam now in the hands of Communist forces. "We do not want . . . to assuage the American conscience by the fact that we are going to adopt 30,000 and forget the other 820,000 that are still over there." But Kennedy made his plea in a hearing room on Capitol Hill, a hallowed hall, to be sure, but the suggestion never went any further. The situation in Vietnam had deteriorated too quickly for such a reasoned response. No matter how farsighted the senator's ideas, few people in Washington were listening.

Chaos and controversy had marked the first days of the Babylift. The mission had begun with Ed Daly's unauthorized flight from Saigon with fifty-something—no one seemed to know the exact number—kids on board. Then came the catastrophe of the Galaxy crash, which destroyed the records of some two hundred children. As the days passed, it became more and more obvious that at least some of the adoption agencies were failing to keep track of the identities of all the children in their care. Still, the U.S. and South Vietnamese governments seemed unable to deal with the problem. New military guidelines—such as the ones that Cherie Clark met by inventing names—were followed, on April 10, by yet another set of protocols from the U.S. State Department. These new requirements, meant to avoid mixing children up, demanded that adoption agencies provide not only each individual child's name, but also his or her place and date of birth. The U.S. government also demanded confirmation that each child was already slated for a particular adoptive family or, failing that, that the child would soon be placed with a family already approved for adoption.

These new protocols sounded promising, but, as Cherie Clark had already demonstrated, there was nothing preventing agencies from simply making up names and birth information. As for the placement requirement, though most Babylift kids were indeed already matched with adoptive families, some were not. Every week, children were arriving in the United States with no place to go. A kind of frenzy developed within some of the adoption agencies. Staff began trolling the country by phone, calling local social service agencies to look for families who already had adoption approval—domestic or otherwise—but had not yet been matched with a child. Would those families be willing to take one from Vietnam?

Clearly, the system couldn't keep up with the arrival of the kids. By April 10, twenty-one flights had departed from Indochina, and 1,318 children—98 from Cambodia and the rest from Vietnam—had already arrived in the continental United States. Some 900 of those children went through processing at the Presidio in San Francisco. While the sickest children had been hospitalized at Clark Air Force Base in the Philippines, those who continued on were weak and malnourished. Some were badly dehydrated, and some had such severe diarrhea that they went through forty-eight diapers per day. The Presidio's medical director, Alex Stalcup, had also begun to notice a troubling psychological problem among the new arrivals. "So many of these children have the orphans' syndrome and suffer severe emotional deprivation," Stalcup, a father himself, told the Associated Press. "They have unusual needs for love."

San Francisco was doing its best. In fact, it sometimes seemed that the entire Bay Area had chipped in to help. Not only did hundreds of citizens volunteer with the effort, but Holiday Inn lent five hundred towels and washcloths. Gerber sent one hundred cases of baby food, and the Salvation Army provided ten thousand diapers. Harmon Hall, with so many toddlers playing in the aisles, looked more like a preschool at recess than a military installation.

On the surface, a sense of happy mayhem reigned at the Presidio. Some staff, though, were disturbed by the disorder. A May 1975 article in the *San Francisco Chronicle* outlined the observations of several people who had worked there. "Everything was in very much disarray, with piles of paper everywhere," one volunteer said. Mai Champlin, who served as a Vietnamese translator, told of a four-year-old boy who continually said in Vietnamese, "Carry me to my Mommy." Champlin said that she found the experience "very painful." Another staffer, a registered nurse, described an occasion on which a doctor asked her to switch the identification bracelets on two children, telling her he'd gotten permission. "I let him do it," the nurse said.

In the end, the new protocols changed almost nothing. Maybe the U.S. government didn't want the responsibility of managing such a situation anyway. USAID's Bob Walsh said as much in the *San Francisco Bay Guardian*. "We're not in the orphan business, we're just in the transportation business," he declared. "We have been assured by the South Vietnamese government and the voluntary agencies that these kids are exportable and ready to move. We are relying on the voluntary agencies. They have responsibility for that child until the kid is turned over to the adopted parent. There's no need for a federal agency to track this down. The agencies are acting 'in loco parentis' [in place of the parent], and you don't have to look over a parent's shoulder to make sure they're doing the right thing."

Medical workers at the Presidio had found, though, that some agencies managed that responsibility better than others. Nurse Janice Stalcup, whose husband, Alex, ran the medical team, came to see that the bigger, more-established agencies—for example, the programs managed by Catholic Charities and World Vision—seemed to move their children through the process most smoothly. These large nongovernmental organizations, she noted, "knew all the little things, like that you actually would need one person per kid. . . . They could make some estimate about how many diapers you would need and how long you could reasonably expect one person to sit with a kid. . . . [they] were really good." For his part, her husband came to regard the smaller agencies, FFAC and FCVN in particular, as "more amateur." Without the long-term experience and administrative infrastructure of the larger international organizations, these smaller groups didn't seem to know what they were doing, either in following international protocols or in handling the enormous numbers of children in their care. Alex Stalcup thought of these smaller agencies as "kitchen-table orphanages" because "they ran their orphanages out of a box on their kitchen table." Though he admired their commitment, he found them "crude and not very skillful" in their ability to keep track of their charges. The kind of frantic last-minute form-filling that Rosemary Taylor and Cherie Clark had engaged in back in Saigon now manifested itself, to the medical staff at the Presidio in San Francisco, as woefully inconsistent information for hundreds and hundreds of children.

On April 11, the phone rang at Lisa Brodyaga's house in Washington, D.C. The thirty-four-year-old feminist lawyer lived in a women's collective called "Self-Reliance." She and her housemates had decorated the walls with antiwar posters and formed a political-study circle to read Mao and Lenin and Marx. Because of her unconventional lifestyle, Brodyaga hadn't expected to win easy approval to adopt a child, and she'd been happily surprised when, a few months earlier, she'd been told she'd receive a referral soon. As a single woman, she expected to adopt a hard-to-place child, either an older one or one with mild disabilities.

The call came from a woman named Carol Westlake in Colorado. Westlake explained that she represented an adoption agency called Friends of the Children of Viet Nam, the organization whose nursery Cherie Clark ran in Saigon. "We have a little girl here from Vietnam," Brodyaga later remembered her saying. "She is about six years old, in good health, and if you want her, we can have her to you tomorrow."

It took Brodyaga a moment before she could even respond. She had never considered international adoption, much less adopting a child from Vietnam. But Westlake needed an immediate answer. "Can I call you back in five minutes?" Brodyaga asked.

Brodyaga got off the phone and hastily called her roommates together for a conference. They had all actively opposed the war in Vietnam and had been outraged by the Babylift, which they considered a misguided response to the crisis of displaced children in a war zone. On the other hand, this child had already arrived in the United States and had no adoptive family waiting for her. As Brodyaga and her roommates talked, they began to see the child's arrival as a fait accompli. They were not responsible for bringing her to the United States, but perhaps they could help her now that she was here. Brodyaga worried that most of the Babylift children would be brought up by "gung-ho military types" and that these children would suffer in that kind of situation. "If I adopted her," she reasoned, "she would be brought up in the kind of environment that we believed in . . . and she would be better off with us than with the alternative." Someone had to take charge of this little girl, Brodyaga reasoned, so it might as well be her.

She called Westlake back. "Yeah," she said. "Go ahead and send her."

The next day, Lisa Brodyaga and her housemates went to the airport to meet the child. As soon as they saw her, they could see that she came from mixed parentage. Though she had the dark hair of a Vietnamese, her features looked Hispanic, or even Native American. And it was hard to tell how old she was. Though the agency had said she was six, she may have been older and merely small for her age. In any case, Brodyaga felt that she was "beautiful . . . perfect. She was absolutely—I couldn't have asked for more."

The child arrived with nothing. FCVN had told Brodyaga her name —Van Thi Ha—but, other than that name, she had no paperwork, no medical records, no birth certificate. Nothing.

For the first couple of days, Brodyaga and her roommates tried to call the little girl by the name that they'd been given. Vietnamese is a tough language to master, and they tried every permutation they could imagine. "Van!" "Thi?" "Ha." No response. She didn't seem to have a hearing problem. What was wrong?

Finally, a few days after the child arrived, Brodyaga located a Vietnamese speaker willing to come to the house and talk with the girl. For the first time, the child could tell her own story.

She was not an orphan, she told them. Her name was My Hang, not Van Thi Ha. She had a mother, a father who worked as a "cook on a ship where soldiers ate," a baby sister, and a baby brother. She didn't know her parents' names because, like so many children, she only knew them as "Mom" and "Dad." She had lived with her mother at an orphanage because her mother worked there. And then, one day, her mother took her to the airport and put her on a plane. She said that her mother had cried when she said good-bye, but she had assured her daughter that, before too long, she would come back to Vietnam.

Speaking through the translator, My Hang announced that she was ready to go home now. She missed her mother, she explained. During her time in the United States, she had collected a few souvenirs and she planned take them home with her and give them to her siblings.

Brodyaga, distraught, called FCVN in Colorado to tell them that the child was not an orphan.

The FCVN staff insisted that she was.

Brodyaga refused to believe them. During the course of that and subsequent conversations, she sensed that the FCVN staff didn't actually care if the little girl was an orphan or not. They seemed to think that, regardless of what she said, she was better off in the United States.

After a lot of phone calls that went nowhere, Brodyaga gave up on calling FCVN and started to look for other ways to help the little girl. She knew it would be a long struggle. In the meantime, she tried to explain to My Hang how hard it would be to find her mother, but the child wasn't convinced.

"She said she knew how to get back home," Brodyaga later remembered. "You go to the airport, take three planes, and then two buses to get back to her mommy."

• • •

Kathy Lawrence wasn't a gung-ho military type. She had opposed the war in Vietnam and had even attended peace rallies while she was growing up. Her husband, Wesley, had actually served as a medical corpsman in the conflict, but his reasons for adopting from Vietnam were more personal than political. Simply put, Kathy and Wesley wanted to become parents and, when they decided to adopt in 1974, they discovered that the easiest babies to get were the ones from Vietnam.

By April 12, the Wakefield, Rhode Island, couple still had no word on their daughter. Over the past week, Kathy had taken many days off from her job in order to stay home and wait for news of the child. That morning, she finally told her husband, "I have to go back to work." Luckily, Wesley was able to stay by the phone and wait for news while Kathy drove to the nearby town of Westerly, where she worked as a nurse making home visits. Every hour or so, she'd borrow a patient's phone and call home. "Any news?" she'd ask. All morning, his answer was the same: Nothing. Disconsolate, Kathy forced herself to concentrate on her work. She didn't pick up the phone again for a long time. Then, at noon, she called again.

This time, her husband said, "Get home. Now."

The agency had called. Their baby girl had made it from Clark Air Force Base in the Philippines to the Presidio in San Francisco. A couple of United Airlines employees had volunteered to fly her to Boston's Logan Airport. "She's coming," Wesley told her, "at six o'clock tonight."

Kathy raced home. After all these months of waiting, the couple now had only hours to get ready. As much as they'd prepared mentally for this moment, they had never known for sure that the child would arrive, and so they had yet to buy diapers, baby bottles, or even a crib. Now, they had five hours to get organized, drive to Boston, and become parents. While Kathy and Wesley rushed north, her mother, who lived in the city, ran out to buy the things they needed most.

By six o'clock that evening, they were standing at the airport gate, watching a 747 taxi toward the terminal. The plane came to a stop and, within another few moments, passengers began appearing. Kathy scanned the crowd for a baby, but she saw nothing. It seemed to take forever for the huge plane to empty out. Kathy could barely contain herself. Then, when she felt she couldn't stand this suspense another minute, an elderly woman approached them. "Are you waiting for a baby?" she asked.

"Yes," the young couple said.

"Oh, my God. She's on the back of the plane and she's beautiful."

Moments later, the escort appeared. In her arms lay a baby girl. The child was tiny, terribly dehydrated, and covered with scabies. One half of her head had been shaved completely bald so that, the Lawrences later discovered, doctors could administer an IV.

Kathy took the baby and stared down at her new daughter. After so many years of infertility, she had lost hope that she'd become a mother. And now, this tiny child had traveled all the way around the world to end up here. Her joy was absolute.

Sarah, as the Lawrences named their new daughter, arrived at Logan Airport with little more than the blanket in which she was wrapped. Among the documents that came with her, the Lawrences found a doctor's assessment from Clark Air Force Base that said, among other things, "Ship to Parents: Severe Orphan Syndrome." Later, the Lawrences asked a Vietnamese speaker to translate some of the other paperwork. That's when they realized that they couldn't count on the accuracy of any of the information they'd received about their daughter's past. Some of the Vietnamese documents that came in the packet from FCVN called the child by a different Vietnamese name than the one they'd originally been given. Kathy was so happy to have her baby, though, that she didn't care.

CHAPTER 10

There Was No One to Take Care of Them

*How much "native culture" does a child get in an institution? Ask the children
if they want to be adopted. Ask the orphans, who never had a chance to have a family.
Which is more important, to have "roots" or to have a family?*

French orphanage volunteer, Ho Chi Minh City, 2005

Rosemary Taylor arranged more adoptions from Vietnam than any
other individual. Many times, as I reread her book, *Orphans of War*, I
found myself flipping to the photographs of her, trying to match the
sweet, slightly wry expression on her pretty face with the more complicated descriptions that came from people who knew her. Her former
colleagues described Taylor as kind, but also profoundly serious, reserved, and intimidating in her single-minded desire to save Vietnamese
children. Some of her Vietnamese staff had found her stern and somewhat distant, but also very generous. One of those former caregivers
told me that, after the war, the Communist government sent many of
her colleagues to the new economic zones in remote provinces. "They
were really miserable," she said. "Over there, they were supplied with
food and money every three months, but their children had no money
to study. Rosemary helped."

The foreigners involved in the Babylift had even more complicated
views of Taylor. "I don't think that Rosemary was aloof," one former

volunteer told me, "but I think she tended to project that, and that might be in part because she was ultimately a very shy person. She was not at all comfortable in the limelight. She just wanted to see children get good homes, basically. That was what her interest was, or what my understanding of her interest was."

I wanted to meet Taylor, but I couldn't even figure out which country she lived in, much less obtain a phone number or e-mail address. I decided to ask her former colleague, Sister Susan McDonald, for help. McDonald, an American nun and nurse, had run Taylor's Newhaven orphanage in Saigon from early 1973 until the end of the war. Before I left for Vietnam, McDonald had offered me contact information for several Vietnamese women who had worked in the FFAC facilities in Saigon. Now I wrote to McDonald to ask if she would put me in touch with Taylor herself.

McDonald's reply was prompt, lengthy, thoughtful, and ultimately disappointing. She had contacted Taylor on my behalf, but Taylor had declined to meet with me. "[Her] work is so involved she is unable to respond to the daily requests for interviews, to be in films, etc. She tells people [that] what she has to say can be found in the comprehensive book she wrote—*Orphans of War*."

McDonald also wanted to make sure, however, that I understood Rosemary Taylor's importance to the story of the Babylift, even if the woman herself refused to meet me. "It is clear from all records of adoptions in Vietnam from 1967–1975," McDonald wrote, that "Rosemary was involved with by far the largest percentage. She is an unusually humble person, was monumental and selfless in giving of herself. I have never in my life met such a truly holy person. And I worked for and met Mother Teresa."

Cherie Clark was easier to find. At the time, FCVN still existed as an adoption agency, and though Clark no longer worked there, she remained in contact with its staff. I sent an e-mail to the agency one day and received a message from Clark herself the next. As it turned out, she had read my first book and traveled frequently to Vietnam. A month later, the two of us were having lunch together at the Metropole Hotel in Hanoi.

While some foreigners involved with Operation Babylift went on to lead relatively mundane lives after the war ended, Cherie Clark has not. She returned from Vietnam in April 1975, traveled to Guam to help with refugees, then went to Colombia and Thailand. By August of that year, she was on her way to India, alone. She and her husband, Tom, had decided to separate. "It was becoming clear that he did not share my restlessness; he was ready to settle down to a career," Clark wrote in her book. "Our lives were taking different directions." A little over two years after the end of the war, she had moved with her eight children to Calcutta, where she opened a charitable organization, International Mission of Hope. She remarried, had two daughters with her Indian second husband, and eventually returned to Vietnam and ran an adoption agency there for many years. By the time I met with her, she estimated that she had been involved in the adoptions of some ten thousand children.

When we got together in 2005, Clark was living the peripatetic life of a fairly constant traveler. She wasn't sure how many times she'd visited Iraq in the last year, and she told me about her trips to Egypt, Oman, Gaza, the West Bank, and Jerusalem, where she'd studied Arabic. "I have to have a Middle East part of my life," she told me. Vietnam no longer held her in thrall as it once had, although she still felt that that country was "where I always say I want to live, work, and die." By this point in her life, however, she didn't want to live there full-time. I sensed that she'd become bored with the place. "It's like living in Colorado," she told me.

We sat in the Bamboo Bar of the Metropole, Vietnam's grand hotel built in 1901. Above us, a ceiling fan turned lazily. Outside the windows, foreigners relaxed beside the sparkling pool. Clark, smartly dressed in black with pearls, looked younger than her sixty years—proof perhaps that it's inertia, not adventure, that can put you in an early grave. There at the Metropole, she blended in well, her face displaying the game hardiness you often see among tourists in Vietnam, but, as we talked, I also saw the tired, somewhat bemused expression of someone who had seen a lot in her life and was very rarely surprised by anything.

She was curious about my research on Operation Babylift, though. I explained that I'd been collecting documents at Vietnamese libraries and archives. Some of the articles I'd found in North Vietnamese newspapers from 1975, I told her, were fiercely critical of the Babylift. At an archive in Hanoi, for example, I had found an article from *Nhan Dan* [The People's] newspaper dated April 8, 1975, in which a coalition of North Vietnamese health-care workers called on the world to "stop the savage, vile, and inhumane actions of the Ford Administration and the clique of Nguyen Van Thieu and his lackeys in kidnapping and mistreating the innocent young children of southern Vietnam, not allowing them the happiness of living in their own native land now undergoing liberation . . ." In recent months, I had become familiar with this kind of language. To me, these articles were interesting, but fairly predictable. After all, the government of North Vietnam had criticized nearly everything the United States did. Clark grew animated when I told her about the accusations, however.

"I can see exactly how [the Babylift] would be perceived by people," she told me. Just after the war, Operation Babylift had led to lawsuits questioning what she and the staff of other agencies had done. At first, Clark disparaged these efforts. "For years, I thought, 'They just don't know what shape these kids were in,'" she told me. More recently, she had begun to look at the events from a broader perspective. "To think that we would just airlift out two thousand of some other country's kids and just say 'Yeah, yeah. We got papers on them, we'll give 'em to you later, I trust this guy.' No, it just seems obscene, legally, to me. And it seems very presumptuous that America would participate and the government would do that."

I looked at her. Cherie Clark had been, after all, one of the most prominent participants in the Babylift. She had been responsible for evacuating hundreds of children out of Vietnam. Now she was calling it "obscene"?

"I'm surprised to hear that from you," I told her.

She nodded again, as if to stress what she'd just said. "I feel that way, strongly," she replied. Then, just as quickly, she added, "I feel that I can vouch for the kids in our care."

"Vouch in what way?"

"That they were genuine," she said. And then, with barely a pause, she returned to her previous assertion. Supporting the Babylift, she told me, would have meant "putting a lot of trust in people who are sticking kids on those planes who don't really know who they were."

I didn't know what to say.

She shrugged. "I've always felt that way."

Three decades after the Babylift, Cherie Clark had found a way to look at it historically. She moved, apparently effortlessly, between faith in her own actions and amazement over the fact that the Babylift occurred at all. It's possible, of course, to both view an event critically and mount a defense of one's own involvement in it. I felt surprised, however, by her honest assessment of what had taken place. She didn't try to defend it wholeheartedly.

Despite her willingness to question the very premise of the Babylift, Clark had reasonable explanations for each of the thorniest issues that had concerned me in my research—namely, the lack of documentation, the destruction of families, and, finally, the controversial question of whether these children would have died had they remained in Vietnam.

In their memoirs about the Babylift, both Rosemary Taylor and Cherie Clark described their efforts to document the children in their care. And yet, in the end, when adult adoptees like David Fisk wanted to find their birth parents, many had absolutely nothing to go on. And others, like Sarah K. Lawrence, arrived in the United States with documents that didn't seem to match their physical characteristics at all. "It's hard for me to imagine how so much could have been so inaccurate," I told Clark.

"We were careful but, you know, documents meant very little. It was the child," she said, reminding me that the problem of abandoned children in Vietnam was enormous, and that most of the children in her care were considered abandoned. She brought up Rosemary Taylor as well. "The certainty that probably Rosemary and I had was: These are orphans. I mean there's no one who's going to come back looking for these kids. In all the years of experience that we had, no one had come back to look for them before. It's not like someone came and was like, 'Oh, gee, I left my baby down in Can Tho at the orphanage.'"

In fact, Clark had very little sympathy for the sad stories that circulated of birth mothers giving up their children. As an example, she told me about "one of the most horrible mothers" who hung around outside the FCVN compound at the very end of the war. Clark had been trying to follow a policy of not accepting children from birth mothers unless those children were Amerasian and, therefore, at risk of persecution by the Communists. This woman's children were not Amerasian, but she "kept hanging around," Clark told me. "And they said she was beating the kids. I did not want to take these kids of this biological mother. And then, all of a sudden one day, she had gotten in and I found the kids sitting next to our van. And we ended up, this was like right at the end, I took the kids out, but I had this mother's name and address." Years later, after the children grew up, they returned and found their mother. As Clark explained it to me, "She basically said, 'I put you inside that gate so that you could go to America and get money and you owe me money.' It was horrible, just horrible. The kids had come over on a fourteen-day ticket. They had brought like two thousand dollars for her. And she basically threw the two thousand dollars back and said, 'That's nothing.' And they left. They only stayed in Vietnam for like forty-eight hours."

Clark wanted me to remember, too, that the decision to evacuate the children had come at a critical moment in the war. Saigon was about to collapse, she reminded me. "It seemed like it was going to be the end of the world, you know? The banks were closed. The city was in chaos. It seemed like there wasn't a tomorrow." The possibilities, she told me, were frightening. "Some of our precious babies . . . if somebody would have told me I had to leave them because I didn't have paperwork, I would have died. Because, leave them to what? Who was going to take care? Where would we have taken them? Where was the milk? I mean that whole sector of babies would have died, because there was no one to take care of them."

• • •

"Our situation was not like Africa," snapped the Vietnamese priest, who had worked with displaced children in Ho Chi Minh City's Go Vap district during the war. "We were very poor, but it wasn't true that they would die."

Thuy and I had gone to visit the priest to ask him about the war years. He was cautious about meeting with us, because relations between the Catholic Church and the Vietnamese government remained strained, so he asked me not to use his real name.

"Call me Mr. Nguyen," he had told me, conspiratorially. I could see that Thuy found this moniker rather amusing, and I, too, tried not to laugh. "Nguyen" is like "Smith" in Vietnam, so it sounded like the name a spy would use. "MR. NGUYEN," I scrawled in bold letters at the top of the page in my notebook.

I was hoping that Mr. Nguyen would offer a different perspective on the plight of parentless children during the war. Again and again during my time in Vietnam, I circled back to the same question: What would have happened to the Babylift children if they had been left in Saigon? From the foreign agency volunteers, I heard one answer. From the Vietnamese who stayed in Vietnam, I heard something else.

Mr. Nguyen, for one, may have had with a tense relationship with his government, but he remained patriotic about his homeland. He came from the Salesian Order of Don Bosco, which had operated a technical school for poor boys in the area. While the foreign-run orphanages concentrated their efforts on evacuating children from Vietnam and placing them with adoptive families overseas, the Don Bosco Technical School raised children to lead productive lives in their own country, whether they had parents or not. Proponents of the Babylift had suggested that there was no hope for the orphans in their care if they had remained in Vietnam. The vast majority of Vietnam's orphans, however—nearly nine hundred thousand children—would never be adopted abroad. Was it really impossible that they could grow up and lead stable lives in their own country?

These days, the priest ran a parish church in a quiet corner of the district. He was a busy man and agreed to meet with us only in the evening, when he had more time. Unlike the center of the city, with its brightly lit shopping centers, crowded restaurants, and lively cafe society, Go Vap became deserted after sunset. It wasn't a threatening emptiness, but rather the emptiness of a working-class neighborhood whose inhabitants have nowhere to go after dark. The parish church itself was substantial and relatively new, a sign of recent warming between the Communist government and organized religion. Now, in the evening, it was so quiet we could hear dogs barking and crickets in the garden. Sometimes, during pauses in our conversation, the lilting notes of the church choir would float down to us from their practice room upstairs.

Aware that I was researching Operation Babylift, Mr. Nguyen quickly differentiated between the Don Bosco school and the nurseries run by foreign agencies who organized adoptions. "I didn't work with the Westerners," he told me. The priest was a hardy, jovial man in his late fifties who spoke a charming French-accented English. He had worked in the school from 1973 until the war ended in 1975. "The children [in Western-run orphanages] lived like rich people, not like orphans," he said.

I'd heard comparisons between foreign- and Vietnamese-run orphanages, of course, but always from a foreign point of view. In her book, for example, Cherie Clark made Vietnamese orphanages sound like facilities in a Dickens novel. In one place she visited, she wrote, "Flies and ants crawled on [the children], gathering at the open sores scattered all over their bodies." Conditions, clearly, were horrific. But, according to Mr. Nguyen, they weren't horrific everywhere.

The orphans in Salesian institutions, Mr. Nguyen explained, went to school. Those who excelled could continue their education, but the Don Bosco Technical School focused primarily on vocational skills. Many of the boys (other institutions provided homes for displaced girls) learned trades so that, by the time they left the institution, they could find work as auto mechanics, for example, or electricians. The goal, Mr. Nguyen told us, was to raise children in a simple, practical way to enable them to become solid members of Vietnamese society. "If they lived rich, then after [they grew up] they wouldn't know how to live by themselves," he told me.

The boys at the technical school didn't "live rich" at all, but I could see the comforts of their routines: wake up at 5 a.m., breakfast at 7, study, play sports. On Thursdays or Sundays, the boys would watch a film or perform a play, sometimes about the lives of saints, sometimes episodes from the French adventure series *Tin Tin*. Out of six hundred children in the school, some two hundred were orphans, but they were never called by that name. They were called "Don Bosco Boys." They looked like all the other children, too, and wore their own individual clothes, not uniforms. Mr. Nguyen explained that uniforms encourage "a mentality of orphans" and the priests wanted to avoid that. "Different colors are beautiful," he told us.

Clearly, the Salesians had very different goals from those of the foreigners, like Cherie Clark or Rosemary Taylor, who focused on getting displaced children out of Vietnam and into adoptive families overseas. He did not dispute the fact that the children who went abroad could do well there. "Vietnamese are very intelligent," he told me. "If they have the occasion to study, they're very successful." Rather, Mr. Nguyen argued that taking children overseas amounted to a waste of resources. "With the cost of bringing one child abroad, you could help three in Vietnam," he pointed out. It was, essentially, the same reasoning that Sen. Edward Kennedy had used when he noted, in the April 1975 congressional hearing he held on the subject, that instead of putting so much effort into international adoption, foreign aid should focus on improving the lives of children in their own countries. In the midst of the crisis in Vietnam, though, Kennedy's argument received very little attention. By the time the senator spoke, America's resources had already been directed toward Operation Babylift and, as the senator had discovered, the U.S. government's attempts to funnel humanitarian aid to Vietnam had been lackadaisical at best.

Indeed, the Babylift seemed, at least to the foreign adoption agency administrators, the only way to save the lives of the children in their care. Cherie Clark had described for me the terrible anxiety she felt over the possibility that, when the war ended, the children would die because no one would be left to care for them. But throughout Saigon, orphanages continued to operate, and some were taking in new children. An Associated Press article published in the English-language *Saigon Post* reported on April 20 that the Hoi Duc Anh Orphanage in that city, which had a population of 635 children, was expanding to take in thousands more.

At the Don Bosco school, too, staff remained in place during this period. While the foreign agencies were airlifting their children to new adoptive families overseas, the students in the Don Bosco school continued their lives without enormous disruption. Three months later, the school did close, but because of bureaucratic brutishness, not because there was no one left to care for the children. In a move that was taking place in similar circumstances throughout the area formerly known as South Vietnam, the Don Bosco Technical School became a victim to the Communist government's effort to consolidate the power it had amassed by winning the war. Always wary of the religious orders, the new administration shut down the Catholic institution and dispersed the students and priests to other places. "[The orphans] were stripped out from our hands," another priest told me, fairly spitting his words. "They were *taken*." Life grew worse for the children then—not dire, perhaps, but worse. The entire economy was deteriorating, though, and that's what happened, essentially, to everyone in Vietnam.

CHAPTER 11

Photographs and Fires and Rage

My country at war for 4,000 years. Never settled. When things bad, kids always get sent to other homes. Then they get sent back. You never give kids away forever.

LAN POPP, Vietnamese mother, 1976

By late April 1975, the refugee crisis was worsening. The Provisional Revolutionary Government, or Viet Cong, had appealed to the United Nations and the International Red Cross for emergency shipments of clothing, food, and medicine to aid the six million displaced people now living in areas under its control. According to the Red Cross's own figures, two million of those refugees were children.

After days of arduous travel, Han and her eight children had finally made it to Saigon, where they were taken in by relatives who lived near the train station. The place had little room for so many new inhabitants, but the family didn't turn them away, and at least they were safe there. All over the city, refugees lay curled up on sidewalks and under trees in parks. Han could feel grateful that she and her children had a roof over their heads.

After Han got the other children settled, she took little Ngoc Anh out into the city. First, they visited a photography shop. Han asked for one picture to be taken of the child alone and another of the two of them together. In those days, photography shops held onto their negatives, which could serve as a source of revenue if customers later wanted copies of their prints. But, after the photographer snapped the pictures of Han and Ngoc Anh, Han made an appeal. "I'm a refugee," she said. She explained that she was taking her daughter to an adoption agency and signing away her rights to the child forever. "Can you let me have the negatives?" She asked, wanting to keep every memento of her daughter. The photographer looked at her. So many rumors were swirling around Saigon about the fate of Amerasian children after the Communists took over. One only had to glance at Ngoc Anh, with her blond hair and Caucasian features, to understand why this refugee mother was giving up her child. The shopkeeper handed Han the negatives.

Han had brought with her the address of the adoption agency. Much later, they would learn that it was called the Holt Adoption Program, but at the time, they knew it only by the name that Vietnamese used, *Mẹ Quốc Tế* (International Mother). By the time they arrived at the office in Saigon, Han and Ngoc Anh were both crying, which they did a lot during those days. At certain points, Han felt that her daughter seemed happy to be leaving. After all, Ngoc Anh's friend Hiep had already gone to the United States and it sounded like an exciting adventure. Now, though, the little girl didn't want to say good-bye.

"You go there and find your father," Han urged her. "If you stay here, I'm afraid they'll catch you."

Holt, which operated out of a large compound near the airport, was crowded that day. Mother and daughter waited for a while until, finally, Han found herself in front of a staff member. She explained why she had come. From here, the process moved quickly. Han signed a few papers. She wrote down Ngoc Anh's name and age and handed over the child's birth certificate. To Ngoc Anh, she gave the photograph of the two of them that they had had taken. This was the only thing she could offer Ngoc Anh that would help the child remember her family in Vietnam. Before Han left that day, the agency staff gave her a receipt.

Over the next few days, Han returned to the orphanage regularly to see her little girl. She returned so often, in fact, that one of the agency staff finally said, "If you love your daughter so much, then take her home." Holt's priority—and one of the reasons that John Williams had decided to work there—lay in preserving families; adoption, they said, should be a last resort.

But keeping Ngoc Anh didn't seem to Han to be a viable option. As everyone could see, the Communists were on their way, and neither the South Vietnamese government nor the United States had tried to discourage people from thinking that a bloodbath would follow, particularly in regard to Amerasian children. Han never truly believed that she could keep Ngoc Anh and so, instead, she kept returning to visit because this separation from her daughter had become too hard to endure. For as long as she could, Han chose the middle ground. She returned to the agency, day after day. Then, finally, Ngoc Anh said, "Tomorrow, I'm going to America." Han told herself that she had to bear the pain so that Ngoc Anh could be happy.

Much later, Ngoc Anh would remember specific moments of those days before she climbed aboard a jet, found herself strapped to the floor, and flew to the United States. She remembered standing on one side of a fence, surrounded by other scared and nervous children. On the other side of the fence stood her mother, looking in at them. Ngoc Anh cried. Her mother cried. "Everything's going to be all right," Han called to her.

And Ngoc Anh would also remember that, just before she left, the adults who worked for the agency built a fire, collected all the photographs and letters that the children had with them, and threw them in. Asked about the incident years later, Holt's John Williams suggested that Ngoc Anh could indeed have remembered fires. The agency staff, like those in so many foreign offices during the last days of war, burned records that might incriminate local employees after the Communists took over. "It is quite likely that the older children might remember seeing things being burned," he explained, but added that, because Holt made careful efforts to preserve important documents, "[it] is extremely unlikely that what she saw being burned were any of the children's papers."

Perhaps, then, Ngoc Anh did not actually see her photo being destroyed. At some point in her future, though, she no longer had it. Her young mind did its best to construct an explanation for this loss. As she later remembered it, the children stood watching their photos and letters go up in flames, trying to understand why the adults had decided to burn them.

By the time Ngoc Anh arrived at the Holt office in Saigon, most of the agency's adoptive children had already been evacuated to the United States. Besides preparing the last few children to leave, Holt's staff was trying to provide refugee relief across the city. Many of the hundreds of thousands of people who had disembarked from the ships at Vung Tau had, by now, made their way to Saigon. Holt and other agencies would identify areas in the city where refugees had congregated and get food to them. If they found a marketplace where hundreds of families had taken shelter, for example, the relief agencies hurriedly distributed rice, milk, and any other supplies that would help ensure that the refugee crisis didn't become a catastrophe. Later, looking back, Holt's John Williams wondered if he slept at all during the entire month of April.

The agency was also making contingency plans. If the Communist takeover seemed imminent, Holt planned to close down operations completely. As the days progressed, Williams began to hear regular fighting on the outskirts of the city. At night, tracers would flare across the sky. He could hear shelling and bombing and see the resulting plumes of smoke. Word spread that a force of South Vietnamese soldiers was holding the line on a bridge that led to Vung Tau. That bridge, right outside the city, now marked the front lines. And still, to Williams's consternation, the U.S. Embassy continued to deny that South Vietnam was about to collapse. Every time Holt staff members ventured over to ask U.S. officials for information, they would hear the same story: "Don't worry," the embassy staff would tell them. "Hang on."

One day, Williams was introduced to a Catholic priest who had just flown into Saigon from Hawaii. "What are you doing here?" Williams asked. It seemed a strange time to be traveling to Vietnam.

The priest had come to Vietnam to meet with representatives of foreign adoption agencies. "I've promised twenty-seven families in Hawaii that I would find them children," he said. He looked at Williams. "Would you please give me twenty-seven children?"

Williams wasn't sure he'd heard correctly. "Excuse me?"

"I promised these families," the priest explained. "I can get them out. Give me twenty-seven children, or however many you can give me. I've got this money here." He proceeded to open a satchel full of bills.

Williams couldn't believe what he was hearing. This kind of thinking contradicted every principle he valued about the work he was doing in Vietnam. He'd arranged adoptions, yes, but he kept his focus on the task of keeping families together. Now this priest was asking him to procure children simply because a group of Americans wanted them.

The priest continued, "Ed Daly has promised that he would put these kids on a flight and take them out for me." He made it clear how much he admired the owner of World Airways.

The reference to Ed Daly, who had been responsible for that disastrous flight out of Danang, finally made Williams explode. "Do you realize that the final flight from Danang *killed* people?" he asked. "There were people hanging out of the wheel wells. They couldn't pull the gear up. People were falling off as they took off. They ran over people on the runway!"

After weeks of trying to address the crisis in Vietnam in some kind of thoughtful, methodical way, the mention of Ed Daly and his cowboy shenanigans made John Williams go blind with rage.

CHAPTER 12

I Wanted to See What Peace Was Like

It seemed like millions of Vietnamese were waiting to see what
would happen, but we didn't know exactly what day. . . .
Although I was walking on the ground, I felt like I was in a dream.

NGUYEN THI NGOC DUNG,
Vietnamese mother and Communist revolutionary, 2006

What might have happened to the Babylift children if they had stayed in
Vietnam? I kept coming back to that question, which made me realize
that I needed more information about what transpired in the orphanages during the days and weeks and months after the Communists took
over. I decided to call Lady Borton, a Quaker who had worked in a
rehabilitation center in Quang Ngai province during the war. She had
written several widely admired books on the Vietnamese and had been
living in Hanoi for more than a decade now. She was the most well connected American I knew in Vietnam.

"I need to hear the North Vietnamese side of this story," I told her. I
didn't mean the propaganda side. I already had numerous articles from
North Vietnamese newspapers that condemned the Babylift while it
was taking place. Now I wanted to speak with people who had fought
for the North but were willing to talk about the Babylift in a more
measured way. And I wanted to know, too, how the North Vietnamese
government viewed its responsibility toward South Vietnam's displaced

children. As the war approached its end, did they have a plan for dealing with the thousands of children who remained in orphanages throughout South Vietnam? Cherie Clark, Rosemary Taylor, and the coordinators of other foreign agencies might have taken all their children out of the country, but the almost twenty thousand kids in South Vietnam's other orphanages weren't going anywhere. Nor were the nearly nine hundred thousand parentless children who didn't even live in such facilities. How the North dealt with the problem of children in general would give me a clue to how they might have handled the Babylift children had they remained in Vietnam.

Borton cautioned me that I probably wouldn't get a lot of information. Many of these people were old, she said, and I was talking about things that had happened thirty years before. More importantly, she reminded me that the Babylift was an ancillary drama to the larger struggle. The evacuation took place at the moment that these revolutionaries were, as they saw it, finally on the cusp of uniting their nation. They couldn't focus much attention on the story of several thousand children being airlifted out of Vietnam. "The energy in Hanoi at that time was directed toward their own soldiers," she explained, "and the end of a long struggle."

Still, Borton gave me several names, including that of Nguyen Thi Loan, who, as a Communist leader, had taken over the care of Saigon's orphans and homeless children immediately after the war ended. These days, Loan was approaching eighty. She lived with her children and grandchildren in a roomy, well-appointed home on a quiet street in Ho Chi Minh City. Despite her age, she was fast-moving and alert, and as soon as we walked through the door, she shepherded us toward a sofa next to a low coffee table, where she invited us to sit down and have tea.

Loan came from a wealthy family in the Mekong Delta, but she joined the revolutionaries as soon as she graduated from high school. It would be thirty years—after the end of the war in 1975—before she returned to normal life. "It's unusual that a girl from a wealthy family would make that kind of sacrifice," I suggested.

Loan shook her head. "At the time of the revolution, everyone rose up to participate," she informed me. "The Vietnamese had been slaves for nearly one hundred years under the French regime, so, when they heard the words of independence and freedom, they went."

On the wall behind her, I noticed a large, blown-up picture of a much younger Loan whispering into the ear of a somewhat bemused-looking Ho Chi Minh. It's an odd sensation, in any case, to see someone you meet in real life posed with one of the most iconic faces of the twentieth century, a sort of "six degrees of separation" proof that that legendary figure was, also, a flesh-and-blood human being. I was equally drawn, though, to the expression on Loan's face in the photo, which had a kind of giddy optimism that helped me understand why the man inspired so many people, rich and poor, to give up everything to follow him.

I glanced back to Loan, who was waiting for me to continue. I was, after all, here on my own mission. "At the end of the war," I began, "did you hear about the children who were taken overseas?"

She raised a hand as if I'd reminded her of something. "I'll talk about that," she said in the tone of a patient schoolteacher.

In April 1975, she explained, she was living in Hanoi, and she heard about the Babylift and, also, the crash of the Galaxy. "I heard that that flight wasn't good because people had arranged it as a screen to take out officers from the CIA and other intelligence people," she told me. "If they had just taken the CIA and people like that, alone on the airplane, it wouldn't have been the best method for them, so they brought along the children as a screen. That's the story, but the plane crashed."

"Do you remember what you thought about it?" I asked.

Loan shrugged. "I don't know much about that story," she said, and her expression told me that she didn't care, either. Her main reaction to events in Saigon was an impatience to travel to the South herself so that she could do something about the problems there. "I was burning to go down there early to have direct involvement with the children," she explained.

Loan arrived in Saigon soon after the war ended on April 30, 1975. Her responsibilities included overseeing care in forty orphanages in the city, both government-run facilities and those managed by charitable institutions. "That was about eight thousand children," she said.

The logistics of taking over an entire government are, of course, monumental. The North Vietnamese–backed revolutionaries, however, had had many years to prepare. They did so by operating shadow ministries in liberated areas. As the military expanded those liberated areas, the ministries expanded their oversight into the new territory. "Everything had to be ready and in working condition," Loan told me, including a broadcasting system, a banking system, a postal system, and women's and youth affairs. As soon as the military took Saigon, Loan's Department of Social Welfare and Invalids moved in to take control of the orphanages.

Despite the panic in the South before the war ended, the takeover proceeded fairly smoothly. Still, the challenge of taking over an orphanage system that housed eight thousand children was hardly as simple as a parent coming home from work and relieving the babysitter. "I still don't understand how you could make such a quick transition to new management in that kind of chaos," I said.

Cherie Clark had described the anxiety she felt over the idea that these children would literally die in their cribs if she didn't get them out of Vietnam. But Loan also reminded me that there were plenty of people taking care of children who had no plans to leave the country. "In the orphanages, both public and private, there were very good, kind people. The nuns were really good. It seemed to me that they did it for the sake of their god. They stayed and took care of the children."

"There was never a time, then, that the children were abandoned and left alone?" I asked.

"No," she said.

A few months before this conversation with Loan, Thuy and I had met a woman named Huong, an orphan herself, who had moved into Go Vap Orphanage in 1972, when she was thirteen years old. Huong had been born in Quang Ngai province, in a village not far from the site of the My Lai massacre. The warfare in this area was horrendous. In some seasons, bombs dropped so frequently that the villagers had no time to plant their crops of rice, and they spent entire seasons running from place to place, ducking bombs. In 1970, one of these bombs fell directly on the hut where Huong and her family had taken shelter, killing her mother. Eventually, the girl made her way to Saigon, which seemed a paradise to her, if only because she could get enough rice to eat and didn't have to fear the bombs.

By the time the Communist forces approached Saigon a few years later, this young girl had become a childcare worker herself, employed by the orphanage that had taken her in. The war that had driven her from her home village was once again closing in on her. "Everyone was scared of the bombs and dying," she told us. But Huong said she felt hopeful as well. Her country had been at war for her entire life. "The most important thing I wanted was peace," she told us. "I wanted to see what peace was like. There wouldn't be any more dying. People wouldn't feel so miserable any more. In peacetime, if people are miserable, it's from hunger or poverty. That's all. But they wouldn't have to be miserable about bombs any more."

In that conversation with Huong, I had been curious to know what happened in the orphanage as the Communist forces approached. At the foreign-run orphanages, of course, fear over the Communist invasion had led to a complete evacuation of all the facilities. Better to take every child—even some not clearly meant for adoption—than risk leaving them to die, alone, in a deserted orphanage with no one left to care for them. I wanted to know what had happened at Go Vap Orphanage on that day in April 1975 when the Communists arrived.

Huong told me that the childcare workers were nervous—so nervous, in fact, that they scraped the polish off their nails because they had heard that the Communists would chop off the fingers of any girls wearing nail polish. They didn't run away, however. They looked out the windows and saw the soldiers marching by, but they didn't leave their posts. "If you were afraid, you were just afraid," she said. "Every room still had dozens of children in it. It wasn't like you could say, 'I'm too afraid, so I quit.' If you were going to die, you'd just die. That's it."

I was coming to see, from my conversations with Huong and Loan, as well as with the Catholic priests, that Vietnam's orphanages remained fairly calm and stable during the crisis that took place in Vietnam at the end of April 1975. The famous photographs I had seen of the panic and despair of "The Fall of Saigon"—the helicopter pulling refugees from the roof of a building, the mobs at the airport desperate to get onto planes—represented only some of the most dramatic images of what happened that day. Most South Vietnamese did what Huong did. They waited and watched. They changed diapers, fed children, cooked food, washed dishes. For almost all Vietnam, life went on. And so, of course, life continued for the orphanage children as well.

Of course, life in the newly reunited Vietnam was not at all easy, as even Loan, the revolutionary, was willing to admit. The war had ended, but the deprivation had not. It would get worse, in fact, over the coming years. Often, she told me, the orphanages had to feed the children sweet potatoes because they didn't have enough rice. They didn't always have enough medicine, either. "We couldn't provide them with everything they needed," Loan said. "We had a lot of troubles."

I saw now that the Babylift children would probably have survived had they stayed in Vietnam. Instead of evacuating more children *from* provincial orphanages, agency administrators could have taken children *to* those orphanages, along with whatever supplies they still had, and left them with the nuns. But even Loan, still a fervent revolutionary, had admitted that the new system had faltered. A child can't thrive in a poverty-stricken orphanage, subsisting on potatoes. What would have been a better fate for these kids—poverty at home or plenty abroad? This question gets to the very point of adoption, in any context. The adoption agencies and the U.S. government believed that the airlift gave these individual children a better chance for their lives. Those who criticized the airlift argued that more comprehensive humanitarian aid would have helped all children in Vietnam, not just a few, and let them remain in their own country.

Once, I asked an American Babylift adoptee what she thought about the evacuation. She had been a six-month-old infant when she was air-lifted from Saigon on April 28, 1975. She grew up—quite happily, she told me—in Oregon. She had never known any other existence than her American life, and consequently, as an adult, she was no more able to engage the question "What if I'd grown up in Vietnam?" than any native-born American could have done. As an observer, however, she could see that the Babylift, which resulted from "chaos and tragedy," as she put it, had created chaos and tragedy of its own. She could easily understand the grief that the Vietnamese felt over the loss of these children. She also saw a kind of national gall in the fact that the United States had airlifted so many of them out of their homeland. If American children had been evacuated and sent to adoptive families overseas, she told me, "the U.S. would have words to say, too."

CHAPTER 13

Hesitation and Resignation

*So might we all [have tears in our eyes] at the spectacle of these orphaned babies
and children hustled out of their country to be scattered around the United States
like so many Easter chicks. How can this possibly be a kindness to children frightened,
hurt, desperate for the security of the familiar? What panicky notions impelled the
Americans in Vietnam to push children helter-skelter onto planes to be shipped to
the country that has been most responsible for the fact that they are orphans?*

Letter to the Editor, *New York Times*, April 15, 1975

On April 7, 1975, the Saigon government ceased to authorize any more
Babylift flights. By April 13, all the children who had previously arrived
at the Presidio in San Francisco had been placed with families or into
short-term care. The facilities at Harmon Hall shut down as the main
arrival center for the evacuation. It seemed, for several days, that Operation Babylift had ended. Then, like a lull that's mistaken for the end of a
storm, the evacuations began anew on April 21. Once again, flights took
off from Saigon, carrying hundreds more children overseas.

Three weeks had passed since the Babylift began. Adoption agencies
and the U.S. government were moving quickly to place children in their
new homes as soon as possible. Social science research on adoption had
begun to show that children could rebound from early traumatic experiences. Researchers John Triseliotis and Malcolm Hill, for example,
noted that studies of children in both adoptive homes and foster care

"demonstrated that the impact of early adverse experiences can 'fade away' with the opportunity to form new positive attachments." From this point of view, settling children quickly seemed essential to avoiding any lasting psychological damage.

But opponents of the Babylift had equally compelling reasons to slow the process down. For one thing, there was precedent. "After the second world war, *no adoption* of displaced children were [*sic*] permitted while the Red Cross searched to bring lost parents and children together," stated a press release put out by the War Resisters League. As the days passed, it had become more and more apparent that many of the children were not, in fact, orphans and were, therefore, ineligible for adoption according to international law. A *Washington Post* reporter visited the facilities at the Presidio and found that, out of ten randomly selected older children, nine so-called "orphans" actually had parents living either in Vietnam or the United States. "They said they had come to the United States to join their parents or uncles, aunts, or other relatives," the article reported. "Six of the children carried papers telling how those parents or relatives could be contacted." It turned out that one boy, who had intended to go to his older sister in Tennessee, instead ended up with an adoptive family in Vermont.

By now, nearly everyone involved in the Babylift acknowledged that the record-keeping had been, to put it mildly, problematic. Maria Eitz, a volunteer with Rosemary Taylor's agency, FFAC, told the *San Francisco Chronicle-Examiner* that it was "apparently correct" that many of the children were not, in fact, orphans. She speculated that Vietnam's powerful and wealthy were using the Babylift as a cover to get their own children safely into exile. "There may have been cases," Eitz hypothesized, "where (a Vietnamese official) said if you take these four children, then you can take these sixty children." She also didn't rule out the possibility that actual orphans "may have been replaced (on U.S.-bound planes) by children from families that had money."

Even some U.S. government officials readily admitted that the humanitarian mission had run into serious problems. In one article that ran in the *Miami Herald*, a State Department official lamented, "I'll tell you what this is turning into. . . . It's starting to become a kidnapping operation by well-intentioned people who are ignoring international law."

On April 21, the U.S. State Department issued a new directive on how to proceed with future flights. By now, though, it was clear that the U.S. government could not monitor the entire evacuation because it could not control all the flights out of Vietnam. The very same day that the State Department issued its new criteria, a World Airways jet took off from Saigon carrying a load of 271 children, illustrating, as one U.S. military history of the Babylift put it, "the lack of military control over commercial airline operations."

Despite these growing concerns over the way that the Babylift was being managed, adoptive families were welcoming their new Vietnamese sons and daughters into their homes: "Larry and Linda Moritz got the son they always wanted," one story read. "Dave and Bobbie Johnson became instant parents of three boys after six years of childless marriage. Tony and Denise Ingram got a new playmate for their two previously adopted Vietnamese girls."

Most adoptive families had spent months or even years anticipating this moment. They had already received names and health information and had merely been waiting for the children themselves to arrive. For these families, the Babylift expedited a process that was already well underway. Some families, however, seemed much less prepared, and ended up with Vietnamese children without having considered the ramifications of their decision. To address some of the many issues that arose, adoption agencies and the U.S. government disseminated information meant to help new parents through the period of adjustment. The Department of Health, Education, and Welfare offered a pamphlet, "TIPS on the care and adjustment of VIETNAMESE and other Asian CHILDREN in the UNITED STATES," much of which was written by the staff of the Holt Adoption Program. The pamphlet offered advice on everything from the transmission of parasites ("Be sure to wash your hands well after changing and cleaning the child") to the

complicated psychological issues that might come up ("One of the areas
of which you need to be conscious is that your new child won't always be
grateful for your efforts. This is also true of one's natural children, but
somehow it seems your special efforts in turning to another country for
a child, along with your financial sacrifices, should guarantee a special
rapport and appreciation from your adopted child. It just can't always
be that way!").

For some families, a bit of counseling or a printed pamphlet was
clearly not enough. After one Florida couple discovered a bump on the
head of their new Vietnamese son, they worried that the child had a terminal disease and rejected the adoption. In subsequent media reports,
the prospective parents expressed their fury that their adoption agency,
the Catholic Service Bureau, had even placed the child in their home.
"It's criminal what's happened," the husband said. "We waited for years
to realize the dream of a child and now it's turned out to be a nightmare."
His wife concurred. "I want a baby that is perfectly normal," she said.
"For such a baby, I can provide a beautiful home." In the end, the boy
turned out to be healthy. By that point, though, he'd been placed with
a new family willing to take a child under any circumstances. Reflecting
on this particular case, the director of Catholic Charities said, "There's
been a lot of unnecessary hysteria involved. I don't know how many
times we explained that these children might be undernourished and
sickly."

At the Presidio, a nurse sent a report to medical director Alex Stalcup detailing certain cases that had come up over the course of the
operation:

"Family #1: Mother and father approx 30 yrs old w/ two sons (3 yrs &
6 yrs old). They were to receive baby A (3 mo. old male). When I placed
the infant in the mother's arms, her reactions led me to believe she was
not prepared for the baby. She immediately started comparing baby
A with baby B (a 2 mo. old male). She made statements such as, 'This
baby (A) is so much smaller than that one (B) and he (A) is older.' 'This
one (A) doesn't smile.' 'It (A) has awful scabs and bumps on his head.'
'You know we really wanted a girl, girls are so much cuter and daintier.'
This mother's mood changed when we went outside. They had brought

along with them their local newspaper men to cover their story. She then appeared happy to have the child, but she changed back again when the newspaper reporters left. Their other children also made some re-marks, 'I don't like him, Mommy, he is ugly.' The parents' reply was 'You will have to like him, now be quiet.' This family appeared to be more concerned with the publicity of adopting a Vietnamese orphan than the infant himself. They continually referred to the baby as 'It' rather than 'he.' The mother did have an appointment with their doctor, but she said, 'I want him to see our doctor right away because I don't want any of us to get anything.'"

"Family #2: Mother and father approx. 30 yrs old, 2 children, girl 3 yrs, and boy 5 yrs. The 3 yr old girl is a Korean child adopted when she was an infant. This family brought baby 'B' to me because he was sent to them by mistake. Their child is 14 mo. old and baby 'B' is 2 mo. old. They explained to me that they had known about their son since he was 5 mo. old. Even though baby 'B' was cute, he wasn't theirs. These parents referred to their baby as 'Adam,' the name they are giving him, and as 'our son.' They appeared at ease, even during a time of tension (their 14 mo. old was missing.). The mother also told me that they had started a scrapbook with all the papers and notes on all the things that happened while they were trying to get Adam. This book would be for Adam to keep. They had done this for their Korean daughter also, so both children will know their own stories and heritage. This family clearly wants their child. They have planned and hoped for him. They appear very stable and would possibly be a good resource for other parents with adopted children in their area.

"Family #3: Mother 26 yrs, Father 29 yrs, no other children. Adopted 3 yr old female. When this child was given to her parents, she was very frightened of her father. It was explained at that time that the child was afraid of men. The father was quite upset, stating, 'We weren't told there was going to be problems like that.' After talking with his wife for a few minutes he appeared calmer. I can't help but wonder how this child will do, especially if it takes her a long time to adjust to her father. The adoption agency has no form of follow up that really considers this type of situation."

• • •

Back in Vietnam, as April progressed, the effort to get these children onto airplanes became increasingly frantic and hard to control. One firsthand witness to the frenzy was a twelve-year-old girl named Phi, who lived with her family just across Tran Ky Xuong Street from Cherie Clark's orphanage. Phi's family had moved to the neighborhood years before, when it was little more than a country village. Even as the city grew up around them, they maintained a fairly normal existence, even though their nation was at war. Sometimes, of course, Phi heard her parents worry that a bomb could drop on their house and hurt them. And she, like most Vietnamese, had relatives who served in the military. But, in general, Phi was a child fortunate enough to be able to focus on childish things—playing outside, eating her dinner, going to school.

Four months earlier, in late December 1974, life for the children of Tran Ky Xuong Street had become a little bit more interesting because the FCVN nursery moved into a large compound halfway down the lane. Several times, Phi and other neighborhood children had ventured through the orphanage gates to play in the spacious courtyard. Phi had peeked through the doors of the villa and seen the tiny babies lying in their cribs inside. For a twelve-year-old girl who knew almost nothing of life beyond her home and school, these developments were intriguing.

But then, in the middle of April, life on Tran Ky Xuong Street changed dramatically. From Cherie Clark's perspective as director of the orphanage, the "quiet lane where my children used to play marbles and soccer with their young Vietnamese friends had been transformed into a scene of bedlam." Over the past few weeks, refugees had poured into the city from all over Vietnam. Lucky ones managed to find room in the homes of relatives or friends. Others slept among the rats and scattered rotting produce on the floors of covered markets, or congregated in parks or in the narrow spaces between buildings. To the residents of Tran Ky Xuong Street, it seemed that thousands had chosen their little corner of the city, and most of them were parents with children. "The narrow lane was literally packed wall-to-wall with bodies," Clark recalled in her memoir, "all trying to get into our compound. The temperature was oppressive and the hot sun beat down on the gathered masses. The clamor was incredible, a primal, throbbing din that continued without letup—babies and children crying, women screaming and sobbing and men shouting towards the Center. It was a living nightmare."

From her house across the street, Phi stood at the window and watched. For days, the panicky crowds stretched in both directions. Some people stayed there all night. Where had these people come from? Why were they here? Sometimes she ventured outside and stood among the crowds. She was too young and afraid to ask questions, but by standing quietly, she could look into the anxious faces of the adults and listen to what they were saying. They had come because of the orphanage, she learned. They knew that the foreigners inside were sending children overseas. These people had brought their own children—Amerasian kids, paraplegic children, weak infants with little chance of survival—to beg the foreigners to take their sons and daughters out of Vietnam. As Phi listened, she heard talk of medical treatment, of hopes for healing abroad. Slowly, the little girl began to develop several firm ideas about what was taking place. First, no one seemed confident about what was going on, or what might happen. Second, in contrast to the children she had seen inside the building in the past, these children on the street weren't orphans. Their parents had brought them here.

These parents, apparently, were desperate. In her memoir, Cherie Clark mentioned a baby boy who died after he was pushed through barbed wire and then allowed to drop to the concrete ground below. Phi never saw anything so horrible or dramatic, but she did see the parents mob the orphanage van every time it emerged from the compound. They would crush against it, yelling, pushing their children forward. Sometimes, the windows of the van were open, and, as the little girl watched, parents pushed their children through, and let them drop inside.

Cherie Clark wasn't the only one who was continuing to take in more children every day. During the second half of April, the population of children in Rosemary Taylor's Saigon nurseries fluctuated wildly. It had become clear to almost everyone that South Vietnam was on the verge of collapse, and debate centered on how much time remained—in terms of days or weeks, not months. Knowing that she would soon be closing her agency entirely, Taylor laid off many Vietnamese staff and began to consolidate her far-flung operations into fewer locations across the city. At the same time, she made arrangements for local people to take over some of her facilities after she and her foreign staff left the country. Children who had not been evacuated were taken to provincial orphanages for resettlement within Vietnam. For a time, then, FFAC's nurseries became considerably more vacant. But the agency was also feeling a pull from a different direction. Many waiting families had still not received the children they had planned to adopt. Suddenly, the empty nurseries began to fill again, Taylor explained in her memoir, because "more children poured in from provincial orphanages, as the Sisters commuted back and forth from the Delta, bringing children who had been promised mostly to families in France and Italy." Soon, Taylor's nurseries reached maximum capacity.

Once again, Rosemary Taylor was in the position of needing to airlift hundreds of children out of Vietnam. As opportunities arose, she was able to get small groups onto planes leaving the country, but by late April, she still had 270 children in her care. Most of those were children who had only recently arrived from orphanages in the provinces. She didn't know them, and they had already been matched with particular families overseas. As days passed, she found herself in the same situation that she and her colleagues had faced a few weeks earlier: Every morning seemed to bring new promises of transportation, which would then disintegrate before the day ended. To make matters more complicated, Taylor's earlier layoffs meant that she was short-staffed, and all but three of her foreign colleagues had either died in the Galaxy crash or left Vietnam on earlier flights. Somehow, Taylor assembled a team of escorts from among the Catholic nuns and priests she knew in the community and from those among her Vietnamese staff who wanted to emigrate overseas. These new escorts had little or no experience caring for children, however. When two new babies came in without nursery names, Taylor and her colleagues had given them ones that fit the mood of that period—Hesitation and Resignation.

Finally, on April 26, the U.S. military authorized a C-141 cargo plane to airlift Taylor's group from Vietnam. By this time, thousands of Vietnamese nationals were mobbing Tan Son Nhut Airport, trying to find seats aboard the refugee flights that were now taking off day and night. Getting the children to the airport demanded the kind of tactical planning that goes into complicated military engagements, but once they got inside, they found that moving the children from the airport entrance onto the plane would be even more challenging. Military and police swarmed the area, rifles in hand, demanding that Taylor's group follow the boarding procedures exactly. One of the registered USAID buses had failed to arrive, however, and the agency's alternative means of transportation, an ambulance, wasn't allowed onto the tarmac. Taylor had no way to get the children the final one hundred yards to the airplane. "When we unloaded the sweltering children and attempted to walk," Taylor recalled, "a police officer drew his gun and leveled it at a four-year-old who was wandering away from the group." Taylor had no one to call because most of the USAID staff had already evacuated. At that moment, she remembered that she had been given a "mystery number" to call in case of emergency. She ran to a phone and called. Eventually, as a result of her call, the military gave the children permission to board the airplane. Still, the group had to go through extraordinarily complicated measures—for example, placing their hundreds of children on buses to travel a few yards to the airplane—simply because officials demanded it.

Once again, Rosemary Taylor faced the fact that she would have to board all these children onto a cargo plane that lacked the most basic amenities. Despite the lessons of the Galaxy crash, this jet was, like that one, completely inadequate to carry such delicate cargo overseas. Many of the children lay in cardboard boxes that had to be carried individually onto the plane and then placed haphazardly on the metal floor. Older children sat on benches along the wall, secured with a single safety belt that stretched across all their laps. Taylor also began to realize just how inexperienced and helpless this new crew of escorts would be. Instead of helping load the children, they stood on the tarmac watching the mayhem, "totally useless and disoriented, clutching their own baggage." Taylor finally grabbed the bags out of the escorts' hands, shoved babies into their arms, and forced them onto the plane. It was impossible to know how these adults would manage with so many children on a flight across the Pacific.

Rosemary Taylor did not take that last flight. She would stay in Saigon for three more days, sorting through photographs, most of which she wouldn't manage to carry out of the country. Finally, on April 29, the day before the Communists arrived, Taylor herself left Vietnam by climbing aboard a helicopter on the roof of the U.S. embassy. The aircraft was crammed with people, many of them journalists. "[V]isibility was poor," Taylor wrote. "The back of the helicopter was left open and we peered out of the gaping hole at the darkening landscape as we headed out toward the sea. There were no lights inside and the high noise level of the engine and rotors made any conversation impossible. We sat tensely, watched, and waited."

On the evening of April 26, not long after Rosemary Taylor sent her last planeload of children out of Vietnam, Cherie Clark left the country on a C-141 cargo plane carrying 184 children and 17 adults to care for them. The previous day, some of Clark's staff had built a bonfire and burned the records of staff and the foster families who had cared for FCVN children, fearing that the Communist forces would later use such information to persecute people who had worked with the American organization. The sight of the flames had indicated to the crowd outside the compound that FCVN was preparing its final evacuation from Vietnam, and the uneasy refugees grew hostile. Day and night now, Clark and her staff could hear the angry yells from the lane. By the time they evacuated the compound on the morning of April 26, the mob had become so threatening that police escorts had to line the road to clear a way for FCVN's staff to carry the cardboard boxes, some with two or three infants in them, out to the buses that would drive them to the airport. Clark herself held in her arms a critically ill infant strapped to an IV, a dying child she couldn't bring herself to leave alone in the compound.

Many of the children in this last group were so weak and malnourished that they risked dying on the flight. Rather than leave them behind in Saigon, Clark remained committed to evacuating her nursery completely. The children wore the same sort of hastily created identification bands that Clark had made for earlier flights. "Some of the names we fabricated made no sense at all," Clark later wrote. "We were too tired to care; at that late stage it didn't matter if we had a boy named Sue." After the baby in Clark's arms did die, on the bus headed to the airport, a U.S. marine who took the body asked Clark the baby's name. "I simply shrugged," Clark explained, "and shook my head."

As the day progressed, other babies would die as well. The group waited hours at the airport, poised to go when and if the pilots finally decided that it was safe to take off from the bomb-damaged runway. Their meager supplies were dwindling quickly. The previous night, Clark and her staff had resorted to boiling used IV needles in an attempt to sterilize them and use them again. "[We] worked with what we had rather than what we needed," Clark explained.

By late afternoon, the escorts were struggling to keep the children hydrated in the scorching heat. It wasn't until early evening that the pilots announced that the plane would take off. Quickly, the FCVN staff loaded the children onto the same type of military jet that Rosemary Taylor's group had boarded earlier that day. Once again, the adults reacted with horror as they stepped onto the plane. The aircraft was a sweltering metal box. It had no seats, only a metal floor on which to set the boxes and boxes of sick children. The adults tried to arrange the boxes in some safe configuration on the floor, then loaded the three crates of supplies—diapers, milk bottles, medicines, and water—that they hoped would last as far as Clark Air Force Base in the Philippines, three hours away.

The head pilot appeared. He was clearly stressed and began yelling orders immediately. Then, he spotted the crates. Thinking that the group had tried to carry on luggage, which was forbidden, he kicked the crates off the plane. Clark watched as the precious supplies fell from the ramp. The glass milk bottles shattered on the tarmac. What had just happened, she knew, "could become a death sentence for these babies." Then the door to the plane closed. A moment later, the aircraft was barreling down the runway. Nothing on board had been secured. As the aircraft took off, climbing at a 45-degree angle to avoid ground fire, the entire cargo—toddlers, adults, infants in their cardboard boxes—slid in a jumble to the rear of the plane.

Slowly, the plane leveled off. In the din, Clark looked around. Children were screaming. The only liquid on board was what remained in the bottles that the adults had in their hands. The group had nearly two hundred children to care for and three hours ahead of them before they reached the U.S. base in the Philippines.

Cherie Clark stood up and carefully made her way to the cockpit of the ascending jet. Inside, the two pilots and flight engineer concentrated on their instruments. The plane remained in danger and they were not interested in talking to a passenger. Clark explained that her supplies had been in those crates and that children would die before they made it to the Philippines.

The pilot turned and yelled above the noise. They weren't going to the Philippines. He told her that they were going to Guam.

Clark stared at him. Guam was eight hours away. The children wouldn't make it to Guam, she tried to explain, but the pilot quickly cut her off. The U.S. airbase in the Philippines was full, he said. They were headed to Guam. Clark could no longer contain herself. This airplane would arrive in Guam, she said, "full of dead babies."

The pilots ignored her. They were Air Force reservists who had been flying nonstop missions in and out of Vietnam. They were exhausted and literally incapable of hearing what she said. Clark and her colleagues continued to plead, but the men wouldn't listen.

Finally, Clark brought one of the babies into the cockpit. The child had turned blue. It was dying in her arms. The flight crew looked up. They seemed calmer now that the plane had reached a safer altitude.

They looked at the baby. One of the crew said to the pilot, "Sir, that baby really is dead."

The pilot looked at Clark, at the cargo hold full of screaming children. He suddenly seemed close to tears. Then he radioed the U.S. military base in the Philippines to say that he had to make an emergency landing.

According to Clark, her group would be the last to fly on a U.S. military aircraft participating in Operation Babylift. The next day, a rocket attack shut down Tan Son Nhut Airport. Looking back, Clark considered "how close we came to being stranded with our babies through the chaos surrounding the fall of Saigon. . . . There was no milk, medicine, medical supplies, or staff to care for the large number of infants through the communist takeover and no matter how gentle the turnover might have been, the children's survival would have been impossible."

Clark never gave an exact number of how many children died on that last flight. "[S]adly," she said, "many."

Rosemary Taylor, Cherie Clark, and the other foreign adoption agency volunteers had suspected for months that they themselves would soon be leaving Vietnam. For the local staff who had filled out the ranks of nursery caregivers, the end of the war meant something much more complicated. During those last days of April, the mood among Saigon's population swung between panic and a somewhat schizophrenic effort to pretend that life was normal. Neighbors passed rumors from house to house: China had invaded North Vietnam; U.S. marines had landed in the South. These were pretty, hopeful notions, but most people recognized them as merely that. The exchange rate for a U.S. dollar, which served as a sign of South Vietnam's economic weakness, shot from two thousand to thirty-nine hundred piasters in the course of four days. Still, shoppers could choose from a wide selection of fruits and vegetables in the market, and the city's famous sidewalk cafes continued to serve their tall glasses of Vietnamese iced coffee, a sweet, bracing brew that probably seemed indispensable at a time like that.

Many local adoption agency staff decided to evacuate, and their positions with the various foreign organizations made emigration easier. Pham Thi Phuong, one of Rosemary Taylor's FFAC staff, had planned to move to Germany with her friend and sponsor, Birgit Blank. After Birgit died in the Galaxy crash, though, Phuong no longer knew what to do with her life. Toward the end of April, another foreign volunteer asked Phuong if she'd like to emigrate to the United States. Phuong considered the offer, but she worried that she wouldn't be happy there. The seventeen-year-old had worked in Hy Vong nursery with an American named Julie, and Julie had often snapped at the local staff. "You're stupid," Julie would tell them. "You're incompetent." Julie's contempt had colored Phuong's view of Americans in general, making her shy away from the United States. "If I went to that country, and everyone insulted me, then how could I survive?" she asked herself. She decided, instead, to remain in Vietnam.

Nguyen Bich Ha (not her real name) was a nurse who worked for Cherie Clark's agency, FCVN. A widow with two children, she was engaged to marry a man who had three children of his own. She and her fiancé had decided to remain in Vietnam because neither of them spoke English and they didn't feel that they would be able to support their family overseas. At first, she felt confident in this decision. In the days leading up to FCVN's final evacuation, she concentrated on her work in the nursery, sleeping on the floor at night to care for the children there. Then, on April 26, things seemed stable, so she went home to see her own family. That day, Cherie Clark received word that the U.S. military jet would evacuate her group. Within hours, they had gone. The next morning, Bich Ha returned to Tran Ky Xuong Street to find the FCVN nursery, once so crowded with children, completely empty. Only Ross Meador, Clark's young American colleague, remained. He, too, had planned to leave with Clark, but he decided to stay in Saigon a few more days so that he could distribute the last of the supplies and ensure the safety of FCVN's remaining local staff.

Bich Ha hurried home and told her fiancé what had happened. He, like her late husband, had fought with the South Vietnamese military. Over the past few days, Saigon had become an increasingly frightening place. News ricocheted like gunfire across the city. It seemed clear that the Communists were about to invade. How would they treat the family of a former soldier of South Vietnam? Late into the night, the couple discussed their options. Finally, they decided that they should leave. The next morning, Bich Ha rushed back to the orphanage, found Meador, and asked him to help them get out of Vietnam.

The Vietnamese nurse and the young American aid worker had been colleagues for nearly a year, but they didn't know each other well. A thirty-something widow with two children simply didn't have a lot in common with a long-haired hippie-type who was barely out of his teens. But Bich Ha liked Ross. He looked strange to her, but she respected him for his hard work, his enthusiasm, and his commitment to the children. Now, she had to ask him to do her a huge favor. Would he be willing to help?

Meador agreed immediately. Over the past few weeks, he and other Americans in Saigon had become experts in the process of getting Vietnamese out of Vietnam. Now he wrote up some documents for her, had her sign them, and told her to meet him the next morning with her entire family. Just don't bring a lot of luggage, he said.

Bich Ha and her fiancé spent the evening carefully deciding which of their precious belongings to take with them overseas and which things they would leave behind forever. Now that she had Ross to help her, she felt more relaxed. They would get out of Vietnam after all. She sorted through clothes, packed bags, carefully made sure that everything was ready.

The next morning, the family woke up and switched on the radio. An announcer was reading the news: The entire city was under twenty-four-hour curfew. No one could leave their homes. Bich Ha and her fiancé looked at each other. In that one instant, they both realized it was too late.

The next day, April 30, 1975, North Vietnamese tanks crashed through the gates of Saigon's Presidential Palace, signaling the end of thirty years of war. It was the Fall of Saigon (or the Liberation of Saigon, depending on your perspective), and the divided opinions within the

city became apparent immediately. Thousands of local residents took
to the streets to welcome the victorious army. Thousands of others
huddled fearfully in their homes.

Phuong and Bich Ha were among those waiting fearfully in their
homes. In the years since foreigners first began to organize adoptions
from Vietnam, hundreds of local staff, most of them women, had kept
these facilities going by cleaning, cooking, soothing infants, changing diapers, offering bottles, and administering medicines. Now, like
the children themselves, these women were scattered across the globe.
Those who had chosen to leave Vietnam would, over the next months,
start new lives overseas. Others would, in coming years, try to escape
their homeland on boats and rafts. The successful ones would end up in
refugee camps and, with luck, new residency abroad. The unsuccessful
ones would end up in jail back in Vietnam, or, worse, as victims of pirates
or drowning. These two local staff—Phuong and Bich Ha—stayed in
their own country. The end of the war marked the beginning of a period
that both women used one particular word to describe: *khổ*, they called
it. Miserable.

At this precise moment on April 30, 1975, however, the North Vietnamese tanks had just begun to roll down the streets of Saigon. Phuong
and Bich Ha could not know what would happen next. They could only
do what so many others were doing—peek out their windows and watch.
The war was finally over.

PART THREE

CHAPTER 14

Resources

The aid worker's life is a constant effort to get supplies or services to those who need them, trying all the while as best he or she can—often, with mixed and sometimes with bitter and unintended results—to, as the doctors say, do no harm, while attempting to mitigate horrors most people in their home countries are at best dimly aware of.

DAVID RIEFF, *A Bed for the Night: Humanitarianism in Crisis*

On April 26, the same day that Cherie Clark and Rosemary Taylor evacuated their last groups of children from Vietnam, the Holt Adoption Program sent a final flight of thirty-two children out of the country. The next day, Holt's remaining American staff flew out on a DC-3 that the agency had hired to transport all its documents back to the United States. Over the two and a half years that the agency operated in Vietnam, it had arranged adoptions for at least seven hundred children. The boxes of these children's records and paperwork filled the entire plane— thousands of pounds of files. In contrast, Rosemary Taylor's FFAC managed to carry out only three hundred pounds of files, and Cherie Clark brought out even less.

When I thought about the chaos that enveloped Saigon during those last few days before the Communist takeover, it seemed incredible to me that one agency, the Holt Adoption Program, actually flew out of Vietnam on an airplane carrying almost nothing but file boxes. How could you value paper over human life? On the other hand, Holt's effort demonstrated a very particular kind of respect for human life. Holt recognized—in a way that few, if any, of the other agencies did—that knowledge was treasure. In the future, when adoptees searched for clues to their pasts, a lot would depend on luck—the luck of having been brought over by an agency that kept good records.

I heard that John Williams now ran the Peace Corps in Thailand. I arranged to meet with him in Bangkok, and a few months later, we were sitting on the porch of the ranch-style home he shared with his wife in a small gated community on the outskirts of the Thai capital, a neighborhood that, by all appearances, could have passed for a suburb of Miami. Williams and I talked about the Babylift for an entire morning, only taking a break for a lunch of the best meat-and-potatoes American food I'd had since leaving North Carolina.

After the Babylift, Williams had gone on to work for Holt for almost thirty years, leading the organization for much of that time. Like so many of the people I'd met who lived through the Babylift, his memories were vivid enough to seem, at times, nearly cinematic. He told me about the "ripe" smell of the 747 that carried four hundred children, most of them infants in diapers, across the Pacific on April 6, and the way the smell "almost knocked back" the ground crew in Seattle when they finally opened the door on arrival. He told me that one of the children died just after the Holt group reached the United States and that he could remember attending the funeral on a cold Seattle day and noticing that a single strand of the child's long black hair had become stuck in the seam of the casket.

Williams had been back to Vietnam in recent years and, using the files that Holt had salvaged on that final flight, had helped a number of adoptees reunite with their birth families. Not all these reunions had gone smoothly, he told me. "A lot of things you fear might come out, come out. Like, 'You're my son, take care of me. It's your responsibility.'"

None of this surprised me. In fact, the acclaimed 2002 American documentary *Daughter from Danang* had focused on the disastrous results of a reunion between a Babylift adoptee, Heidi, and her birth family in Vietnam. Heidi had never really bonded with her adoptive mother in Tennessee, and when she traveled to Vietnam, she hoped to kindle the kind of family love she had not experienced in the United States. At first, the reunion went well, but it eventually deteriorated when Heidi's Vietnamese siblings asked her to help them care for their aging mother. The young American took this request for support as a sign that the family only wanted money from her. She left Vietnam and eventually cut off all contact with her family there. Although I never had any contact with Heidi, I met her birth mother when I was in Danang—she's the mother named Kim whose story I tell in this book—and saw how deeply the woman continued to grieve over the original loss of her daughter and the more recent debacle of the family reunion. I knew that things could go wrong. On the other hand, I had also seen how desperately many adoptees and birth families yearned to have the chance to reunite, regardless of how the meeting might turn out.

Williams and I exchanged stories about searches. I told him about David Fisk's endless, fruitless quest to find any clues about his family. Williams told me about an adoptee on one of his reunion trips (though not an adoptee from Holt) who returned to the country and found information about his family within fifteen minutes. Fifteen minutes! I was flabbergasted. Apparently, his agency had collected thumbprints from birth mothers, which made searches easier. I wanted to understand how the procedures of different adoption agencies could differ so markedly from one another.

Williams shrugged. Some agencies, he told me, "didn't care." Then he laughed a little and added, "I shouldn't say that."

I smiled. Williams had written to Holt for permission before he even agreed to speak with me, so I knew how conscious he was of the delicacy of our conversation. Carefully, I pushed on. "It's hard for me to understand what's so different," I said, "that you could find somebody in fifteen minutes and David Fisk—a thirty-eight-year-old man who was seven years old at the time and had clear memories of Vietnam—doesn't know the name of anything, or even where he was."

I did have sympathy for the predicament of the adoption agencies, but I still wondered if they could have done a better job of keeping track of the children in their care. I looked at John Williams and said, "People tell me, 'We *had* to do it this way.'"

He took a moment to reply. Perhaps it was his years of experience as head of Holt that had made him so diplomatic. Then, quietly, he said, "In my opinion, it did not *have* to be that way."

The firmness of his voice surprised me. I saw now that, even after thirty years, he remained as engaged in this debate as he had ever been. "We had kids who were abandoned and we didn't have a lot of information," he said. "But whatever you have, you document. You do tracing. It requires time and resources to be able to do that. You've got to ask the questions and you've got to be willing to invest the time. And a lot of people—." He paused. After a moment, he continued, "I don't want to paint everybody with the same brush," he said, "but there were some people who—again, depending on the mission of the organization and all sorts of things—there were people who were out to 'save' children, either for, in some cases, religious motivations and, in some cases, because they somehow believed that life in the United States is better than life in Vietnam."

In Williams's view, you had to make a distinction between necessary and unnecessary adoptions. "Holt's philosophy," he explained, "is that life in a family, if it's a reasonably good and wholesome family, is the best place, no matter what country it is and no matter how poor the surroundings. If the child is loved and has some opportunity to get by in life, he should have that opportunity to be with his parents—his birth parents."

In all my conversations with adoption agency staff, none had ever spoken so forcefully on the sanctity of the birth family. In a practical sense, I had heard so much about what the agencies did do that I didn't know what they didn't do to help preserve these families. "Would you send investigators around to search for birth parents if a child was abandoned?" I asked.

He nodded. "That's what the social workers did."

"They would try to find women in a neighborhood who might have been pregnant at a particular time?"

"Sure."

"I haven't heard of people doing that."

"There are limits to how much you can expect to do," he admitted.

Actually, Holt's methods, as Williams explained them, were based not on absolutes, but on practicalities. "To me, it's not one or the other," he said. "I've always looked at it as, like, if you're going to take off in an airplane, you have a checklist of the things you consider. The list is usually in some kind of priority order—1, 2, 3, 4—and you check your ailerons and fuel. You have your checklist: Does the child have birth parents and is it a reasonably safe and secure environment for the child to remain with the birth family or to be returned? If the child is in an orphanage, do you know who the birth parents are? Is there a way to return the child to the birth family? If there is no way, then you look, okay, what's the situation with domestic adoption? Is adoption a concept in this particular country that is acceptable? What could we do to promote it? You go through a list of options, but the options are all equal in a way."

I thought about the difference between a big agency, like Holt, with its well-established headquarters in Seattle, and smaller ones, like FCVN and FFAC, the "kitchen-table ladies," as Alex Stalcup called them, agencies that operated on shoestring budgets. "But Holt also had the resources to do that kind of investigation, which some of these smaller organizations didn't have," I said.

Williams looked exasperated. "If you don't have the resources, you shouldn't be doing it," he told me.

CHAPTER 15

Baby in a Burning Building

The State Department, Senate Refugee Subcommittee, and news correspondents agree that there has been no indication of anything resembling a massacre by the victorious North Vietnamese.

The Washington Post, August 5, 1975

"I'll bet the tulips are coming up in Danang now," thinks Kim, a newly adopted Vietnamese baby, in a June 1975 installment of Garry Trudeau's comic strip *Doonesbury*. Kim's adoptive mother and grandmother talk nearby. "Why do you think the adoption was such a mistake?" the younger woman asks the older one.

The grandmother, her head covered in curlers, sits with a cup of coffee at the kitchen table, a cigarette dangling from her hand. "I just think you're taking on more than you can handle," she says.

"Mother," her daughter replies. "I'm perfectly capable of—"

"I *know* you're capable of raising a *child*, honey—it's the fact she's a Vietnamese war orphan that worries me!"

"What do you mean, mother?"

"There won't be any escaping. For the next twenty years, you're going to turn around and see a face that'll do nothing but to remind you of the most *grotesque* war in our nation's *history!*"

The new adoptive mother looks over at the baby, who sits nestled in

184

an armchair, smiling up at her. "Yeah, but she'll be in school a lot of the time," she finally says.

"Well, it's your life, honey," replies her mom.

In the real world, the Babylift children were settling in with their new families in places as disparate as Germany, France, and Australia, as well as the United States. By the time Saigon fell to the Communists on April 30, nearly three weeks had passed since the day that Kathy and Wesley Lawrence rushed from their home in Wakefield, Rhode Island, to Boston's Logan Airport to meet their little girl. After months of being completely focused on the war in Vietnam—and consumed with worry over the child they hoped to adopt from there—they had now become absorbed by issues much closer to home. They had entered the twilight world of the newborn. Time revolved around diaper changes, feeding schedules, and lack of sleep. The baby went by the name of Sarah now, and when she woke every morning at 5 a.m., Kathy would set her in the playpen, switch on "Future Farmers of America" or whatever else was playing at that hour on TV, then lie down and try to doze. Kathy wasn't just tired; she was also queasy. Not long after they'd picked up Sarah at the airport, the long-infertile couple discovered that they were going to have a biological child as well. Kathy's first reaction to her pregnancy was worry: would someone find out and take little Sarah away from them? Once she felt confident that she could keep her new daughter, the realization that she would soon be the mother of two children made her even happier.

In the feminist collective called "Self-Reliance" in Washington, D.C., lawyer and activist Lisa Brodyaga experienced no such contentment. The little six- or seven-year-old girl who had arrived so suddenly from Vietnam still talked about her birth family on the other side of the world and expected to return to them. Brodyaga and her housemates wanted to help, but FCVN, the agency that had carried the child out of Vietnam, offered no information on where the girl had come from. As the days passed, Brodyaga developed a horrible conviction that her worst fear had been accurate, that Operation Babylift had, after all, been a kidnapping.

In Georgia, Colleen Ballard, who had suffered from infertility for such a long time, was now learning how to care for her new son. According to the doctor's best guess, the baby was about six weeks old when Colleen and her husband, Jerry, picked him up on May 7. The new mother knew nothing about infants, had never even babysat, and looking back later, it seemed to her that, in those first few weeks, she had nearly killed him several times. Her infractions, as she remembered them, were numerous: "Fed him cold milk out of the fridge as soon as I got him. Didn't know how to bathe him. I knew nothing, absolutely nothing. And he was very sick, as were a lot of the babies."

The Ballards had signed up to adopt a Vietnamese child through an agency called Tressler-Lutheran Service Associates, based in Pennsylvania. As the war approached its last weeks, they had gotten a call to go to Fort Benning, not far away from them in Georgia. An American woman named Betty Tisdale had, almost single-handedly, carried out of Vietnam some two hundred children from Saigon's An Lac Orphanage and settled them temporarily in a schoolhouse on the army base. Hundreds of volunteers were working around the clock to care for the kids, who, though not officially part of the U.S. government's Operation Babylift evacuation, had ended up in the country anyway.

Colleen and Jerry first visited the An Lac children in mid-April, just after the group arrived from Vietnam. Colleen cried when she saw them. "There were kids with no legs. Kids with huge sores and no hair. Crutches. It was horrific. It was just terrible," she later remembered. The young couple didn't ask for a healthy child, but they did ask for a baby rather than an older child. It seemed too difficult to begin the task of parenting by dealing with the language barrier and probable culture shock from which an older child would likely be suffering.

On May 7, a few weeks after their first visit, they received another call to come down to Fort Benning. A staff member gave them a number —58—and the young couple waited nervously in a hallway until that number was called. Then, together, they filed into a room. Within moments, a doctor handed Colleen a baby. The child was wrapped in a quilted yellow jacket with a hood. Colleen peeked under the diaper and saw that it was a little boy. He was so small that his entire body fit in the crook of her arm. "Oh, God," she said. "He's so tiny."

The doctor told them that the baby weighed six pounds and was probably about six weeks old. "All these children are little," he said.

The new parents signed a few papers, so few, in fact, that later, in retrospect, Colleen felt like she'd merely signed a receipt. In return, they received, along with their new son, a box of clothes, some baby food, and a few pages of information on what to do next. Betty Tisdale's husband, Patrick, a medical doctor and colonel at Fort Benning, provided a list of possible medical conditions the new parents might encounter, including chicken pox, scabies, lice, bronchitis, and intermittent diarrhea ("*Intermittent?*" Colleen later thought. "That's an understatement!").

The staff at Fort Benning had also provided translations for some basic Vietnamese words, but the list seemed more appropriate for soldiers on the ground in Vietnam than American parents trying to get to know their new children. It included the phrasing for "Do you speak English?" and "harvest time" and the number 45, for example, but not "Are you hungry?" or "Are you sad?" Luckily for the Ballards, they'd adopted an infant so they needed no translations. Oddly, though, in the coming months, some of the Ballards' neighbors would stop Colleen on the street, look down at the baby in the stroller, and ask, "Well, does he speak Vietnamese?"

"No," Colleen would have to answer. "He's not even a year old. He doesn't even speak English yet."

If the Ballards were uncertain about how to raise their son, whom they'd named Robert and called "Bert," they were even less certain about how to finalize their adoption. Their adoption agency, Tressler, seemed equally confused, even writing to say that "we'll be in touch about Immigration procedures on these kids as soon as someone tells us what they are!"

Normally, adoptions are preceded by a "referral," which provides information on the particular child offered to a family to adopt. The adoptive family must also complete a "home study" that prepares them for the arrival of the children and confirms their qualifications as parents. The Ballards, however, had never received a referral for their new son and had never completed a home study to prove themselves eligible to adopt a child. As soon as they returned home with Bert, Colleen went to the local social services office. "I've got this baby," she told them, revealing the obvious, that she and her husband were going through the adoption process backward.

She had to complete the home study anyway, staff members replied. But, no problem. "We'll treat it as if you don't have a child," they told her.

At first, Colleen and her husband tried to move forward as if, in some more comprehensive way, the entire process made sense. "I must have been really naive," she later reflected, "because I just thought this was normal." The Ballards soon realized, however, that Operation Babylift adoptions were not normal at all. Even their baby's name made no sense. The forms listed him as Vu Tien Do II. Number Two? What did that mean? They wrote to Betty Tisdale and later received a reply that told more about Betty Tisdale's method in evacuating the An Lac children from Vietnam than it revealed about the background of their new baby. "Let me try to explain about the name Vu Tien Do," Tisdale wrote.

> When I was at An Lac for the three days it was almost impossible to do the evacuation in that time—but we tried. I had a list of 350 children which I took to the Minister of Social Welfare—he told me that I could not take all of the children—so I had to revise the list and pare it down to those under 10 (I took a lot over 10 but didn't say anything). There was one little baby named Vu Tien Do. As I checked the list and those being put into baskets to make the trip by bus to the airport—I was told by one of the little girls that Vu Tien Do was not going to be allowed to go—he was too sick or something—and since we were pressed for time—I picked up another baby and asked Mme. Ngai [the director of the An Lac Orphanage] if this was OK and it was. It would take hours to tell you of the confusion at the airport—and again at Clark Field [in the Philippines]. Anyway—when we finally got on the plane from the Philippines to L.A. I practically walked across the

Pacific—checking to see if I got all the An Lac children from the base at Clark Field. Lo and behold—I found the first Vu Tien Do—and the one I replaced—soooo—two Vu Tien Do's but only one name on the list—so yours is Vu Tien Do II. He indeed was at An Lac—an abandoned baby like the rest—and now he is yours —by the simple fate of being "added" to a list. In fact, I "added" and "changed" to get more and more on the plane. All of which Tressler [the adoption agency] and the Army could not and would not know anything about.

Tisdale's explanation did little to help Colleen and Jerry Ballard move closer to legalizing the adoption of their son. As time passed, it became clear to Colleen that the baby had been "brought here illegally. We had no green card. We had no residency. We had nothing. And then we started fighting for two years to get him citizenship." Legally, they had no real rights to the boy, but emotionally, he was their son and they were determined to keep him. "I'm pretty strong-willed," Colleen explained, and she was ready to fight for her baby.

And fight she did. Once, when Bert was about five months old, a man came to the door, handed Colleen his business card, and identified himself as a government official working on the Babylift case. He wanted to examine Vu Tien Do II, he said.

"He's asleep," Colleen replied.

"Well, wake him up."

The new adoptive mother assumed that this visit was part of the legalization process. She went into Bert's room, pulled off his diaper, and brought him back to where the agent was waiting.

The man began to examine the baby, carefully moving from hands to feet to back to legs. "I need to see if he has any identifiable marks," he explained, "so that at some time later a mother could say, 'Oh, that's my child.'"

When she heard that, Colleen grabbed her son and pulled him from the agent's arms. Then she looked at him. "I'll move to Canada," she screamed. "You can't have him. He's mine!"

• • •

On every level, then, from the original decisions about which children would be airlifted to the protocols for finalizing adoptions, Operation Babylift suffered from acute disorder and a nearly complete lack of oversight. Around the same time that Colleen and Jerry Ballard picked up their new baby in Georgia, an effort began in San Francisco to assert some control over what had become, by many accounts, a fiasco. On April 29, 1975, as the Communists were poised to complete their takeover of South Vietnam, a group of attorneys filed a class-action lawsuit seeking to halt the Babylift adoptions. The title of the lawsuit offered the first indication of its expansive goals:

NGUYEN DA YEN, NGUYEN DA VUONG, and NGUYEN DA TUYEN, on their own behalf and on behalf of all others similarly situated, by their guardian ad litem, MUOI MCCONNELL, Plaintiffs, v. HENRY KISSINGER; JAMES SCHLESINGER; EDWARD LEVI; COL. ROBERT KANE; COL. JASPER HORN; MARIO OBLEDO, Defendants.

Obviously, the case aimed to incriminate those in the highest echelons of power in Washington.

But its mission was also concrete and specific. One of the attorneys, Thomas Miller, had, with his wife, the one-time Presidio interpreter T. T. Nhu, helped organize the Babylift protest at San Francisco's Glide Memorial Church a few weeks before. Despite growing concern over the disarray of the evacuation, planeloads of children had continued to take off from Saigon. By the end of April, more than two thousand children had arrived in the United States and, as the staff at the Presidio, among others, had discovered early on, there was considerable evidence that many of them were not orphans and were not eligible for adoption. In response to the situation, Miller banded together with other Bay Area attorneys and the Center for Constitutional Rights in New York to file the lawsuit. Calling themselves the Committee to Protect the Rights of Vietnamese Children, the group aimed to force the U.S. government to investigate each individual case to determine which children were actually eligible for adoption.

Three siblings—Nguyen Da Yen, Nguyen Da Vuong, and Nguyen Da Tuyen—served as the named plaintiffs in the case. These two sisters and their brother, ages three, six, and seven, had arrived at the Presidio early in the month. There, they told a Vietnamese nurse, Muoi McConnell, that they were not orphans. In the chaos that had overtaken South Vietnam during the final days of the war, they had become separated from their parents and ended up in an orphanage. A few days later, they were placed on an airplane and flown to the United States. Now, they told McConnell, they wanted to go home. McConnell tried to help, but not long after that discussion, the children disappeared from the Presidio. U.S. government officials and adoption agency staff refused to give McConnell any information about where the children had gone. Anxious about their situation, McConnell agreed to serve as the plaintiff of record in the suit. "[All] we're asking is enforcement of laws on the books," Miller told the *New York Times*, "and to slow everything down until we can check what is happening."

Though the plaintiff's attorneys were moving ahead with the lawsuit, they also lacked one important piece of information. They planned to argue that the birth parents of any non-orphans should be contacted and, if possible, reunited with their children, either in Vietnam or, if the parents had emigrated, overseas. No one knew the Hanoi government's stand on the issue, however, and there was little point in pursuing a lawsuit if Vietnam refused to repatriate any children that the court decided should go home. Behind the scenes, Miller used the contacts he had made during his years of working in Vietnam to approach high-level officials there. Obviously, it wasn't a good time to bother them. The new government was just beginning the arduous process of merging two former adversaries into one nation. Hundreds of thousands of refugees and former soldiers had to return to their homes and try to rebuild their lives in the country at peace. In Saigon alone, as many as twenty thousand children remained in orphanages, desperately in need of care. Faced with these nearly insurmountable challenges, the Vietnamese might have simply ignored the niggling issue of several thousand children who had, in the last days of war, ended up overseas.

But Hanoi had never resisted a chance to condemn its old neme-
sis, the United States. By May 9, just over a week after the conflict
ended, the new government's ambassador in Paris sent a cablegram to
Miller's group in San Francisco. "We demand that the United States
government return to South Vietnam children illegally removed by
Americans," the message read. "We will assist in the placement of these
children in their families or foster homes."

Miller and his colleagues now had what they needed to move the
lawsuit forward.

Meanwhile, despite the lawsuit, more and more Babylift children were
being placed in their adoptive homes. One of those children was Ngoc
Anh, the light-skinned Amerasian child from Danang whose mother
had carried her south on a teeming refugee ship to get her out of Vietnam. Ngoc Anh's photograph reached the home of Syd and Norm
Gelbwaks in early May. For weeks, the couple—as well as their three
sons—had been anxiously awaiting news of the little girl who would join
their family. The child in the photograph was very, very blond and terribly thin. She was seven years old, only forty inches tall, and weighed
thirty-three pounds. In the photo, she wore a plaid jumper that hung on
her body "like a sack," Syd thought, and shoes that looked way too big.
In her arms, she held a sign with her name and a number on it. Although
the adoption agency presented a couple of girls as choices, including a
Spanish-speaking child for a domestic adoption—both, to Syd's mind,
"absolutely heartbreakingly gorgeous"—when the Gelbwaks saw the
picture of Ngoc Anh, "there was no other child for us from that moment
on." The Jewish couple found the image of this forlorn little Vietnamese
girl too familiar to ignore. "She looked like some of the pictures that we
had seen of people in the camps during World War II," Syd thought.
"It brought her so close to us because of our remembrances."

At that moment, Ngoc Anh, or Anh, as she would come to be called,
was in the midst of an experience that, for anyone, would feel cata-
clysmic but which, for a child of only seven, probably seemed not only
terrifying but also utterly incomprehensible. In the course of only a

few weeks, she had left her tiny home on the banks of the Han River in Danang, cowered among the thousands of refugees crammed on a ship headed south along the coast of Vietnam, made her way overland from Vung Tau to Saigon, said good-bye to her mother and siblings, and flown with a planeload of strangers across the Pacific. Somewhere along the way, she received treatment for worms and the mumps. She also acquired a dress and a very fancy pair of white patent leather shoes. Finally, in May, she ended up in an orphanage in Philadelphia. She didn't mind the orphanage at all. In fact, she liked it. There were other children to play with, and a trike that she could ride. Plus, she loved her fancy shoes, even though they were two sizes too big. She loved them so much that she refused to take them off.

In late May, the entire Gelbwaks family drove down to Philadelphia from Connecticut to meet her. When they first saw Anh, she was riding the trike. Her face was swollen from the mumps and she looked so funny that Syd began to laugh. When the little girl saw the two adults and the three boys who had come with them, she grabbed the closest thing around, a water fountain, and clutching tight, began to scream. For the next two hours, the Gelbwaks family sat with her. Anh screamed the entire time. At one point, Syd and Norm sent their boys away, hoping to calm her. Anh screamed and screamed. Norm tried to put her on his lap and the child pulled away in a panic, ripping the buttons off his shirt. Finally, Syd and Norm retreated. The family drove to a Holiday Inn, spent the night, and returned the next morning. Anh still didn't want to leave with them. Finally, they managed to load everyone into the car— Syd, Norm, the three boys, Anh, and the family dog—and drove the four hours back to their farm in Connecticut. Anh had grown quiet now. She sat on Syd's lap the entire drive. "She was probably scared stiff," Syd later remembered. Anh kept those fancy shoes on her feet until her new parents finally took them away.

After saying good-bye to her little girl, Anh's birth mother, Han, had taken her remaining children and slowly made her way back north to Danang. She didn't try to leave Vietnam, but other birth mothers did.

One such mother, a woman named Doan Thi Hoang Anh, arrived at the refugee resettlement center at Camp Pendleton, California, in early August 1975, four months after the war ended. The thirty-two-year-old Hoang Anh had relinquished all seven of her children at the FCVN compound during the final days of the war. Now, as she acclimated herself within the teeming Marine Corps complex, she was, effectively, alone.

Camp Pendleton, which lay in the middle of the California desert, had been designated one of the primary receiving centers for Indochina refugees, more than 113,000 of whom had left Southeast Asia and were now "under American protection." At Camp Pendleton, refugees received food, shelter, clothing, counseling, and resettlement support. The U.S. government supplied the facilities and conducted immigration screenings, and a group of voluntary agencies—among them the U.S. Catholic Conference, International Rescue Committee, and Traveler's Aid–International Social Services—searched for new homes for the immigrants in communities across the country and in foreign countries that had agreed to accept certain quotas.

Within days of her arrival, Hoang Anh made her way across the sprawling refugee camp to the offices of the Red Cross. There, she told her story. She came from the Central Highlands of South Vietnam, she explained. Her husband had been killed by the Communist forces, leaving her to care for their seven children alone. When the Spring Offensive began in March, she gathered her children and a few belongings and joined the masses of terrified refugees heading south toward Saigon. At one point, fearing that one of her sons would die of thirst, Hoang Anh used her own saliva to keep him alive. Somehow, the family made it to Saigon, but Hoang Anh had come to believe that this, alone, was not enough to ensure their survival. She had heard of an agency, FCVN, which would take unaccompanied children to safety overseas. Hoang Anh and her children made their way to that address, pushing through the crowds outside the gate and managing to find Ross Meador, Cherie Clark's young American colleague. Meador listened to Hoang Anh's story and agreed to take the children to the United States. Carefully, the young mother recited the names and ages of each of her children, making sure that Meador understood which was which. To her children, she explained that she could not travel by plane with them, but that she would try to get to the United States to find them. Although FCVN typically required birth parents to sign a release, Hoang Anh refused, and she never consented to her children's adoption. Instead, she told her oldest daughter to keep the entire family together for two years.

Once she had settled her children at the orphanage, Hoang Anh left the compound and went back into the city to plan her own way, alone, out of Vietnam. The children flew on FCVN's final calamitous April 26 flight out of Saigon, the one on which infants began to die and Cherie Clark had to beg the pilots to make an emergency landing. Hoang Anh found passage on a fishing boat, which took her across the South China Sea and landed, eventually, in Singapore. From there, over the course of the next few months, she made her way to the Philippines and Wake Island before finally reaching California, and Camp Pendleton, in August. There, she announced to the staff at the Red Cross that she was ready to get her children back. The Red Cross agreed to help.

The United States operated three major refugee processing centers—at Camp Pendleton in California, Eglin Air Force Base in Florida, and Fort Chaffee in Arkansas. As more and more refugees arrived, international voluntary agencies were hustling to find sponsors for them, either individuals or groups who were willing to help the immigrants adjust to their new lives. Within a month of her arrival, Hoang Anh received word that three Methodist churches had agreed to sponsor her, and that she would be living in a place called Montana. By September, she had moved into a small apartment in Great Falls, a city that lay on the Missouri River about a hundred miles south of the Canadian border.

As Hoang Anh was finding a home for herself and, she hoped, the rest of her family, the Red Cross began searching for her children. At first, the process went quickly. When the agency contacted the Denver office of FCVN, they discovered that four of Anh's children were right there in the city, staying at the home of one of the adoption agency staff. On September 28, five months after she left them in Saigon, Anh regained custody of those four children. According to court documents, they yelled, "Mommy! Mommy!" as soon as they saw her.

With four of her children back in her care, Hoang Anh began her search for the other three. FCVN disclosed that two had been placed in foster care but did not reveal their location. As for the third, a little boy named Doan Van Binh, Hoang Anh learned that an Iowa couple, Johnny and Bonnie Nelson, had taken him in. Hoang Anh contacted the Nelsons immediately.

Here was the nightmare that so many adoptive parents of Babylift children dreaded, especially during those early months: A birth mother wanted her child back. The Nelsons, who had accepted the boy with the understanding that they would file for his adoption, were devastated. They wrote to Hoang Anh, imploring her to reconsider. The boy had been in their home for months already. In their letter, they didn't question Hoang Anh's claim that she was Binh's mother, but they did send their minister to Great Falls to try to determine whether the story was true. The immigrant mother apparently impressed the clergyman. He described her apartment as small, but clean and nicely furnished. He also expressed a conviction that Hoang Anh was, indeed, Binh's mother.

FCVN, apparently, had given Binh to the Nelsons because the agency considered him eligible for adoption. Cherie Clark, acting in her role as overseas director of FCVN, would later sign an affidavit stating that the mother had "verbally and physically" released her children to Ross Meador. But Hoang Anh herself disputed that.

The Nelsons refused to return the boy to his birth mother. On February 6, 1976, Hoang Anh filed suit in Iowa courts to regain custody.

Cherie Clark also had an explanation for how the three young children named as lead plaintiffs in the gigantic class-action lawsuit—siblings Nguyen Da Yen, Nguyen Da Vuong, and Nguyen Da Tuyen—had ended up in the United States. The lawsuit claimed that they were not orphans, and Clark admitted the truth of this allegation. The children were, rather, relatives of a Vietnamese social worker on FCVN's staff. Like Doan Thi Hoang Anh and her family, these three children and their parents had fled their home in the Central Highlands during the last few weeks of the war. By the time they arrived in Saigon, the parents were exhausted, weak, and terrified of what would happen when the Communists took power. Frantic, they turned to the only person they thought might help them: Cherie Clark. "[They] didn't want their children to suffer any more," Clark later explained, "and begged me now to take the children out and give them to a good family for adoption."

Clark was torn. FCVN policy specifically limited the agency's mission to arranging adoptions for "true orphans" or, in some cases, Amerasian kids. These three children were neither, but their plight made her waver. Finally, "after much soul-searching," she agreed to evacuate the children, provided that the parents legally relinquished their rights and cleared the way for adoption.

In any case, FCVN now had a major lawsuit to deal with. The three named plaintiffs were merely the most visible in a case that included every child carried out of Vietnam during Operation Babylift—between two thousand and three thousand kids. Although none of the adoption agencies were named as defendants (the case laid blame, instead, on high-level U.S. government officials), they all had a stake in the outcome. FCVN, for one, petitioned for inclusion as "friends of the court" in order, as Clark put it, "to present a more balanced picture." The move also put FCVN in a position to defend the rights of its adoptive families. As Clark later explained it, her view of the lawsuit centered on the fact that

[Despite] numerous affidavits by [birth]family members, these children were portrayed as an example of children "lost" or "stolen" from Vietnam by the agencies working there in those last days—apparently because they had cried at the Presidio in California when they were evacuated, asking for their parents. . . . I was not alone in my belief that the lawsuit was politically motivated and had nothing to do with the children.

But, of course, the lawsuit had emerged from more than anecdotal recollections about homesick kids at the Presidio. In fact, it drew some of its primary arguments from international protocols on the protection of children in time of war. Three articles from the 1949 Geneva Conventions, in fact, took a clear position on the issue, and that position differed markedly from the notion that these displaced children should be evacuated and put up for permanent adoption overseas. Article 24 stated that orphans should be cared for and that "[their] education shall, as far as possible, be entrusted to people of a similar cultural tradition." Article 26 dealt with the reunification of families: "Each Party to the conflict shall facilitate enquiries made by members of families dispersed owing to the war, with the object of renewing contact with one another and of meeting, if possible." And Article 49 recognized the occasional necessity of evacuating civilians, but stipulated that "[persons] thus evacuated shall be transferred back to their homes as soon as hostilities in the area in question have ceased. The Occupying Power undertaking such transfers or evacuations shall ensure, to the greatest practicable extent, that . . . members of the same family are not separated."

The Geneva Conventions, though, were only one facet of the debate that raged over Operation Babylift and influenced public opinion about the lawsuit. People who opposed the evacuation, for example, argued that Vietnamese could take care of themselves, offering glowing examples of age-old Vietnamese cultural traditions in which neighbors or relatives would take in orphaned children and raise them. Helen C. Steven, who had worked in Vietnamese orphanages for two years, published an article in *Capitol Hill Forum* stating that 97 percent of Vietnamese orphans are cared for by family members. "Child abandonment is unnatural and a last resort for Vietnamese people," she wrote. Vietnamese émigré T. T. Nhu, the young Presidio interpreter whose husband, Thomas Miller, was a plaintiff's attorney in the lawsuit, mentioned a Vietnamese proverb, *sẩy cha còn chú, sẩy mẹ bú dì*, which, she explained, means, "If you lost your father, you still have your uncle; if you lose your mother, your aunt will still nurse you."

Rosemary Taylor offered a much more brutal view of Vietnam's traditional society. She had made it out of Saigon just before the city fell and she had a strong reaction to the lawsuit. More than any other single person involved in Operation Babylift or, for that matter, adoption from Vietnam, Taylor had developed a well-reasoned justification for her efforts to find new permanent families for displaced children in that country. The vast majority of her children had been abandoned at birth, she argued, which made the calls for their reunification with family members irrelevant. Moreover, from her perspective, Vietnam was a place where children could be "abandoned and sacrificed to appease angry gods; infanticide was practiced; children who were malformed and who would only be an economic liability were left to die; the extended family, spoken of so reverently by our sociologists, might sometimes take in a poor relation as a cheap way of acquiring a servant." Taylor reserved particular vitriol for Vietnamese immigrants like T. T. Nhu, who, she believed, perpetuated a romanticized picture of their homeland. "The whole idea of a devoted extended family is now propagated by well-to-do expatriates who naturally wish to stress the noblest practices of [Vietnamese] society." In Taylor's view, it took the arrival of the church, during the colonial era, to install in Vietnam an orphanage system that, while flawed, at least acknowledged the fundamental value of every human life. "Christianity certainly believed," she wrote, "that it was right to free men from the manacles of hostile gods and an enslavement to fate, and uphold the unique preciousness of each human being."

Such debates revealed a profound disagreement about the nature of Vietnamese society, and, predictably, they echoed the far-ranging animosities that had flared throughout the war. By the summer of 1975, however, such arguments had become, fundamentally, academic. What mattered now was not Vietnam's cultural traditions, but the fate of these thousands of children (about six hundred of whom went to countries other than the United States) who had been brought out of South Vietnam in the last weeks of war. On that matter, the adoption agencies differed in their opinions of what should happen next. John E. Adams, the executive director of the Holt Adoption Program, expressed a surprising public sympathy for the demands of the lawsuit. "We must focus on one question," he said. "In those final weeks, were there children mistakenly separated from families and brought to the U.S., or relinquished in an emotional situation such that the family should now be given the opportunity to reconsider?" If so, Adams stated, those children should be returned to their families, and as quickly as possible.

Other adoption agency personnel, however, were more hostile to the lawsuit. When Cherie Clark discussed the case in her memoir, she focused on the cost her agency incurred ("in excess of $150,000 attempting to show the true story of this humanitarian effort") and on the fact that, in her eyes, "the lawsuit never took into consideration the pain and hardship that the [birth]parents endured in voluntarily relinquishing their children." She did not, however, address the question of whether, now that the war had ended, these birth parents should be given the chance, as the Geneva Conventions stipulated, to change their minds.

In fact, some adoption agencies went so far as to block birth parents from gaining access to their children's records, and to the children themselves. For example, in the case of Doan Thi Hoang Anh, the mother who had made her way alone to Camp Pendleton, FCVN argued that giving her information about her children's current living situation would undermine the privacy of adoptive parents, even though Hoang Anh had never signed a release for adoption. In another case, this one involving FFAC, a birth mother tried to regain custody of her sons, whom she had relinquished in the last days of the war. After leaving the children with foreigners who promised to take them to the United States, this mother stood in line for two days before getting herself on a flight out of the country. Once she made it to the United States, it took her months to find the children, and when she did, and asked for them back, adoption agency officials had little sympathy for her situation. In an interview with the *New York Times*, FFAC's Wende Grant tried to show the birth mother's effort to follow her children to the United States as a sign of selfishness. "Take a hypothetical example. Would you stand in line for two days to get yourself out of a country when you don't know where your children are?" Grant asked.

Some Babylift children were returned to their birth families without appeals to the courts. In her memoir, Rosemary Taylor refers to seven such families. In Nebraska, a state senator returned to their birth mother the children he had hoped to adopt. The disarray of the Babylift put strains on the relationships between agencies and their adoptive parent clients. Lisa Brodyaga, the feminist lawyer who was trying to help her Babylift child find a way to return to Vietnam, was so infuriated with her adoption agency, FCVN, that by early May she became involved with the class-action lawsuit—on the plaintiff's side of the case. The resentment went both ways. In Rosemary Taylor's criticism of the lawsuit, she never mentions the emotional pain that adoptive families endured when they had to give children back to their birth parents, but she does say that the "considerable financial cost of those transfers was borne by the agency that had brought them from Vietnam." She added, too, that "all the [birth]mothers admitted lying to the agency." Clearly, some adoption agency staff had come to believe they were being attacked from all sides.

For generations, child custody decisions have been based on assessments of "the best interest of the child." Individual lawsuits stemming from Operation Babylift were no exception. For the adoption agencies, however, their stated allegiance to the children sometimes conflicted with their need to defend the rights of adoptive families. In one Michigan lawsuit, for example, a Vietnamese mother named Duong Bich Van filed to regain custody of her son who had left Vietnam during Operation Babylift. The judge, Richard D. Kuhn of the Sixth Judicial Circuit Court, specifically concentrated on the question of the child's best interest. The mother, who had relinquished her son but never signed a release for him, made it to the United States herself, found the boy, and appealed for his return. The adoptive family, acting on the advice of their lawyer, continued to argue and delay, despite the fact that they had no release, because doing so might complicate the birth mother's attempt to regain custody. The case was not decided until June 1976, almost a full year after the birth mother began her efforts to get her son back. An apparently irritated Judge Kuhn asked in his opinion, "Who really was concerned about the child in question in this case?" If the adoptive family, he wrote, "really had the best interests of this child in mind," they would have brought the case to court for a decision quickly, rather than "stonewalling."

With that, Judge Kuhn awarded custody to the birth mother.

As the class-action lawsuit and the individual custody trials slowly moved through the court system, the responsibility of unraveling the tangled knots of the Babylift fell on the shoulders of judges like Kuhn, who could see how the evacuations, born of tragedy, were causing new tragedies on all sides. In a California case, Superior Court Judge Bill Dozier employed a creative means of determining custody in the case of an eight-year-old boy called "Tuan Anh" by his birth mother and called "Dean" by his prospective adoptive parents. The birth mother, Le Thi Sang, had worked for the adoptive parents, William and Elizabeth Knight, in Vietnam. At the end of the war, fearing for his well-being because he was Amerasian, she gave the boy to the Knights, whom she believed could save him from possible persecution at the hands of the Communists. As it happened, Sang managed to escape from Vietnam and made it to the United States at around the same time that her son did. She then found the Knights and asked them to return the boy to her. The Knights, who had believed that they could adopt the child, refused, and the boy, who had grown to like his new life with his new parents, refused as well. Sang sued, and the case dragged through the courts for twenty months—so long, in fact, that the boy, who had taken up baseball, no longer remembered or cared about Vietnam. Judge Dozier focused his decision on a single question: Would it harm the boy to return to his birth mother? To find out, he sent the child to Ohio for three months to live with Sang. If she could prove during that time that the boy loved her, the judge would award her custody of her son.

As Judge Dozier later noted,

The first six weeks of the visit were a shambles. Tuan Anh talked to his mother only through his aunt, informed her that he hated her, and kicked the walk [*sic*] or threw tantrums whenever his mother thwarted his wishes.

The mother was faced with the formidable task of reestablishing her mother-son relationship with the boy and also setting some limits to his behavior despite his repeated threats to "tell the judge" or run away to the Knights.

In this guerilla war, the mother LOST 14 pounds in the first two months. Significant as an insight into Tuan Anh is the fact that he GAINED six.

Through some magic elixir of patience, resilience, and mother love, plus an inner need in the 8-year-old boy not theretofore perceptible, the mother won the battle. He began to communicate with his mother, call her "Mom," appreciate how hard she was working, how tired she was, and how much she loved him.

In this case, as in many of the cases filed across the country, the judge awarded custody to the birth parent. Judge Dozier also noted that a "bitter aspect of this whole tragic drama is that toward the Knights, who cared for Tuan for two years and who have been put through this harrowing experience of deprivation and legal expense, Tuan Anh exhibits an attitude basically of indifference." In fact, Dozier did not seem to expect *any* positive result to come out of this sad dispute. He called the boy "handsome and likable but clever, materialistic, self-willed, and of the strong bent to look after No. 1." Ultimately, the judge predicted, "He will be a management problem to any parent and has a flattened capacity for affection so that disappointment awaits any parent who anticipates the reward of deep filial love."

As for Doan Thi Hoang Anh, who had started to search for her seven children as soon as she arrived as a refugee at Camp Pendleton, it took eighteen months of court battles to regain custody of her son, Binh. In March 1976, an Iowa district court found in her favor. The adoptive parents, Johnny and Bonnie Nelson, however, refused to relinquish the boy. Instead, they appealed all the way to the Iowa Supreme Court and, six months later, the high court affirmed the lower court decision, awarding Doan Thi Hoang Anh custody of her son. To make its decision, the State Supreme Court relied on an earlier court's definition of "abandonment" as "a total desertion. It includes both the intention to abandon and the external act by which the intention is carried into effect." By that measure, the court said, "We are wholly unable to see how [Hoang] Anh's relinquishment of her children to FCVN could be construed as an indication to abandon them. On the contrary, her relentless search for them in this country affirmatively manifests her intention to meet her parental duties and obligations."

Somewhere between ten and twenty birth families eventually filed individual lawsuits to regain custody of their children. In most of these cases, the birth parents won. The enormous class-action lawsuit, however, was not so successful.

Thomas Miller, one of the plaintiffs' attorneys, sometimes compared the predicament of the Babylift birth parents to that of a mother in a burning building, who throws her child to someone down below to save its life. Once she gets out of the building herself, she wants her baby back. Typically, the person who rescued the child would acknowledge a moral obligation to return it. In the Babylift case, Miller said, the rescuer decided to keep it. "One of the basic ideas of our lawsuit," he later explained, was that "if the family wants the child back, you make an effort to find the family. You return the child to the family."

Again, certain basic questions arose: Which children were legitimate orphans? Which were not? Which parents wanted their children back? Because so much of the documentation had been based on admittedly fraudulent paperwork, it wasn't clear how such questions could ever be answered. Miller's burning-house analogy made sense in a purely moral way, and, no doubt, anyone who heard it would have agreed that the rescuer had an obligation to return that child to its mother. However, the Babylift case involved between two thousand and three thousand children, and no one—not the doctors at the receiving centers, not the government officials who had authorized the airlift, and certainly not the adoption agency staff—could sort it all out. The plaintiff's attorneys demanded that they do just that.

At an early hearing in the class-action case, on May 21, 1975, it seemed that all sides were working together to untangle this mess. The "defense" in this case included such high-level U.S. officials as the secretary of state, the secretary of defense, and the attorney general, none of whom appeared in the courtroom. Practically speaking, though, the defense attorney, Assistant U.S. Attorney John Cooney, represented the wing of the U.S. government most responsible for investigating what had happened, the INS. At the May hearing, Judge Spencer Williams requested that the INS "commence immediately and conduct a record check on all the children," a process that had been one of the primary demands of the lawsuit. Cooney readily agreed. "That is acceptable to the defense," he said. The first hearing seemed to go so smoothly, in fact, that, in concluding it, Judge Williams noted, with apparent satisfaction, "that all parties to this litigation were in my view working jointly with a uniform purpose."

Already, though, there were signs of problems ahead. Contrary to the judge's observation, the different sides were not actually working with uniform purpose. In fact, they had very different goals. The government wanted to straighten out the immigration status of the children to close the files on what had become a bureaucratic nightmare. The plaintiffs' attorneys wanted to find out which children weren't eligible for adoption and, if possible, return them to their birth families. And the adoption agencies—some of which would eventually become "friends of the court" in the proceedings—wanted each child legally and permanently settled with its new adoptive family.

For the plaintiffs' attorneys, each month mattered. Everyone acknowledged that the longer the children spent with their new families, the more difficult it would become to move them should their birth parents be found. As Joseph H. Reid, the executive director of the Child Welfare League of America, explained in a letter to Judge Williams, "We are sure that the court is aware of the fact that time is of the essence. Very young children's sense of time is very different than that of adults. Two months in the life of a five-year-old can be equivalent to years in a twenty-year-old. It is imperative that the Court, or its agent, carefully oversee this operation to make certain that unnecessary delay does not further injure the children."

But the case continued, with hearings and appeals and counter-appeals, well into 1976. While the plaintiffs needed speed, the adoption agencies and adoptive families could see just as clearly the advantage of delay, which would solidify the children's roles in their new families and make it ever more difficult to move them. And the government in the middle? The government rarely changes its speed for any reason, so the government lumbered on.

Slowly, the INS investigators—like the one who had knocked on Colleen Ballard's door and tried to find distinctive birthmarks on her baby boy—went about collecting data across the country. From the adoptive parents' perspective, the INS represented a government willing to tear from their arms the children they had so desperately wanted. From the perspective of the birth parents who wanted their children back, however, these investigations, however superficial and inept, provided the only chance that they might one day find the sons and daughters they had lost.

Meanwhile, the courts had allowed the plaintiffs' attorneys access to many of the children's files, and they were accumulating evidence. By late February 1976, ten months after the lawsuit began, attorney Thomas Miller filed a deposition claiming that the INS used standards of determining adoption eligibility that were, in Miller's words, "highly questionable and self-serving, as well as inconsistent." He provided numerous examples, among them:

> In some 40 percent of files reviewed, the INS reversed the burden of proof normally used to determine eligibility for adoption. Investigators would assume a child was eligible unless they saw evidence that the child was not. A child with no documentation, therefore, would be assumed eligible for adoption.

> The INS failed to interview many of the children who were old enough to speak. When officials did conduct such interviews,

they often approved adoption eligibility even if the children said that they had been accidentally separated from their parents during the war. In one case involving FFAC, the oldest of three children told the INS that she and her siblings were not orphans, then provided her parents' names and street address. The INS investigator, who believed the child's story, approved them for adoption anyway.

In the case of the children of An Lac Orphanage, brought to the United States by Betty Tisdale, all 212 children had, according to their documents, the same family name. An INS inter-agency memo attached to the file on these children read, "Subject: Orphans Reported as Not Being Eligible. I received a telephone call from investigator Hulsey, San Francisco. He said that they had received instructions from Central Office that all An Lac orphans we had reported as not eligible were eligible. Hulsey is changing the copies he has of our reports to read that they are eligible."

The INS ignored obvious factual discrepancies in children's records. In one example, an adoptive couple had personally chosen their child from the Good Shepherd Orphanage in the town of Vinh Long, but the child's release came from the Providence Orphanage in Can Tho. In another case, a child's documentation gave an older age than was possible for that child. Because of the discrepancy, the INS deemed the child ineligible. The adoption agency, FCVN, submitted an affidavit explaining that it had originally offered a false identity on that child. The INS decided that the child was, after all, eligible.

Using the investigation of the court-appointed expert witness, the plaintiffs' attorneys came up with a breakdown of adoption eligibility for all the Babylift children. Out of 2,242 children who had arrived in the United States, the plaintiffs argued that 1,511 were ineligible for adoption, either because of inadequate or fraudulent documentation, because no release had been signed, or because a release had been signed "during the final weeks of the war (after March 14, 1975) when panic spread throughout the population within the areas controlled by the Saigon Government causing persons to use any means possible to remove their children from danger, including the signing of adoption papers under conditions of such severe panic and duress as to negate their validity." The INS would disagree with this large number, but, significantly, the INS' own investigation would find that 263 children— over 10 percent of the evacuees—were not eligible for adoption.

The case was becoming unmanageable, however, and, after ten months of wrangling, Judge Spencer Williams threw it out. As he wrote in his decision, his reasoning did not consider the facts of the case. Rather, he focused on the question of whether or not the adoption eligibility of these several thousand Vietnamese children could be argued as a group, a necessary requirement for a class-action lawsuit. On that point, the judge responded definitively. "If there ever were a 'Frankenstein monster posing as a class action lawsuit,'" he wrote, "this is it. It is the opinion of this court that the problems of managing some two thousand individual determinations of both illegal conduct by defendants and interveners and the right course of future action for each plaintiff would overwhelm this court's abilities." He saw only one way to get to the truth of the matter: "Each child's case must be factually and legally reviewed independently of every other case," he said. "A decision in one instance will have no effect on a decision in another."

Later, in her assessment of the lawsuit, Cherie Clark, whose agency, FCVN, received the largest share of criticism for its conduct in the airlift, would assert that the case had been thrown out because it was "without merit." In fact, the "merits" of the plaintiffs' claims were never considered. As the judge explicitly stated, there was "no basis in the context of a class certification hearing to inquire into the merits." His role was to decide if these two thousand cases could be grouped as a class and, on that point, he decided they could not. The judge did not, however, make any ruling at all on the plaintiffs' attorneys' claims of adoption agency failures.

Still, though the victory might, for the adoption agencies, have lacked that certain sweetness, it was a victory nonetheless. There was no way that the plaintiffs could have fought each adoption individually. These cases would never be fully investigated, and the children— except the ten or twenty whose birth families pressed their own cases —would eventually be adopted. Appeals over the class-action lawsuit continued to wind their way through the courts for years. The argument, though, had lost its momentum. By the time the case finally died, in the early 1980s, very few people likely noticed.

As for the three children named in the lawsuit, Nguyen Da Yen, Nguyen Da Vuong, and Nguyen Da Tuyen, the International Red Cross did attempt to contact their parents in Vietnam, and it failed to find them. The siblings were deemed eligible for adoption, and their case was dismissed.

As months and then years passed, the children of Operation Babylift became more and more American, less and less Vietnamese. Those who had arrived as infants tended to settle in more easily than the older children, who could remember more and therefore had more troubles moving on.

For a long time, little Anh Gelbwaks, the blond child from Danang, kept a bottle of *nước mắm* nearby at mealtime. The Vietnamese fish sauce, she found, imbued her food with the comforting flavor of the dishes her birth mother used to make for her in Danang. On the Gelbwaks' farm in Connecticut, she tried other ways to make this strange new world more familiar as well. She constructed a traditional Vietnamese altar in her bedroom by draping a hand towel over a footstool and placing upon it a mirror, a picture, and a tiny Buddha, which she had managed to carry with her from Vietnam. Still, her new mother could see that Anh was suffering. The child would steal food from the cupboards and stash it under her bed. She wanted to nurse as well, and Syd would have to feed her with a spoon. Although Anh was seven or eight by the time she arrived in the United States, "emotionally, she was only about two years old," Syd later said. The child was clearly traumatized.

Often, she would disappear, and Syd would find her curled up alone in a closet.

In California, feminist lawyer Lisa Brodyaga had testified in the class-action lawsuit about her efforts to find the birth family of My Hang, the little girl who had arrived so suddenly and continued to believe it was possible to return to Vietnam. Those attempts ultimately failed, and Brodyaga began adoption proceedings. Within a few years, she and My Hang moved to Texas, in large part so that the child, whose features looked somewhat Hispanic, could grow up in a place where she resembled the people around her. Eventually, My Hang announced, "I don't want to be Vietnamese any more. I want to be Mexican." Her mother replied, "Well, you really can't change who you are, but you're more than welcome to learn Spanish and kind of fit into that culture if you like." Soon, My Hang gave up her Vietnamese name entirely, preferring instead to go by the more normal-sounding name of Lynn.

When little Bert Ballard—whose adoptive mother had once shielded him from the prying hands of an INS investigator—turned two and a half, his father's job with the Army Corps of Engineers took the family from Georgia to Alabama, then later to Utah, Arizona, and, finally, Colorado, just as he started second grade. He stayed there through high school, a healthy boy who, his mother said, "didn't like his skinny wrists and nose."

On the East Coast, Kathy Lawrence gave birth to a baby boy, a little brother for Sarah, who had arrived at Boston's Logan Airport weak, malnourished, and covered with scabies. Within a few years, Kathy and Wesley divorced. Wesley, who had served as a medic in Vietnam, married a Vietnamese immigrant. As an adult, Sarah added "Kim" as a middle name. It was a name she'd found on the birth certificate that arrived with her.

In Great Falls, Montana, Doan Thi Hoang Anh—the mother who had shown up, all alone, at Camp Pendleton four months after the war ended—had managed to reunite with five of her seven children, perhaps the most of any birth mother who relinquished her children to the Babylift. The adoption agency, FCVN, never told her what had happened to the other two children. One, they speculated, may never have made it out of Vietnam. And the other? That boy's fate was unclear. Within a few years, the story of the Babylift itself fell from the attention of the national press, and Doan Thi Hoang Anh receded from the pages of the newspapers and slid into the anonymity of a typical Vietnamese refugee in America. Perhaps she stopped looking for her children, perhaps not. Sometime in the early years of the twenty-first century, more than three decades after the end of the war, a small post appeared on the "Looking For . . ." page of a Web site called Vietnambabylift.org:

> I am assisting my Vietnamese friend, Doan Thi HOANG ANH, in finding her son who was adopted by a French couple in May, 1975. He was adopted from "Friends of Children of Vietnam" based in Denver, Colorado, sometime in 1975. Her son's name is CHO LON Doan THAN Phong and his birth date is July 15, 1974. My friend wishes very, very much to be reunited with him. She went to France to look for him in July, 1981 without luck. Her message to him is "I wait for him for 30 years. I wish I can see him or a picture of him. I never forget him and I pray for him. I know he has been well taken care of but I am sick for 30 years from missing my son." May God Bless you all!!!!

Apparently, at least one mother was still searching.

CHAPTER 16

Belonging

Each new morn new widows howl, new orphans cry,
new sorrows strike heaven on the face.

WILLIAM SHAKESPEARE, *Macbeth*

Rosemary Taylor concluded her memoir *Orphans of War,* published in
1988, with a chapter titled "The Children Now." In it, she offered updates on many of the Vietnamese children for whom she had found
adoptive homes overseas. By 1988, most of these adoptees were teenagers or young adults. One, a young woman called Nathalie who had
grown up in Belgium, had written to Taylor "wanting to express her satisfaction with her life and thank me for the part I had played in making
it possible." She had "grown up like any Belgian on this earth," she said.
Another adoptee, also Belgian, had written, "I feel more like a Belgian
than a Vietnamese though I am not rejecting my origins; I am proud to
have been born in Saigon."

Taylor reported some problem placements as well, including "perhaps twenty" who needed to be removed from their adoptive homes and
matched with new families. For the most part, though, the children she
described had adapted well. As the years passed, Taylor would receive
unexpected letters from them. Some asked her for information about
their past; others wanted to thank her or offer her news about their lives.
"Only one of these letters," Taylor wrote, "has expressed a great need to

know about her biological parents—'I can't live with this empty feeling for the rest of my life'—though she does not want her adoptive parents to suspect such feelings in her. All the other letters," Taylor continued, "have expressed a sense of total belonging with no trace of anxiety about their origins. The children know that they came from Vietnam but for the most part they do not identify themselves as Vietnamese but as American, or French, or Australian, and so on—as belonging to the country where they have grown up."

It is likely that many, even most, Vietnamese adoptees have done well in their new homes. In particular, the ones whose adoptions occurred before the Operation Babylift evacuations of 1975 benefited from the fact that their adoptions took place under calmer, less controversial circumstances. From my own research, however, it seems that Taylor's confidence in this sense of "total belonging" was premature and, most likely, distorted by her involvement in these adoptions and an understandably ardent hope for their success. In the early and mid-1980s, the Vietnamese adoptees were still young, and probably they were unable to express adequately their complicated feelings about their history. I met and corresponded with a number of Vietnamese adoptees during the course of my research, which has taken place since they entered their thirties and forties. Many, as I have noted, experienced happy childhoods and have grown into healthy, well-adjusted adults. Others, however, have suffered. Some experience depression and have a troubled sense of their own identity. Some developed bulimia and other eating disorders. Such psychological issues may not be the norm, but they are not unusual among these adoptees, either. The adoptive mother of one Babylift child told me that her daughter had become estranged from her as a teenager and had spent most of her life trying, unsuccessfully, to find a new family. There were disrupted adoptions, kids shuttled from foster family to foster family, and cases of sexual abuse.

Alienation, abuse, and depression occur in many families, regardless of circumstances, but it seems that a significant number of the Operation Babylift adoptees, in particular, have suffered trauma, either from their early displacement, the events that took place during the evacuation, experiences in their post-adoptive lives, or all these things. The only generalization I could make about the experience of these adopt-ees—and there were thousands of them—was that those who were old enough to remember their lives in Vietnam seemed more likely to have trouble adjusting to their new situations overseas. They knew, most clearly, what they had gained by leaving, but they knew what they had lost as well. In any case, not a single adoptee ever expressed to me the sense of "total belonging" that Taylor described. Several told me that they were happy now and felt content with their lives and very grateful to have been adopted, but most also recognized the complex nature of what had happened to them. They valued, especially, the sacrifices that their birth parents had made in giving them up.

Given all that I had seen and heard, it was easy to let my mind become tangled by the what-ifs: What if the U.S. government had devoted more of its wartime budget to improving the lives of children and families in Vietnam? What if the evacuations had taken place earlier, when the situ-ation in Saigon was less chaotic? What if USAID had not only funded the airlift, but also demanded adequate record-keeping and oversight? What if the U.S. government had conducted an active search for birth parents and made an effort to reunite displaced families? And, of course: What if these children had stayed in Vietnam?

One weekend during my months in Vietnam, Thuy and I traveled to Danang, where we met a couple of Amerasians whose mothers did not send them away on Operation Babylift. One of these young adults, a man named Phung, had done fairly well. His mother, a quiet and re-served woman, told us that she had heard about the efforts to evacuate Amerasian kids, and that some people even tried to persuade her to send Phung away. She refused, but the fear she felt for her son was enormous. "People spread rumors that whoever had a mixed-race child would have their stomach opened up and their eyes and heart taken out," she told me. "We were scared." Still, despite the risk, she kept her boy with her. To protect him, she burned any records that suggested his father was an American soldier. Ultimately, although they were too poor for the boy to get much of an education, he ended up marrying a woman from a family that was stable financially. When I met them, Phung and his wife were trying to emigrate to America through a U.S. policy that accepts the Amerasian children of U.S. soldiers who fought in the war.

I also met an Amerasian woman named Thuy. Her mother had worked in Saigon during the war and, after her daughter's birth, sent the child to Danang so that relatives would care for her. No one did. Thuy couldn't even tell me who had raised her from her infancy until she was eight years old. After that, she pretty much took care of herself, though she had an uncle who would check on her now and then. She worked as a maid in various households throughout her neighborhood, living life as a scavenger. The reason that Thuy didn't fly out of Vietnam on the Babylift was not that her mother couldn't part with her. Rather, no one cared enough to sign her up. As a result, she lived the life of a waif in a Dickens novel: hungry, beaten-down, homeless, and afraid. In short, her life supplied a perfect example of what adoption proponents, like Rosemary Taylor and Cherie Clark, were trying to help these children avoid. Finally, when Thuy was a teenager, a woman in the neighborhood made a proposition to her. This woman had a deaf-mute son whom no one else would marry. What if Thuy married him? The girl agreed. It would, at least, give her a family and, with any luck, provide her with a roof over her head. By the time I met Thuy, some twenty years later, she and her husband had three children of their own. None of them had made it past the sixth grade. Her husband worked odd jobs in construction or the fishing industry, if he could get them. Thuy earned money by trolling the empty streets from midnight to dawn, collecting discarded bottles and papers for resale. She didn't make much, and she was so embarrassed to be a trash-picker that when people asked her how she made her living, she told them she worked in "recycling." Like Phung, Thuy talked about emigrating to the United States. Was this, then, the life that David Fisk and Steve George and any of the other adoptees I met had given up by leaving Vietnam? Sure, there is misery and unhappiness among the Babylift kids overseas, but would they have been happier in their homeland? No one can answer such questions.

• • •

In the summer of 2007, I traveled to the YMCA's Snow Mountain Ranch, in the Rocky Mountains of Colorado, to attend a reunion of Vietnamese adoptees called Vietnamese Heritage Camp. The group included Operation Babylift kids, a few adult adoptees who came to the United States before April 1975, and a new generation of Vietnamese children who had arrived in recent years, after the U.S. and the current Vietnam governments signed contemporary adoption agreements. Hundreds of people attended the camp, most of them these younger children and their families, who had come because they wanted to use the camp as a way to help the children learn about the culture and traditions of their birth country. During the day, the kids split into groups, marching off behind their Vietnamese-American college student counselors, who would teach them Vietnam-themed arts and crafts and songs and dances. At night, the whole camp came together for big events—a fashion show in which the children filed through wearing bright silk *áo dài* (traditional dress), a lion dance, an aerobatic performance by a local troupe that practiced Shao Lin kung fu. The adults spent their time in workshops discussing such topics as raising international adoptees, facing their child's adolescence, or maintaining relationships with birth families. During downtime, they could wander through a "Vietnamese market" that sold handicrafts, folk music, imported silk, and books that ranged from biographies of Ho Chi Minh to histories of the war and how-to guides on Vietnamese cooking.

This year, the Heritage Camp included a reunion for the Vietnamese Adoptee Network (VAN), that group of adult adoptees whose meeting I had attended in Boston two years earlier. The VAN members had come to camp, in part, to act as a resource for the younger generation of Vietnamese adoptees and their families. When adoptive parents wondered how to talk with their young children about adoption, or whether or not to find a tutor to teach them Vietnamese, they could ask someone from VAN for an opinion. One evening, VAN hosted a private dinner for the oldest of this new generation, preteen and teenage adoptees.

Together, young people and their now-adult fellow adoptees tried to hash out what it meant to grow up as a Vietnamese person in a non-Vietnamese family.

A fairly small group of eight or ten VAN members had come to Colorado. They invited me to stay with them in the rambling bunkhouse that overlooked the hills and valleys of the Snow Mountain Ranch. One day, I happened to mention to one of the adoptees, Bree Sibbel, that I had read Cherie Clark's memoir, *After Sorrow Comes Joy*. Sibbel sighed. "I try to read Cherie's book," she said, "but I can only get through a bit at a time. When I read about those babies in the orphanage, I think, 'That could have been me.'" Sibbel was adopted through Catholic Charities when she was six months old and grew up in a close-knit family in rural Oregon. She was married now, and the mother of a toddler. The experience of pregnancy and giving birth had been a revelation for her. "Never before had I felt so close to my birth mother," she would later explain. "My pregnancy was the first experience I had ever had that I knew for certain my birth mother had experienced, too." Having a child had also given her a biological connection to family, something completely new to her. "It is amazing for me to look at my son and see my eyes and to see him wrinkle his little nose that looks so much like mine. Having a blood relative has been indescribable and something best understood by those who have never had one."

Like Bree Sibbel and all the other Babylift adoptees who attended the Heritage Camp, Bert Ballard has, by many measures, lived a successful life. The malnourished infant that Colleen and Jerry Ballard picked up at Fort Benning, Georgia, in May 1975 had grown into a healthy, bright, and outgoing adult. Married and the father of two little girls, he was finishing up his doctorate in communications studies and looking for academic positions in his field. Perhaps because of his scholarly training, Ballard had a nuanced view of Operation Babylift, and he talked about the evacuation not only in terms of how it affected his own life, but also in terms of public policy with regard to adoption. During Operation Babylift, he told me, "There was a lot of 'objectifying' or 'commodifying' of the children, as opposed to them being real human

beings." Ballard understood the difficulties that faced the Babylift organizers. He knew that the war had presented enormous logistical challenges to simply keeping these children healthy and safe. In fact, he, like
so many of the Babylift adoptees I'd met, had a deep affection for the
people who had carried him overseas. "God, we *love* the caregivers," he
told me. Still, he also believed that the organizers had plenty of time to
think through the ramifications of what they were doing. "Absolutely,"
he told me. "There was this conscious choice: 'Okay, we're just going
to evacuate these children and we're going to feel good about what's
going on. We don't really care about their past or anything else that
was happening.'"

In Bert Ballard's own life, the effect of those choices has been tre-
mendous. He knows absolutely nothing about his past—not his name,
his birth date, or even how he ended up on an airplane. Essentially, his
history begins with a name that appeared on a roster of the children
from An Lac Orphanage, but no one knows for sure where that particular child came from, or even if he ever lived in the orphanage at all. It's
possible that someone—a birth parent perhaps?—placed this undocu-
mented infant, who was only about three weeks old, on the airplane at
the very last minute. Ballard simply doesn't know.

Bert Ballard had no interest in blaming anyone for the blanks in his
life, but he did insist that someone learn from the failures of Operation
Babylift. Since the evacuations ended in 1975, interest in international
adoption has grown tremendously. According to the U.S. State Department, over two hundred thousand children were adopted from overseas
between 1998 and 2008. As Ballard saw it, every effort should be made
to maintain birth records for these children, as well as for domestic
adoptees and kids in foster homes, so that they can have these records
when they grow up. He and so many of his fellow Babylift adoptees
have "gone through our lives with absolutely no information, with no
way to recover the information, sometimes through conscious choices,
sometimes as a result of it being chaotic, sometimes as just a conse-
quence of what happened or [it] not even being thought of at all." Even
today, more than thirty years after the war ended, he told me, "conscious

choices are being made to forbid adoptees from looking into some of their past records." For Bert Ballard, access to information is a moral issue. "It's our eyes and our identities, our stories," he told me, "and that's really all that we have."

Epilogue

After reuniting the country in 1975, the Vietnamese government insti-
tuted a set of disastrous economic reforms that left the nation close to
ruin. By 1986, Vietnam's leaders had made a major policy shift, called
đổi mới, or "renovation," and begun to open the country to entrepre-
neurism and investment from the outside world. With the opening of
the economy, foreigners from all over began to visit Vietnam and move
there to work. By the early 1990s, the foreign population had grown
considerably. Even in Danang, the most remote of the nation's largest
cities, it became more and more normal to see foreign faces around
town.

By the early 1990s, one particular group of women began to see an
opportunity for themselves. Nearly twenty years had now passed since
the war ended and scores of frantic Danang mothers sent their children
overseas. For many of these women, the wounds had never healed. Now,
seeing the change coming to their country, some began to pull the hidden boxes from under their beds. They dug into the deepest recesses of
their drawers to the places they kept their most treasured possessions.
There, they found the documents and photos they had hidden so many

years ago, evidence of their children who had flown away. Papers in hand, they went out into the streets, looking for foreigners who could help them.

Ho Thi Han, who had given up her youngest child, the tiny, blond Ngoc Anh, walked up and down the streets of Danang regularly. Han was old now, but persistent. She approached every foreigner she could find, even though she had forgotten most of her English. "Please," she would say, "Can you help me?" For a long, long time, no one could.

And then, one day in 1994, she spotted a tall Caucasian man approaching on the sidewalk. He was walking with a couple of Vietnamese women. Han stopped in front of him. "Please, can you help me?" she asked.

The women looked at her. "What do you want?" they inquired in Vietnamese.

"I sent my daughter to America," Han said. Quickly, she showed them her papers and photos. She explained that she'd given up Ngoc Anh in Saigon at the end of the war. "Can you help me find her?" she asked.

The Vietnamese women looked at each other and gasped. "Oh, my God!" they said. "You're so lucky!" It turned out that the Western man worked for the Red Cross. He might, in fact, be able to do something. For a few minutes, Han spoke with the man while his Vietnamese colleagues translated.

"You'll have to give him your documents," they said.

Han looked down at the papers in her hands and hesitated. These were the only things she had that connected her to her daughter. If she lost them, what could she do? On the other hand, she had never before met anyone willing to help her locate the girl. She decided to risk it. She handed the man her papers.

By 1994, Anh Gelbwaks had gotten married and changed her name to Hansen. These days, she lived in Superior, Wisconsin, with her husband, Jon, and their two daughters. With her fair complexion, she fit in well in the northern reaches of the United States, though she didn't like the long winters. Anh was twenty-six now, or so she thought. Her adoptive parents had never been able to tell her exactly how old she was. In fact, her history had left a number of holes in her life and, except for one brother, Dan, with whom she remained close, she went through long periods during which she had almost no contact with her adoptive family. Over time she had come to consider her in-laws, Jon's parents, as the family she could count on.

Then, one morning, while she was taking a shower, her mother-in-law ran upstairs and banged on the door. "You have to come down!" she yelled. A young woman from the Red Cross had arrived at the house. "You have to meet this girl. Somebody found your birth mom! Found *you!*"

Within minutes, Anh had raced downstairs, her hair still dripping. A young woman stood looking at a picture that Anh and Jon kept on top of their television set. It was a photo of a little blond-haired girl holding a card on which was written the name: "HO THI NGOC ANH." It was the only picture that Anh had from her past. The young woman from the Red Cross pointed to the photograph. "This," she said, "is who we are looking for."

Together, they hurried down to the Red Cross office, where staff members showed her a file that contained two or three more photographs, pictures of Anh as a child that she could not remember ever having seen. They also showed her a photo of her birth mother. Anh began to cry. In her dreams of the past, she had always seen her own face clearly, but the face of her mother was nothing but a blur to her. "Now I know what she looks like," she sobbed.

The mother and daughter wrote to each other for the next seven years. Anh desperately wanted to see her mother again, but she soon had three young daughters of her own. The family lived on a tight budget and she couldn't see how she could get the money to fly halfway around the world. Then, over the Christmas holidays of 2001, a stranger called from Michigan. He had just come back from Danang, he told her, and he had met her mother there. "She's very nice," he said. "She really wants you to come over." By now, nearly eight years had passed since that first visit from the Red Cross. Anh found herself imagining the effort that her mother had made to tell this man their story and to ask that he call her. "You need to go back," the man said.

Anh got off the phone and looked at her family. "I have to go," she told them. She knew that it would be impossible for the entire family—Anh, Jon, and the three girls—to make the trip, but maybe, she thought, she could scrape together the money to fly there herself.

Her adoptive brother, Dan, was visiting them for the holidays. He had watched the entire telephone conversation transpire, and now he saw the look of resolve on his sister's face. "Well," he said. "I'll go with you."

Eight months later, Anh and Dan flew to Danang. Her entire birth family—Han, eight brothers and sisters, all their spouses and kids—showed up at the airport to meet them. In a photograph that Dan took, Anh and her mother stand together in front of the airport terminal, holding each other. Anh's eyes look red from tears. Han's expression reveals not only joy but also, perhaps, a feeling of victory achieved after a long, long struggle.

The first few days in the city felt "very eerie" for Anh. She could vividly remember her life there, and it was a life of war: soldiers marching through the streets, the sounds of bombs and shelling, military jeeps roaring past her house. Now, the air, the smells, the sounds, and the light all brought those memories back into her consciousness. "I could feel the soldiers walking around," she said. "Just being there at night, just closing my eyes, I could picture back then."

Nearly thirty years had passed since Anh—Ngoc Anh then—had been part of this family. She was, after all, the child who had disappeared. In all practical ways, these people were strangers to each other. Anh was an American now. She made her home on the snowy shores of Lake Superior. With her blond hair and Western fashion sense, she stood out more in Vietnam than she ever had as a little fair-haired girl in the midst of a dark-haired family. To make matters even more complicated, she couldn't speak Vietnamese and had to rely on a single English-speaking older half-brother to translate.

Still, the language gap didn't really matter. These people had known her since the day she was born, had played with her, sheltered her, fed her, loved her, and carried her, their little sister, all the way to Saigon because they were convinced it was the only way to save her life. Intellectually, they could all understand the strangeness of this meeting, but they felt comfortable, and comforted, to be together, too. Anh had heard of cases in which Vietnamese families demanded large sums of money from family members returning from abroad. One sister did ask for money, but Anh explained that other than some funds she had brought for their mother, she had nothing left to give. "And that was it. There was no—I didn't take it the wrong way and they didn't take it the wrong way," she later remembered. Asking her for help, she knew, didn't mean they didn't love her, too.

At the center of all of this, Han beamed with joy. She was now in her sixties, and she hunched a bit when she walked. She still had energy, though, and the same determination that had, three decades earlier, propelled her entire family the length of South Vietnam to get that one vulnerable daughter out of the country. During the two weeks that Anh spent in Vietnam, Han rarely left her side. She showed her daughter baby pictures and a few pieces of Ngoc Anh's clothing, now almost rags, that she had saved all these years. Han would stay at Anh's hotel late into the night before going home, and then she would rise early the next morning to rush back to her daughter's side. "Even though I couldn't understand what she was saying," Anh said, "there was this connection and closeness. She always said, 'I love you!' Even if my half-brother wasn't there to translate and we couldn't understand each other, she was holding my hand." It was as if, during the panic of those last awful days of war, the frantic mother had held her daughter in her hands, then set her aloft to make her own way in the world, like a fledgling bird. Now, after years of grief, she had lifted her hands again, and pulled her child back toward her.

Acknowledgments

Dozens of people took the time to speak or correspond with me about aspects of this research or their experiences during the Babylift. Every single communication—whether it appears explicitly in the book or not—helped further my understanding of what happened to these children during those chaotic weeks in 1975 and in the years that followed.

I thank the Fulbright Foundation for seeing the value in this project and for providing me with the resources to spend a year conducting research in Vietnam. Fulbright staff—including Tran Xuan Thao, Do Thu Huong, Jessica Needham, and David Adams—offered regular assistance and good cheer. Nguyen Ngoc Hung, vice-director of the Vietnamese Language Center at the Hanoi University of Foreign Studies, gave me a home within that country's university system.

Three people contributed to this project with a passion and diligence that continually moved me. Phung Thi Nguyen Thuy, my assistant in Ho Chi Minh City, approached the challenge of unearthing a lost history with humor, cleverness, and unbounded energy. I felt grateful for her company and her partnership every single day. Likewise, my

Vietnamese-language teachers, Nguyen Thu Nga and Pham Thi Mai Thanh, worked with me to translate dozens of hours of Vietnamese interviews into English. Thanh is responsible, too, for the transcription of nearly all the Vietnamese voice recordings, a muscle-wrenching task about which she never complained.

I must mention several people whose enormous efforts have added immeasurably to my ability to tell this story. I was never able to speak with Rosemary Taylor, but her book *Orphans of War* gave a detailed and insightful explanation of her work in Vietnam. I relied on it for both factual information and as a window into her ideas about adoption. Wende Grant, too, through her collaboration on that book, aided me in this project. Cherie Clark, whose memoir, *After Sorrow Comes Joy*, offers a vivid picture of these events, spent hours talking with me about the Babylift, and we have corresponded now for years. I am grateful not only for her generosity toward me but also for her honest reflections on what happened back then. Through my previous work in Vietnam, I have known attorney Thomas Miller and his wife, T. T. Nhu, for many years. In addition to sharing their recollections of the Babylift and its aftermath, Tom loaned me his extensive collection of files on the subject, which included newspaper clippings, personal correspondence, and documents from many of the legal cases. This material was a treasure. For her part, Nhu put me in touch with the birth mothers in Danang, which gave me the ability to tell that side of this story.

There are two adoptees whose experiences, to my mind, lie at the center of this book: David Fisk and Anh Hansen. I feel honored by their faith in me and by their willingness to share their stories not only with me but also with the wider world. Other adoptees, too, have been extremely helpful. Bert Ballard's wise comments on my manuscript enabled me to make this a better book. Steve George, Trista Goldberg, Sarah K. Lawrence, Sarah Lotchin, Daniel Preusse, Jared Rehberg, Bree Sibbel, and several members of VAN all shared with me information or reflections on their experience as adoptees. I also thank Le Nhan Phuong for telling me his story of *almost* being adopted (he reunited with his birth mother first), Kevin Minh Allen for allowing me to use his beautiful remark to open chapter 8, and Indigo Willing, whose group "adoptedvietnameseinternational" on Yahoo! helps to unite adoptees all over the world. I must mention, too, that Trista Goldberg's Web site, operationreunite.com, supports Vietnamese adoptees trying to find their birth families.

The parents of the Vietnamese adoptees—both their birth parents and the mothers and fathers who raised them—have also added enormously to my understanding of this subject. Thanks, especially, to Colleen Bonds, Lisa Brodyaga, Syd Gelbwaks, Don and Kathy Peters, and Kathy Lawrence in the United States; and in Vietnam, to Ho Thi Han and Mai Thi Kim. Adoptive mother Lana Noone has provided an essential service to the Babylift community with her Web site, vietnambabylift.org.

In addition to those mentioned previously, a number of former caregivers have offered valuable advice and information, among them Sister Susan McDonald, Ross Meador, LeAnn Thieman, John Williams, Nguyen Thi Hong, and the women I refer to as Bich Ha, Huong, Phuong, and Tuyet. In particular, I'd like to thank Christine Leivermann for her willingness to speak with me not only about her experience as a nurse in Vietnam but also on the difficult subject of the Galaxy crash. For telling me about the relief effort at the Presidio, I thank Col. Bob Kane and Alex and Janice Stalcup. The Stalcups also shared with me their extensive personal files from that period.

In Vietnam, I received assistance from the staffs of the Vietnam National Library and the Institute of Social Sciences Information, both in Hanoi, and from the staffs of the General Sciences Library and the Vietnamese National Archive II, both in Ho Chi Minh City. In the United States, I benefited from the resources of the Dartmouth College Library; the Directorate Information Management at Fort Benning, Georgia; the Gerald R. Ford Presidential Library and Museum; the National Park Service Golden Gate National Recreation Area Archives; the Presidio Trust; the archives of the U.S. District Court for the Northern District of California, and the Library of Congress. I owe particular thanks to Steve Maxner and his colleagues at the Vietnam Center at Texas Tech University and to Liza Palmer, Rebecca Kemp,

Madeleine Bombeld, and the other librarians at Randall Library of the University of North Carolina at Wilmington, who were not only skilled but also enthusiastic.

In Vietnam and in the United States, many people gave me help and encouragement: Greg Auberry, Sarah Bales, Karen Bender, Ruti Ben-Artzi, Lady Borton, Robert Brigham, Amy Damutz, Ginger Davis, Dan Duffy, Clyde Edgerton, Nga Erdman, Janet Ellerby, Sherry Goodman, Molly Hartman-O'Connell, Gerry Herman, Carolyn Jones, Amy Keith, Natasha Kraevskaia, Nguyen Thanh Lam, Nguyen Thuy Lan, Rebecca Lee, Andrew Lund, Duong Thi Ly, the late Shirley Peck-Barnes, Sarah Messer, Stephanie Meyers, Nathalie Miller, Gabrielle Miller, Hope Mitnick, Tenley Mogk, John Tue Nguyen, Bob Reiss, Robert Siegel, John Sullivan, Ronnie Suozzi-Auberry, Vu Dan Tan, Pham Bich Thuy, Tran Khanh Tuyet, and Kathryn Winogura. Judy Goldman read this manuscript at a critical moment and responded in just the ways that helped me most.

Thanks to my wise and patient agent, Douglas Stewart, who saw that I was desperate to write this story and encouraged me to do it. Thanks to everyone at Beacon Press, including Joanna Green, Tom Hallock, Sarah Laxton, Susan Lumenello, Pamela MacColl, Susan McClung, and, especially, my editor, Gayatri Patnaik, who, with intelligence and kindness, helped me turn my manuscript into a book.

This is a book about family, in all its many forms, and so, here, I return to mine. I am thankful for the support of Oliver and Ginny Berliner, Barbara and Norm Namerow, Annabelle, Evan, Adam, and Madison Sachs, Tracy and Ron Smith, Mark Street, Boris Torres, and Bob Vidulich. My grandmother, Rose Sachs, taught me what it means to persevere. My brother, Ira Sachs, and my sister, Lynne Sachs, gave me not only love, but also friendship and inspiration. My mother, Diane Sachs, and my father, Ira Sachs, taught me, in their own particular ways, how to think and to love. I thank my sons, Jesse and Samuel Berliner-Sachs, who, with courage and curiosity, spent a year away from their American childhoods to take up residence in Vietnam. And my deepest gratitude goes to my husband, Todd Berliner: great love, partner, best friend.

Notes

For more information on The Life We Were Given, *including a bibliography and photographs, please go to www.beacon.org/thelifeweweregiven.*

INTRODUCTION

The photograph comes from the Web site adoptvietnam.org. As for the number of children evacuated in the airlift, estimates range widely, which testifies to the disorder that marred the operation. The Department of Defense Commander-in-Chief Pacific Command History "1975 Appendix III—Babylift" (hereafter called the "Command History report"), for example, claims that 2,926 children were evacuated from Indochina (Command History Branch, Office of the Joint Secretary; accessed through Texas Tech University's Vietnam Center and Archive). The U.S. Agency for International Development's "Operation Babylift Report" (henceforth called "the USAID Babylift report") puts the number at 2,547, with 1,945 of those settling in the United States. The information on children during wartime comes from a number of sources: "Spartan Society: Structural Ritualization in an Ancient Social System" (J. David Knotternus and Phyllis E. Berry; *Humboldt Journal of Social Relations*, Vol. 27 ([1], 2002, pp. 1–41); "Children at War" (P. W. Singer, *Military History*, Vol. 24 ([6], 2007, pp. 52–55); *Case Closed: Holocaust Survivors in Postwar America* (Beth B. Cohen; New Brunswick, N.J.: Rutgers University Press, 2007); *The Lost Apple: Operation Pedro Pan, Cuban Children in the U.S., and the Promise of a Better Future* (Maria de los Angeles Torres; Boston: Beacon Press, 2003); "Refugee Children Return to Lagos" (William Borders, *New York Times*, November 10, 1970, p. 11). The University of Oregon's Adoption History Project provided the information on the history of adoption legislation. Quotation about the Babylift offering atonement: "The Orphans: Saved or Lost?" (*Time*, April 21, 1975, p. 10). The USAID Babylift report estimates that 20 percent of the children were adopted in countries other than the United States. My account of the 2005 VAN conference comes from my notes and a recorded interview with David Fisk. An article about David appeared in the *Miami Herald* on April 9, 1975.

CHAPTER 1: WHERE THEY CAME FROM

Opening quotation: Michael Bilton and Kevin Sim's *Four Hours in My Lai* (New York: Penguin Books, 1992, p. 21). Information on the Spring Offensive and subsequent refugee crisis: Michael Maclear's *The Ten-Thousand Day War: Vietnam: 1945–1975* (New York: St. Martin's Press, 1981) and March 1975 editions of the *Saigon Post* (the newspaper ceased publication at the end of the war, and copies are not widely available; I relied on the set of copies in Ho Chi Minh City's General Sciences Library), including Nguyen Tu's dispatches and Richard Blystone's "Survivors of Incredible Saga Lose All But Life" (March 25, 1975). Rosemary Taylor's quotations appear in her memoir *Orphans of War: Work with the Abandoned Children of Vietnam 1967–1975* (written in collaboration with Wende Grant; London: Collins Publishers, 1988). Judith Coburn's descriptions of Go Vap Orphanage appear in "The War of the Babies" (*Village Voice*, April 14, 1975, pp. 14–17). The explanation of adoption agency procedures: Taylor's book and Sister Susan McDonald's *For Children Cannot Wait* (privately published in 1980). Excerpt from the FFAC newsletter: *Orphans of War*, page 110. Statistics about Vietnamese families taking in orphans: South Vietnamese government report titled "Child Welfare in the Republic of Vietnam," which was part of a larger investigation called "Vietnam Children's Basic Problems" (Texas Tech's Vietnam Archive). Statistics on how many FFAC children had left, on average, in previous months appear on page 89 of *Orphans of War*. The number of children FFAC was attempting to evacuate appears on page 152 of that book. Cherie Clark describes her trip into the Mekong Delta in her book, *After Sorrow Comes Joy* (Westminster, CO: Lawrence and Thomas Publishing House, 2000, pp. 112–17). Information on the atmosphere in Saigon in mid-March 1975 was published in "Saigon Under Siege" (*Time*, April 14, 1975, p. 12). Chris Hedges outlines his ideas about the attractions of war in *War Is a Force That Gives Us Meaning* (New York: Anchor Books, 2002; quotation on p. 3). Information about training for adoption professionals: Marshall D. Schechter and Doris Bertocci's "The Meaning of the Search" (*The Psychology of Adoption*, eds. David M. Brodizinsky and Marshall D. Schechter; New York: Oxford University Press, 1990, p. 87). I learned about the term *radio miệng* ("mouth radio") through a September 2008 correspondence with Harvard University historian and professor Hue-Tam Ho Tai. The birth mothers Han and Kim spoke with me in Danang in March 2006. Allegations of Communist brutality appear, for example, in numerous reports in the *Vietnam Press* and *Saigon Post* published in March 1975. Description of the National Security Council meeting on March 28, 1975: National Security Council Minutes and the Ford Daily Diary (Gerald R. Ford Presidential Library and Museum). Bernard Weinraub's March 28, 1975, *New York Times* front-page story: "Communist Force Is Surging South; Danang Holds On." Excerpts from Secretary of State Henry Kissinger's press conference appeared in the previous day's edition of the *New York Times*. Information on the Military Sealift Command comes from "By Sea, Air, and Land: An Illustrated History of the U.S. Navy in Southeast Asia" (online; the Department of the Navy's Naval Historical Center). The description of Han's journey south is based on my 2006 interview with her and, later that year, with her daughter, Anh Hansen, in Superior, Wisconsin.

CHAPTER 2: ALL AMERICANS GO HOME NOW

P. W. Singer's quotation comes from the above-noted article "Children at War." David Butler's description of the boy on the bike is in *The Fall of Saigon: Scenes from the Sudden End of a Long War* (New York: Dell, 1985, p. 119). My meeting with "Tuyet" took place in Ho Chi Minh City in September 2005. The history of Rosemary Taylor's nurseries comes from *Orphans of War* and *For Children Cannot Wait*, which also provide photos that helped me describe these facilities.

CHAPTER 3: A SEA OF HUMAN NEED

George Will quotation: *San Francisco Chronicle* (April 10, 1975). The corporate Web site of World Airways supplied the assessment on the success of the Danang mission and the figure for how many planes flew that day (there are conflicting reports). Jan Wollett and Joe Hrezo, World Airways employees who accompanied Daly on the flight, recounted their experiences in Larry Engelmann's *Tears Before the Rain: An Oral History of the Fall of South Vietnam* (New York: Oxford University Press, 1990). Wollett's quotations appear on pages 5 and 8, Hrezo's on page 16. The history of the Caravelle Hotel comes from Caravelle promotional literature. The story of Wende Grant's meeting with Daly appears on page 153 of *Orphans of War* (on which Grant collaborated); her account of her experience in Cambodia is on page 146. That book serves as the source for all the information about Taylor and Grant in this chapter (see, particularly, pp. 1–15, 53–54, 71–78, 87–88, and 155), except on the points that follow: the views of former FFAC staffers about Rosemary Taylor and Margaret Moses are based on interviews I conducted in Vietnam and the United States between 2005 and 2007; I supplement Taylor's account of the split between FCVN and FFAC with information from *After Sorrow Comes Joy* and Shirley Peck-Barnes's *The War Cradle* (Denver: Vintage Pressworks, 2000). The allegation that Ed Daly called U.S. ambassador Graham Martin "nothing but a used-car salesman" (to his face) comes from Joe Hrezo in Engelmann's book (p. 13). Butler's *The Fall of Saigon* discusses U.S. government policy on the large-scale evacuations from Saigon. Alex Stalcup's recollection of the initial Presidio efforts come from our 2007 interview in California. *After Sorrow Comes Joy* contains the text of Phan Quang Dan's controversial letter on pages 127–28. The accusation that the Babylift was used to "turn American public opinion" was widely debated. For example, Malcolm W. Browne's article "Opposition Charge Denied" (*New York Times*, April 8, 1975). *After Sorrow Comes Joy* provides detailed information on that first evacuation flight out of Vietnam. Ed Daly's boast about evacuating fifteen hundred children, including his taunt to the U.S. and South Vietnamese governments—"Let 'em stop us"—appeared in an Associated Press story published in the *Miami Herald* (April 2, 1975). The exchange between World Airways pilot Ken Healy and air traffic control came from the *San Francisco Chronicle* (April 3, 1975).

CHAPTER 4: IF YOU ARE OUT THERE, WE LOVE YOU AND WE ARE LOOKING FOR YOU

Introductory quotation: "A Fear-Swept Saigon is on the Brink of Chaos" (Bernard Weinraub, the *New York Times*, April 3, 1975). Cherie Clark's description of mothers throwing their children over the fence comes from *After Sorrow Comes Joy* (p. 181). The bulletin board messages appeared on the "Looking For . . ." pages of vietnambabylift.org, last accessed June 3, 2009. My discussion with the friends of the birth mother, Le, took place in Ho Chi Minh City in October 2005.

CHAPTER 5: LOST IN THE SHUFFLE

Herb Caen's comments: the *San Francisco Chronicle*, April 4, 1975. The article about Daly's arrival in California, "52 Viet Orphans Land in Oakland," appeared

April 3 in the same newspaper. Descriptions of the medical staff triage and pro-cedures: Alex and Janice Stalcup interview. My account of the relief effort at the Presidio comes from media reports and a variety of other sources. The Stalcups shared a wide range of material from their personal files, including correspon-dence, volunteer and agency reports, and procedural documents. From the Pre-sidio Trust archives, I obtained a copy of "OPERATION SPOVO: Support of Vietnamese Orphans," an unpublished account of the effort that was written by Col. Robert Kane, the post commanding officer. I also interviewed Col. Kane in his home in California in 2007. The National Park Service Golden Gate National Recreation Area Archives provided me with photographs and plans of Harmon Hall and the extremely thorough Department of the Army report titled "Support Plan for Vietnamese Orphans" (Collection Number GOGA 35292 F2), which of-fered details on such things as the number of sinks installed, the size of washroom signs, and Shirley Small's earnings. Additionally, in 2007 I visited the Presidio and Harmon Hall myself. The three different numbers given for how many children flew into Oakland on the World Airways jet come from the April 3 *San Francisco Chronicle* article that opened this chapter; the Department of the Army report; and "Red Cross and the Children from Vietnam," a report by the American National Red Cross Golden Gate Chapter, which I obtained from the Stalcups (henceforth referred to as "Red Cross report"). My account of the Gelbwaks family and their decision to adopt comes from an interview with Syd Gelbwaks in April 2008. Both Taylor and Clark mention "nursery names" throughout their books, though some of the more evocative can be found in *Orphans of War*, pages 108 and 125. Taylor writes about her difficulties finding transportation for her children in numerous passages of the same book, but she discusses them in particular detail between pages 149 and 159. The statement that only 20 percent of Babylift children were considered mixed-race is based on the USAID Babylift report, page 5. My ac-count of the Galaxy C-5A flight and its crash comes from many sources, including *Orphans of War* (chapter 14 includes Christine Leivermann's official statement to the Air Force, given after the accident). Rosemary Taylor's extended descrip-tion of the children on the plane appears on page 162 of *Orphans of War*. In July 2006, I met in San Francisco with Christine Leivermann, who spoke about the crash and her experiences working in Vietnam. I also obtained information on the flight from the account of another survivor, Dr. Merritt W. Stark (David Butler files at Dartmouth College Rauner Special Collections Library). Specifica-tions about the C-5A aircraft come from the Federation of American Scientists. No one knows how many children were on the Galaxy jet. My estimate comes from "Baby Bottles, Toys, Bodies All Over" (*Miami Herald*, April 5, 1975). I heard about the friendship between Pham Thi Phuong (whose name I have changed for privacy reasons) and Birgit Blank during my October 2005 interview with Phuong in Ho Chi Minh City. As for the number of dead, again, no one knows for sure. The immediate reports of deaths ("Bodies of Orphans Hunted: 199 Feared Killed in Plane Crash" in *Miami Herald*, April 5, 1975, p. 1) gave higher numbers than later estimates. The USAID Babylift Report says that 228 children were on the jet and that 78 died and 150 survived (p. 3). The Command History report estimates that 230 children were aboard, with 66 adult escorts. This report gives no overall statistics for the number of deaths but tries to explain the confusion in numbers by stating that FFAC failed to keep track of which children boarded and which did not. As for how many adults died in the crash, the number seems to fall somewhere between ten and twenty. The Command History report admits the obvious by noting, "None of the sources cited here nor those in the subsequent narrative agree on the statistics relating to either the C-5 crash or the total numbers of orphans evacuated" (p. viii). Information on the Lockheed lawsuits comes from Rosemary Taylor's account in *Orphans of War* (pp. 238–50) and the troubled history of the C-5A aircraft comes from various press accounts, including "Two Democrats Urge Grounding of All C5s Till Cause is Found" (*Miami Herald*, April 5, 1975) and Richard Witkin's "Crash of Galaxy is Puzzling to Experts (*New York Times*, April 5, 1975). The information on the internment of remains appears in the Command History report (pp. 13–14). Reactions of adoptive parents to the crash come from interviews with Kathy Lawrence (now Kathy Tirrell) in 2008 in Rhode Island, Colleen Ballard (now Colleen Bonds) in 2007 in Colorado, and, by telephone, with Lisa Brodyaga in 2008.

CHAPTER 6: STANDING ON TWO LEGS

The Web site wikimapia.org shows the clear shift between urban and rural that one experiences in crossing the Ben Cat River (search for: "The An Phu Dong Ferry, link between Go Vap district and An Phu Dong Isle"). By making the image somewhat more distant, one can also see the runways of Tan Son Nhut Airport, which demonstrates the proximity between the crash site and the airport that the jet was trying to reach. My interview with Mrs. Tram took place in February 2006 on the Go Vap side of the river in Ho Chi Minh City. I learned the history of An Phu Dong from conversations with local people. The lyrics to the song "An Phu Dong" appear on the Dac Trung Web site; the translation is mine. Several Vietnamese told me about the Viet Cong soldiers who were killed when the Galaxy crashed, but I have never seen any published accounts of their deaths. My interview with Steve George took place in Hanoi in November 2005.

CHAPTER 7: GOOD INTENTIONS

President Gerald Ford's statement: "Ford Sends Condolences" (*New York Times*, April 4, 1975). *New York Times* reporter Malcolm W. Browne's article quoting the South Vietnamese army lieutenant was widely noted as evidence of South Vietnamese antipathy toward the United States (I cite the wire service version: "The Vietnamese Left Behind," *San Francisco Chronicle*, April 7, 1975). The *San Francisco Chronicle's* editorial commendation of Gerald Ford appeared in "Rescue Operations" on April 4, 1975. The anecdote that the San Francisco Red Cross office switchboard "lit up": Red Cross report. Statistics on calls coming into Washington, D.C., during the evacuation: "Emergency Indochina Humanitarian Relief Committee A.I.D. Public Inquiry Telephone Center" (Alex and Janice Stalcup's files). The comment from political scientist Lucien Pye: Richard Flaste's "Airlift Evokes Emotional Debate in U.S." (*New York Times*, April 9, 1975). Taylor and several of her colleagues, including Wende Grant, describe the Pan Am flight on April 5 (*Orphans of War*, pp. 178–92). The passages about Christine Leivermann's experience on this flight are based on our interview in 2006. Wende Grant's comments about adoption bureaucracy appear on pages 37 and 75 of *Orphans of War*. My account of President and Mrs. Gerald Ford's participation in the arrival of the April 5 Pan Am flight comes in large part from my interview with Alex and Janice Stalcup, although details also come from media accounts ("Fords in S.F. to welcome Viet Orphans," the *San Francisco Examiner*, April 6, 1975, for example). Additional material on the Fords' activities that day: the Ford Daily Diary (Gerald R. Ford Presidential Library and Museum). I base my account of the experience of the young Vietnamese interpreters at the Presidio on interviews and e-mail correspondence with T. T. Nhu and Tran Khanh Tuyet, as well as on court documents in the case of *Nguyen Da Yen, et al., plaintiffs, v. Henry Kissinger, et al., defendants*. The health of the children on arrival at the Presidio was described to me by Alex and Janice Stalcup and was also discussed in Douglas E. Kneeland's "Many Children Found Ill on Arrival from Vietnam" (*New York Times*, April 7, 1975). (That article, by the way, puts the number of children arriving on the Pan Am flight at 313, while Wende Grant, in *Orphans of War*, says 324 had boarded the plane in Saigon and two had been hospitalized in Japan. I have no explanation for this discrepancy.) The April 8, 1975, exchange between Sen. Edward Kennedy and USAID administrator Daniel Parker appears in the transcript of "Indochina Evacuation and Refugee Problems, Part I: Operation Babylift & Humanitarian Needs, Hearing Before the Subcommittee to Investigate Problems Connected with Refugees and Escapees of the Committee on the Judiciary, United States Senate" (Texas Tech University's Vietnam Center). When we spoke in 2008, Col.

Robert Kane, former commanding officer of the Presidio, described to me Senator Kennedy's visit there. My description of the protest at Glide Memorial Church comes from "Kidnap claim is leveled at Viet babylift" by Dexter Waugh (*San Francisco Examiner*, April 5, 1975), as well as from discussions with T. T. Nhu and Thomas Miller. The *Miami Herald* published Kevin Leary's "Anguish Terrible as S. Floridians Await Viet Waifs" (April 3, 1975). Quotations from Shirley Jenkins, Jane Barton, and Howard Wriggins all appeared in the same April 9 *New York Times* article by Richard Flaste that I cite earlier in notes for this chapter, as does the quotation from the spokesperson for the Holt Adoption Program. The statements I quote from Rosemary Taylor defending adoption appear in *Orphans of War* (pp. 221–23). The account of the agency staffer who says that callers to her office only want to adopt comes from Coburn's "The War of the Babies" (*Village Voice*, April 14, 1975, p. 17).

CHAPTER 8: MEMENTOES AND SCARS

The quotation from adoptee Kevin Minh Allen comes from his Web site, misplacedbaggage.wordpress.com. My account of the day I spent in Ho Chi Minh City with David Fisk is based on notes I took at the time. Adoptee Sarah K. Lawrence's thoughts on her experiences growing up are derived from our correspondence in 2008 and 2009. In retelling the history of Go Vap Orphanage, I benefited from information provided to me by the scholars Tuan Hoang and Peter Hansen. Judith Coburn's description of Go Vap Orphanage appears in "The War of the Babies." Phuong's story about her life after the war is based on our 2005 interview in Ho Chi Minh City. The quotation from Rosemary Taylor about "comforting that one child" appears on page 222 of *Orphans of War.*

CHAPTER 9: SHIP TO PARENTS: SEVERE ORPHAN SYNDROME

The young lady's message to foreigners: *Saigon Post* collection, Ho Chi Minh City's General Sciences Library. The information from John Williams comes from our 2006 interview in Bangkok. The history of Holt comes from Williams and from the University of Oregon's Adoption History Project, which is also the source of Harry Holt's 1955 letter about adoption as a "mission for God." I obtained Max Bader's letter, which compares the receiving centers in Seattle and San Francisco, from the personal files of Alex and Janice Stalcup. (I have not been able to determine if that letter was ever published in the *New England Journal of Medicine* but, based on information in the scholarly research database Web of

Science, it seems likely that it was not.) Information on the attack on Saigon's Presidential Palace appeared in Malcolm W. Browne's "Thieu Seems Well in Control Despite Palace Attack" (*New York Times*, April 9, 1975). Ho Thi Han's account of arriving in Vung Tau is based on our interview. Malcolm W. Browne's "A Refugee Barge Leaves 50 Dead at Vietnam Pier" (*New York Times*, April 7, 1975) provides details on the failures of the relief effort. My description of Kathy and Wesley Lawrence waiting for the arrival of their daughter comes from my interview with her. Cherie Clark describes her efforts to prepare her children for departure on pages 155–157 of *After Sorrow Comes Joy*. Her quotation about Communist killings of mixed-race children appeared in "Major Orphan Airlift Ends—Pace Will Slow" (the *Miami Herald*, April 8, 1975). The examples I cite of "adoption mania" appeared in the *Miami Herald* on April 3 and April 4, 1975. Pat Steger wrote the "Social Scene" column in the April 9 edition of the *San Francisco Chronicle*. Betty Ford's discussion of the emotional impact of photographs of orphans appeared in "'Tragic,' Mrs. Ford says," a United Press International story (*New York Times*, April 3, 1975). W. A. Wilson's "Snatching Viet Orphans is 'Madness'": the *Vancouver Sun* (April 4, 1975). Sen. Edward Kennedy made his comments about U.S. adoption policy during the April 8, 1975, Senate hearing (hearing transcript, Texas Tech University's Vietnam Center, pp. 27–30). The new State Department guidelines are outlined in the Command History report, pages 6–7. Statistics on numbers of children transported by April 10 come from "Fact Sheet on Orphans & Refugee Relief in Indochina," a press release from USAID's Office of Public Affairs (April 10, 1975). The report that nine hundred children had already gone through processing at the Presidio appeared in "Orphans Express Great Love Need" (*San Mateo Times*, April 9, 1975), which also includes the quotation by Alex Stalcup in the same paragraph. Statistics on diaper use at the Presidio come from the Red Cross report (p. 2). Examples of disarray at the Presidio appeared in Jerry Carroll's article "Witnesses Say 'Viet' Orphans Have Families" (*San Francisco Chronicle*, May 20, 1975). The quotation by USAID's Bob Walsh: Katy Butler's "Behind the Babylift" (*San Francisco Bay Guardian*, April 19–May 2, 1975). Alex and Janice Stalcup made their comments about adoption agencies in our interview. Lisa Brodyaga's story is based on my interview with her in April 2008, an affidavit she wrote for the class-action lawsuit (files of Thomas Miller), an essay she published in *Harper's Weekly* ("My Daughter Belongs in Vietnam," December 1, 1975), and "Prospective Parents, Vietnamese Children Lost in Legal Limbo" (Elizabeth Becker, the *Washington Post*, April 25, 1976), in which appeared My Hang's directions about how to "get back to her mommy." Kathy Lawrence's story is based on my interview with Kathy and e-mail correspondence with her daughter, Sarah K. Lawrence.

CHAPTER 10:
THERE WAS NO ONE TO TAKE CARE OF THEM

The quotation from the French orphanage volunteer is based on notes from our meeting in Ho Chi Minh City in 2006. The observations about Rosemary Taylor come from interviews I conducted with former colleagues in Vietnam and the United States. Sister Susan McDonald's comments about Taylor were sent to me by e-mail on February 9, 2006. Cherie Clark wrote about the dissolution of her marriage on page 208 of *After Sorrow Comes Joy*. Other quotations from Clark come from my interviews with her, which took place in Hanoi in November 2005 and in Colorado in August 2007. I obtained the April 8, 1975, *Nhan Dan* newspaper article from the Vietnam National Library in Hanoi. The translation is mine. My interviews with two Vietnamese priests took place in Ho Chi Minh City in 2005. Cherie Clark's description of children in Vietnamese orphanages appears on page 48 of *After Sorrow Comes Joy*. Information about Hoi Duc Anh Orphanage appeared in "Large Orphanage Rejects U.S. Appeal for Evacuation" (*Saigon Post*, April 20, 1975). The end of this chapter mentions what happened to the children in the Don Bosco Technical School in the months and years following the Communist takeover. Unfortunately, other than what I heard from the priests, I was not able to collect any more information on the fate of these children.

CHAPTER 11:
PHOTOGRAPHS AND FIRES AND RAGE

The quotation from Lan Popp (known in court records as Hao Thi Popp), a birth mother suing to get her children back, was published in Barry Siegel's "Repercussions of the Babylift" (*Los Angeles Times*, December 26, 1976). The quotation from the Viet Cong appeared in "Plea for Aid" (*San Francisco Chronicle*, April 4, 1975). The story of Han and Ngoc Anh in Saigon is based on interviews with both of them. In my interview with John Williams, he told me about Holt's activities in Saigon in April of 1975, and he also recounted his experience of meeting the Catholic priest.

CHAPTER 12:
I WANTED TO SEE WHAT PEACE WAS LIKE

My interview with Nguyen Thi Ngoc Dung took place in Ho Chi Minh City in 2006. Lady Borton's comments about the Babylift are based on e-mail communications in 2006. The statistics on displaced children come from Part One of the

South Vietnamese government report mentioned in the notes for chapter 1. My interview with Nguyen Thi Loan took place in Ho Chi Minh City in 2006. The story of Huong, the orphan who became a caregiver, comes from an interview I conducted with her in 2005. Bree Sibbel is the Babylift adoptee I quote at the end of the chapter. Her comments came as a response to a list of questions I sent to her via e-mail in 2008.

CHAPTER 13: HESITATION AND RESIGNATION

The letter to the editor in the *New York Times* was written by Carol Bernstein Ferry of Scarsdale, New York, and was published under the title "The Misused Children" (April 7, 1975). The information on the pause in the airlift comes from "Saigon Ends Orphan Airlift" (*San Francisco Chronicle*, April 7, 1975). The Red Cross report includes a timeline of events, from which I've taken the information on the placement of children. The psychological studies of children and adoption were discussed in "Contrasting Adoption, Childcare, and Residential Rearing," by John Triseliotis and Malcolm Hill (*The Psychology of Adoption*, p. 115). The War Resisters League statement appeared in an April 14, 1975, press release titled "Committee Calls for Reuniting Families; Not All Children Are Orphans" (files of Thomas Miller). The *Washington Post* reporter's account of finding many children who weren't actually orphans appeared as a wire service story, "Confusion over Orphans Didn't End in Vietnam" (*Miami Herald*, April 14, 1975). The quotation from FFAC volunteer Maria Eitz appeared in Robert Hollis's article "Many Non-orphans Reported Airlifted" (*San Francisco Chronicle-Examiner*, April 14, 1975). The State Department official's comments appeared in "Administration Split over Orphans—Did Airlift Become a Kidnapping?" a *Newsday* wire service report published in the *Miami Herald* (April 16, 1975). Information on the April 21 State Department directive and the World Airways flight that day comes from the Department of the Army report, which is also the source of the quotation about military control over commercial airlines. Grace Lichtenstein's "For Childless Couple, Three Instant Sons" (*New York Times*, April 5, 1975) offers the examples I mention of adoptive families welcoming their new children. I quote from pages 4 and 11 of the "TIPS" pamphlet (U.S. Department of Health, Education, and Welfare, DHEW Publication No. ([OHD] 75–72; Stalcup files). Information about the couple who refused to adopt a child they considered ill comes from two articles in the *Miami Herald* by Andy Rosenblatt: "Fears Put Their Orphan in Second Family's Arms" (April 17, 1975) and "2nd Chance for a Child" (April 18, 1975). The nurse's letter to Alex Stalcup is dated June 7, 1975 (Stalcup files). My interview with Phi (whose name I have changed for privacy reasons) took place in Ho Chi Minh City in 2005. Cherie Clark's comments about the situation on Tran Ky Xuong Street appear on page 178 of *After Sorrow Comes Joy*. The anecdote about the baby being pushed through barbed wire appears on page 181 of the same book. Rosemary Taylor describes the events of the last few weeks of April from pages 193 to 216 of *Orphans of War*. Cherie Clark's account of her flight out of Vietnam appears on pages 193–204 of *After Sorrow Comes Joy*. My description of the mood in Saigon during those last days of April is based on "Saigon: A Dreamlike, Twilight Mood" (*Time*, May 5, 1975, p. 21). Phuong outlined for me her reasons for remaining in Vietnam during our 2005 interview. My interview with Nguyen Bich Ha (whose name I've also changed for privacy reasons) took place in Ho Chi Minh City in 2005.

CHAPTER 14: RESOURCES

David Rieff's quotation: *A Bed for the Night: Humanitarianism in Crisis* (New York: Simon and Schuster, 2003, p. 22). John Williams told me about the plane carrying Holt's files during our interview. In *Orphans of War*, Rosemary Taylor discusses how she got three hundred pounds of files out of the country (p. 197). In a June 4, 2009, message, Cherie Clark told me, "Everything I brought out, including all of our belongings and personal effects, I hand carried on the [April 5] flight the day after the crash." The documentary *Daughter from Danang* was directed by Gail Dolgin and Vincente Franco.

CHAPTER 15: BABY IN A BURNING BUILDING

Introductory quotation: George C. Wilson's "No Vietnamese 'Bloodbath' Is Found: 100 Days After Fall, U.S. Fear of Massacre Unrealized" (*Washington Post*, August 5, 1975). The *Doonesbury* comic strip character Kim, the Vietnamese adopted baby, has grown up to become, according to Doonesbury.com, a "Vietnamese-Jewish-Southern-Californian-American" who works as a computer hacker and is married to the strip's title character, Mike Doonesbury. The information on the Lawrence family is based on my interview with Kathy Lawrence (now Tirrell). Lisa Brodyaga's recollections come from our interview. Colleen Ballard (now Bonds) described her son's arrival when I spoke with her. Information on the An Lac children at Fort Benning comes from the April 18, April 25, and May 2, 1975, issues of the *Bayonet*, the base newspaper at Fort Benning (Fort Benning Garrison Command Directorate of Information Management). The glossary of Vietnamese terms was a brief, untitled handout from Fort Benning (Colleen Ballard's files). Tressler's message about Immigration comes from

"Check List for People Adopting Vietnamese Children" (Colleen Ballard's files). Betty Tisdale's undated letter is also from Colleen Ballard's files. Tracy Johnston wrote about the class-action lawsuit in "Torment over the Non-orphans" (*New York Times Magazine*, May 9, 1976). The class-action lawsuit was filed in the U.S. District Court Northern District of California (Case Number C-75-0839-SW). Unless otherwise noted, I obtained copies of all of the legal documents mentioned in this chapter from the files of Thomas Miller; I also procured files from U.S. District Court archives in California. I attempted to contact John F. Cooney, Jr., who served as Assistant U.S. District Attorney representing the defense in this case, but received no response; I also received no response to my attempts to contact representatives of FFAC and FCVN, other than those individuals already mentioned in this book. Because accurate statistics about the Babylift are impossible to determine, I've given an estimate here on how many children had arrived in the United States by the end of April. The Command History report (p. viii) states that 2,894 children arrived in the U.S. mainland, but several hundred were in transit to other countries. Douglas E. Kneeland tells the evacuation story of the three named plaintiffs in "U.S. to Review Refugee Orphan Status" (*New York Times*, May 9, 1975). My estimate on the number of internal refugees in Vietnam is based on reports of mass displacements that had reached crisis levels by late March. For example, Pham Tran's "Stranded Refugees Remain Highlight" (*Saigon Post*, March 25, 1975) describes a "flow of refugees numbering about 200,000." The estimate of the number of children in Saigon orphanages is, again, based on the South Vietnamese government's report on child welfare (see notes for chapter 1). The Communist government's response to Thomas Miller's query appears in "Saigon is Said to Demand Refugee Children's Return" (*New York Times*, May 10, 1975). My description of Anh's arrival is based on my interview with Anh Hansen in Superior, Wisconsin, in 2006, and on a telephone interview with Syd Gelbwaks in 2008. The story of Doan Thi Hoang Anh is based primarily on records in the case of *Doan Thi Hoang Anh, Plaintiff, v. Johnny Nelson and Bonnie Nelson, Defendants:* District Court of Iowa in and for Winnebago County (Case Number 12004) and the Supreme Court of Iowa (Case Number 229/3-59318). A U.S. House of Representatives' hearing "Enabling the United States to Render Assistance to, or on Behalf of, Certain Migrants and Refugees" discusses the refugee relief effort (Texas Tech University's Vietnam Center online archive, article number 2185202012, pp. 2–4). Cherie Clark's explanation of the evacuation of the named plaintiffs in the class action lawsuit appears on pages 142–43 of *After Sorrow Comes Joy*. Clark states her opinion of the lawsuit on pages 207–8 of the same book. I have reproduced the Geneva Convention articles—"Geneva Convention Relative to the Protection of Civilians in Time of War," Adopted August 12, 1949—from the official Web site of the United Nations Office of the High Commissioner for Human Rights. Helen C. Steven's "Babylift or Babysnatch" appeared in the *Capitol Hill Forum* (June 30, 1975). T. T. Nhu's comment comes from her affidavit in "Appendix for Plaintiffs" in the class-action lawsuit (filed April 29, 1975, p. 21). Rosemary Taylor's assessment of the lawsuit appears on pages 229–37 of *Orphans of War*. I quote her thoughts on Vietnamese attitudes toward children from pages 218-19 of her book. Statistics on the number of children evacuated during the Babylift, once again, come from the Command History report and the USAID Babylift Report. John E. Adams's remarks concerning the investigation were published in *Focus on Children and Youth*, a publication of the National Council of Organizations for Children and Youth (October 1975, vol. II, n. 10, p. 11). Cherie Clark's discussion of the financial cost of the lawsuit appears on page 208 of *After Sorrow Comes Joy*. Further details on the Doan Thi Hoang Anh case appear in the above-mentioned court records. Here I also describe the case of *Hao Thi Popp v. Richard Lucas, et al.* (Under the name of Lan Popp, her quotation marks the beginning of chapter 11 of this book.) The story of Hao Thi Popp (this time, her name is spelled "Lon Popp") waiting in line for two days, and Wende Grant's reaction to it, appears in Tracy Johnston's "Torment over the Viet Non-orphans" (citation above). Rosemary Taylor recounts the occasions of adoptive families returning children to birth parents on page 231 of *Orphans of War*. Custody cases involved various adoption agencies. Examples include the above-mentioned cases of Doan Thi Hoang Anh, which involved FCVN, and the case of Hao Thi Popp, which involved FFAC. *Nguyen Thi Hua, child of Lan Baker, Petitioner, v. Joseph Scott, et al., Respondents* (Court of Appeals, Eighth Judicial District, Cuyahoga County, Ohio, Case Number 38455; Thomas Miller files) involved the Holt Adoption Program. Court records from the files of Thomas Miller include information on cases involving other agencies. As for cases of returned children, the Nebraska state senator is mentioned in Katy Butler's "Who Owns the Babylift Kids? The Tragic End to Operation Babylift" (*San Francisco Bay Guardian*, February 20, 1976). In our interview, Lisa Brodyaga told me that in her testimony in the class-action lawsuit, she asserted that the child she had received was not an orphan. Taylor's comments about the financial cost of the lawsuit appear on page 231 of *Orphans of War*. The information on *Duong Bich Van v. Michigan Department of Social Services and David and Barbara Pederson* is based on court documents (Sixth Judicial Circuit Court, County of Oakland, State of Michigan; File No. 76–140499-AH) and the opinion released June 21, 1976 (pp. 10–12). Information on the case of *Le Thi Sang v. William Knight and Elizabeth Knight, Respondents* (Superior Court of California, County of San Joaquin, Case Number 125898) is based on court documents. Thomas Miller made his comparison of Operation Babylift to the rescue of a child from a burning building during our interview in Hanoi in 2006. The dialogue between the judge and attorneys in the class-action lawsuit appears in the transcript of a May 21, 1976, hearing. Joseph H. Reid's letter to Judge Williams serves as Exhibit 19 in the class-action lawsuit (filed June 25, 1975). Thomas Miller's deposition on the INS was filed February 27, 1976 (I quote from pp. 2, 4, 5, 6, and 7). Statistics on eligibility appeared in a March 19, 1976, certificate of attorney. Judge Spencer Williams's decision appears in Federal Rules Decisions (70 F.R.D. 656 (1976), pp. 656–73). Quotations cited appear on pages 660, 663, and 668. Cherie Clark's comment is taken from page 208 of *After Sorrow Comes Joy.* Information on attempts to find the family of the class-action lawsuit's three named plaintiffs comes from a petition for rehearing submitted to the U.S. Court of Appeals for the Ninth District (July 24, 1979; No. 76–1833, p. 6) and from information provided to me by Thomas Miller. Later information on the adoptees comes from my exchanges with Syd Gelbwaks, Lisa Brodyaga, Colleen Ballard, and Kathy Lawrence. The Internet message from Doan Thi Hoang Anh was accessed most recently on June 4, 2009.

CHAPTER 16: BELONGING

The quotation from *Macbeth* is taken from act IV, scene 3, lines 4–6. The quotations from Rosemary Taylor's book *Orphans of War* appear on pages 253 and 254. My interviews with Phung, his mother, and Thuy took place in 2006 in Danang. Details about the Vietnamese Heritage Camp are based on my notes and later interviews with Bree Sibbel and Bert Ballard. The U.S. Department of State Office of Children's Issues releases statistics about intercountry adoption on its Web site every year.

EPILOGUE

The story of Anh's reunion with her birth mother is based on my 2006 interviews with Han in Danang and with Anh in Superior, Wisconsin.

Index

Adams, John E., 199–200

adoption: best interest of the child, 201; Clark's philosophy of, 143–44, 147–48, 157; class-action lawsuit seeking to halt Babylift adoptions, 190–92, 196–201, 204–10; controversy surrounding Operation Babylift, regarding orphan status of children, xiv, 53–56, 88, 98–99, 102–5, 130–31, 135, 136, 162–63, 185, 190–92, 207–8; finalization of, 187–89; Holt Adoption Program's philosophy of, 182–83, 200; and individual custody trials concerning Vietnamese adopted children, 201–4; international adoption for Vietnamese children, 26, 56, 130, 136, 144, 150–51, 159, 197; international adoption as last resort for Vietnamese chil-

dren, 102–3; lay persons involved in international adoption, 10–11; Massachusetts law on, xiii; of mixed-race children, 14–20, 85–86, 144; and Operation Babylift placement requirement, 132, 161; problem placements of Vietnamese children, 212–13; purpose of, xiv; referral and home study before, 187–88; research on impact of, 161–62; standard procedures for international adoption, 92; statistics on overseas adoptions, 218; Taylor's philosophy of, 26, 36, 37, 55, 104–5, 118–19, 143–44. *See also* adoptive families; adult Vietnamese adoptees; Operation Babylift; Vietnamese orphans and displaced children

adoption agencies. *See specific agencies,*

245

oir of, 53, 200, 217; on need for
evacuation of Vietnamese children,
53; negative views of, on Operation Babylift, 142–43; on refugees,
166–67; Sachs's meeting with,
140–44; travels of, after leaving
Vietnam (1975), 141; on Vietnamese adoptees' happiness, 98. *See
also* Friends of the Children of Viet
Nam (FCVN)
Clark, Tom, 10, 43, 45–49, 128, 141
Clark Air Force Base, 132, 137, 138,
171, 188–89
Coburn, Judith, 6
Colby, William, 17–18
Committee to Protect the Rights of
Vietnamese Children, 190
Communists: and Catholic Church,
145–48; fear of, 12, 56, 126, 129–
31, 151; media coverage of, 130–
31; and mixed-race children in
Vietnam, 12, 65, 126, 129–30,
144, 214–15; orphanages in Vietnam after takeover by, 148, 154–
60; and orphans under Communist
government, 88; takeover of government of South Vietnam by,
157
Congress, U.S., 100–102, 131
con lai. See mixed-race children
Cooney, John, 205
crash of Galaxy airplane: and adoptive families, 79–80; casualties
from, 77, 83, 92, 168, 174; description of, 73–85; lawsuits on, 78–
79; and Leivermann, 73–77, 112;
Nguyen Thi Loan's memories
of, 156; and loss of identification
records for children, 128–29, 131;
memorial services at site of, 107,

113–14; Mrs. Tram on, 81–85;
public response to, in U.S., 89,
95–96, 102–3; site of, 81, 111–14;
and Taylor, 77, 78–79, 168
Cuban children. *See* Operation Pedro
Pan

Da Lat, 119–20
Daly, Ed: and evacuation of Vietnamese children from Friends of the
Children of Viet Nam (FCVN)
orphanage, 45–49, 57, 60, 63–64,
69–70, 90, 131; evacuation of refugees from Danang by, 27–31, 40,
153; and Friends For All Children
(FFAC), 31–34, 39–40, 45, 63; and
Holt Adoption Program, 123; as
owner of World Airways, 27–34,
41; relations between U.S. government and, 40
Dan, Phan Quang, 43–44
Danang: Daly's evacuation of refugees from, 27–31, 40, 153; mothers
of mixed-race children in, 12–
20; reunion of Ho Thi Han and
her daughter Anh in, 222–25;
Thuy (Amerasian woman) in,
215; during Vietnam War, 12–20,
125
Daughter from Danang, 180–81
deaths of Vietnamese children, 25–26,
77, 83, 92, 167, 171–73, 180, 195
diseases. *See* illnesses of Vietnamese
children
displaced children. *See* Vietnamese
orphans and displaced children
Don Bosco Technical School, 145–48
Doonesbury, 184–85
Dozier, Bill, 202–3
Dung, Nguyen Thi Ngoc, 154

opment (USAID), 44–45, 64, 76, 89, 100, 133, 169, 214
United States aid to Vietnam, 6, 101, 131, 147
U.S. Army Mortuary, 77–78
U.S. Catholic Conference, 194
U.S. Department of Health, Education, and Welfare, 163–64
U.S. Immigration and Naturalization Service (INS), 92, 93, 205–8, 210
U.S. Military Sealift Command, 19
U.S. State Department, 131–32, 162–63, 218
University of California, San Francisco (UCSF), 40–41, 60
Ursula, Sister, 77
USAID. *See* U.S. Agency for International Development

VAN. *See* Vietnam Adoptee Network (VAN)
Van, Duong Bich, 201–2
Vancouver Sun, 130–31
VC. *See* Viet Cong (VC)
Viet Cong (VC), 82–84, 114, 149
Vietnam: economy of, in 1980s and 1990s, 221; U.S. aid to, 6, 101, 131, 147
Vietnam Adoptee Network (VAN), xv–xix, 21, 216–19
Vietnambabylift.org, 53–56, 211
Vietnamese children. *See* Vietnamese orphans and displaced children
Vietnamese Heritage Camp, 216–19
Vietnamese orphanages. *See* orphanages in Vietnam
Vietnamese orphans and displaced children: controversy surrounding adoption of, xiv, 53–56, 88, 98–99, 102–5, 135, 136, 162–63, 185,

190–92, 207–8; and Communist takeover, 148, 154–60; deaths of, 25–26, 77, 83, 92, 167, 171–73, 180, 195; definition of orphans, xii–xiii; evacuation of, from Mekong Delta, 8–12; identification records for, 58, 62–63, 66, 93, 128–29, 131–32, 134, 143, 171, 179–83; illnesses of, 25–26, 41, 66–67, 91–92, 94, 95, 99–101, 109, 132, 138, 164–65, 171, 187, 193; informal fostering network for orphans, 8, 198; international adoption for, 26, 56, 130, 136, 144, 150–51, 159, 197; international adoption as last resort for, 102–3; medical care for, 40–41, 57–60, 91–92, 94–97, 99–100, 133–34, 164–65; names of, 62–63, 129, 135–36, 138, 188–89, 210; photographs of, 149–52, 223; remaining in Vietnam after war, 145–48; return of, to birth families after evacuation, 196, 200–201, 210–11; South Vietnamese government approval of evacuation of, 43–45, 63; statistics on, 5–8, 43, 145, 155, 157, 191; Taylor on, 36, 104–5; visas/exit authorization for, 42, 63, 122. *See also* adoption; adoptive families; adult Vietnamese adoptees; birth families; mixed-race children; Operation Babylift; orphanages in Vietnam
Vietnam War: casualties of, 4, 9, 65, 158; in Central Highlands of South Vietnam, 3–5; Danang during, 12–20; duration of, 3; end of, xii, 3–5, 175–76; evacuation of local adoption agency staff from Saigon at end of, 173–76; and fall